JERSEY : 'That Nest of Vypers'

*Cover: 'Re-building of Havre Neuf (South Pier), St Helier'
by General Thomas Remnent Charleton, c. 1814.*

The old Harbour Works at La Collette

'Geography matters; it makes people who they are.'
Jeremy Paxman

JERSEY

'That Nest of Vypers'
But were we?

Alec Podger

Société Jersiaise

Published in 2007 by
La Société Jersiaise
Pier Road
St Helier
Jersey

Origination by Seaflower Books, Jersey

Printed in Britain by
Cromwell Press
Trowbridge, Wiltshire

ISBN 0-901897-42-6

© 2007 Alec Podger

Contents

	Dedication	7
	Acknowledgements	9
	Foreword	11
	What's it all about?	13
1	The Maritime Situation of Jersey in the early 13th Century	15
2	Pirates around the Channel Islands	24
3	St. Peter's Marsh (Goose Green Marsh)	29
4	Living in precarious times: Jersey, 1300-1450	39
5	Two cases of Deodand	52
6	Disaster at St. Ouen	55
7	A brief glimpse of the Maritime History of Jersey	71
8	Privateering: a general history	81
9	Smuggling by Channel Islanders	93
10	Was your Ancestor a Smuggler?	99
11	The Social Ladder in the 17th Century	105
12	Fishing and Agriculture in the 17th Century	119
13	Manufacture and Trade in the 17th Century	129
14	Blake's attack on Jersey, 1651	141
15	Jersey Trade in the late 18th Century	147
16	Jersey Privateers in Napoleonic times	161
17	St. Helier Harbours to the beginning of the 19th Century	171
18	Shipbuilding in Jersey	187
19	Life at sea in the 19th Century	197
20	Land reclamation in Jersey	203
	Postscript	208
	Notes	209
	Bibliography	213
	Index of People	217
	Index of Ships	220
	General Index	222

This book is dedicated to Rita, who proof-read and commented on almost all of these pieces at the times they were originally created. She died fifty-five years after our marriage, in 2004, but would have been so happy to have seen this work.

Acknowledgements

B T Binnington, OBE, former President, States of Jersey Harbours and Airport Committee; Jurat E J M Potter, ISO, former States' Greffier; Jurat R M Bullen, MBE, former Harbourmaster; Capt. C L W Page, RN (Retd.), Director, Naval Historical Branch, Ministry of Defence, Portsmouth; Mr G Drew, former Curator, Société Jersiaise; Miss J Arthur, local historian; Mrs. M-L Backhurst, local historian and members of the Publications Committee of the Société Jersiaise; Mr G Syvret, Photographic Archivist of the Société Jersiase; the Librarians of the Société Jersiaise (now the Lord Coutanche Library) over the period of my adult lifetime; the Librarians, especially of the Reference Section, of the States of Jersey Public Library (now the Jersey Library) over the same period; the Historical Committee (now Section) of the Société Jersiaise.

Because much of this work was written many years ago, the following are no longer with us: Major N V L Rybot, DSO; E F Guiton and Reverend G R Balleine. These three men were the leading lights in the Société Jersiaise for many years, but nevertheless could still give the impression to a teenager that what he said mattered. My interest in the study of local history stems largely from their encouragement.

Mrs S B Le Brocq, former Chief Executive, Jersey Chamber of Commerce; Mr G Vowden, former Registrar, Jersey Shipping Register; Dr G A Body, Senior Lecturer, Weymouth College of Education; Mr P J de Veulle; Mr R Cox, local historian; Mrs J Stevens, local historian; Miss M Syvret, local historian. Finally, my wife, Mrs M J Podger (Rita), who helped make this work possible.

I have little doubt that I have omitted names that should be included, due to the long period over which these works were compiled. To them I offer my genuine apologies.

Foreword

Some years ago a series of public lectures on Jersey's history was started by the History Section of the Société Jersiaise. These lectures, given by members of the Section, were wide-ranging pieces of research. The chairman of the Section remarked that it was a shame that so much work was not published so that it could be enjoyed by a wider audience.

In approaching Alec Podger, one of the Section's longest-serving members and a retired history teacher of considerable experience, we hoped that he would have one or two of his talks still available, which we might be able to include in a publication. It was with considerable delight, however, that we learnt that he had some twenty talks and essays already written up, and it, therefore, seemed quite natural to publish them as a collection. Alec has mainly looked into the very rich maritime history of Jersey over a period of the last thousand years and his research is original and thought-provoking.

The title of this book, which is attributed to Oliver Cromwell, represents the difficult position that Jersey found itself in during the 17th century, being a Royalist stronghold during the English Civil War.

The Société Jersiaise is pleased to be able to publish this book and hopes its contents will be enjoyed by all those interested in the fascinating history of a small island, of more importance than its size might suggest.

Marie-Louise Backhurst

What's it all about?

The following pages are not chapters in a story, they are all individual items. They have been arranged chronologically as far as possible, but can be read in any order. There is also a small amount of repetition, as a talk given after a study will naturally include some of that study, but it is limited and infrequent.

There is no pretence whatever that this book is a history of Jersey. It is almost wholly history, and about Jersey, but it is rather like a wander through a shopping arcade, passing some places unnoticed, hesitating at something that catches one's eye, and spending long in one or two shops of one's choice. It spends time in admiration at the organised way of life of the people in what is known as the Later Middle Ages, tries to find a lost manor-house of the period, and is then found looking on in helpless distress as the Channel Islands become the shuttlecock between England and France during the Hundred Years' War.

Suddenly life becomes so peaceful that it is simply a quick stroll through the Tudor period – no mention of King Henry VIII and only a brief nod towards Queen Elizabeth – before stopping for ages to really find out what life in Jersey was really like at the time of the Stuarts. Then off again after an argument with King William III because he is not allowing things like brandy or tobacco to be smuggled into England!

A quick jaunt through the next century, the eighteenth, when the North Atlantic Ocean is rapidly becoming home from home for Jerseymen, until Napoleon comes on the scene, and the game of shuttlecock begins again, but this time the Islanders, although not quite ready, were prepared to look after themselves – not that they had much choice in the matter.

Apart from one or two sideline visits both during and at the end of this collection of talks and essays there is no more. All of us have varied interests, this shows what interests me most – the Middle Ages, the seventeenth century, and the huge influence that being an island has had on its population, so that ships seem almost always to be in sight.

A P   October 2007

1

The Maritime Situation of Jersey in the early 13th Century

The shape of the island

Why should the very middle of St. Ouen's Bay be called 'Le Port?' It seems to make no sense, but the name is centuries old.

In a document dated 1685 and attributed to Jean Poingdestre, former Lieutenant-Bailiff, he states (in translation):

> It is a well-known fact, and contemporary documents tell us, that the sea has encroached upon the richest part of the soil in the Parish of St. Ouen during the past 350 years.

He goes on to describe a valley 'commencing from l'Etacq and proceeding as far as St. Ouen's Pond, while the land protruded well into the sea.'

And there is an old saying in St. Ouen to the effect that disaster occurred 'when the great bank at Le Port broke'.

The National Meteorological Library has only one record for the English Channel area in the 1300s, and that was 23rd November, 1334, when major flooding occurred all along the south coast of England. As it is well known that strong storms were frequent in the 1300s this very specific date suggests that it was extra special enough to stick in people's memory.

Poingdestre's document, dated 1685, says 'during the past 350 years' (not exactly 350 years ago), and 350 from 1685 is 1335. I am satisfied that the hurricane of November 1334 broke the great bank at Le Port and flooded the l'Etacq valley, leaving a long peninsular running south, which degenerated, probably over a period of several decades, into the reef that we see today.

So what is the point of this story? In the early 1200s, which is the period of this chapter, and until the winter of 1334/5, St. Ouen's Bay was a totally different shape from today. Le Port was not a built harbour as we know the word, but it apparently was a harbour then, a place where boats could be beached safely in normal weather conditions. These conditions were mild, with few storms before the 1330s, when there was a rather sudden and dramatic change.

As for the remainder of the island we know of no sea walls, but sand-dunes sheltered most bays, with semi-tidal estuaries, or mud-flats, at the mouths of streams. There was a large low-lying plain in St. Clement, flooded at extra high tides, which made a useful salt marsh (Samarès), and maybe some parts of the St. Clement/La Rocque reefs were larger and greener islands than today, but we cannot say so for certain.

Who owned the foreshore?
According to GFB De Gruchy, in his book *Medieval Land Tenures in Jersey*, the foreshore belonged in medieval times to the seigneurs of the adjoining fiefs, but the public had ancient right of use. Because of this a seigneur had rights to wreckage on his fief, and while the early situation is unclear, by the 15th century, and probably earlier, he had to have any wreckage guarded and not moved until 'viewed' by the Bailiff as Chief Magistrate, after which everything except perishables was kept for a year and a day to allow a claimant to appear. It was then publicly sold, the money going to the seigneur, partly as one of the profits of his position, and partly as a means of recovering expenses incurred, such as paying a guard. But the king, as duke of Normandy, had all rights to gold and silver, bales or cloaks of scarlet cloth, and hunting hounds if found with the vessel.

Writing in 1957 De Gruchy adds 'The Crown now claims full ownership, including the right to sell and close against the public.' This was disputed by Les Pas Holdings with their contentious but ultimately successful claim for ownership of part of the new reclamation site in St Helier, said at the time to be worth £10,000,000.

The Ecréhous, the Minquiers and the Chausey islands
These groups of islets were all under Jersey administration from very early Norman times, if not before, and, of course, the Ecréhous and

The Maritime Situation of Jersey in the early 13th Century

the Minquiers remain so today. The Chausey islands were administered from Jersey only until 1499, when they were seemingly left to look after themselves, so the French took them over. It is possible, though unproven, that the Jersey authorities had found them too expensive to maintain in money and manpower, for these islands and the Minquiers were often the bases for pirates. While the Minquiers were on the direct route between Jersey and St. Malo, the Chausey Iles were not on a direct sea-lane, and were closer to France, so that, in my view, they could safely be abandoned to the French. Trade with Normandy died temporarily after its conquest by the French in 1204, but soon recovered, mainly because Norman abbeys were still holding lands in Jersey, as they still did in England for generations more, but trade was with the northerly port of Carteret rather than with Granville, which is much more liable to shipping delays unless the wind and tide are in the right direction.

In 1203 the Ecréhous had been granted to the Norman abbey of Ste Marie de Valricher, though remaining a dependency of Jersey, to build a chapel dedicated to God and St. Mary, and a mass to be said every day. It was manned by a prior, a monk and one servant, whose job it was to keep a candle burning at night to warn mariners – clearly a large candle. It is virtually certain that this priory was intended as a 'lighthouse' from the start, administered by the Church, and so able to offer up prayers for the mariners, in addition to the more material safeguard. The fact that it was financially well supported from Jersey, Guernsey and Normandy seems to bear this out. The light remained until the confiscation of alien priories during the mid-16th century.

Naval events

At the period which we are considering no European country had a permanent navy, though these did exist in the Indian Ocean countries. When there was a need for ships to make an overseas attack requisition orders were sent to all ports likely to have vessels large enough to be of use, and these were then taken on a hire basis.

There were two such attacks on the Channel Islands at this time, the first in 1205 when John sent 30 galleys to recover the islands from the French, and the second in 1216 when the French tried to get them back, but were unsuccessful.

What sort of boats or ships did they have?

Primitive men were using sealskin canoes in the area of the Channel Islands before they were islands, but obviously there is no record of when and how men began to build ships in Jersey. Nevertheless the construction of small rowing or sailing boats has been so universal in every part of the world, whether developed or 'savage', as our forefathers would have put it, that they must have been boat-building here several thousand years ago. How else would the substantial prehistoric population of the island have survived for so long? Then, over two thousand years ago, there is no doubt that they received some influence from the Veneti, a maritime tribe inhabiting the western area of modern Brittany, and so, relatively speaking, just around the corner. The Veneti were building vessels for trade with Britain, which had oak planking several inches thick, large leather sails, and iron chains for anchoring, and which even the ships of the Roman Empire did not challenge lightly. (Iron chains did not come into general use in the British navy until the late 18th century!)

Later came the Vikings, who were visiting Jersey well before the tenth century. They certainly knew how to build very fine ships, and once some of them had settled here, as we know that they did, the locals would undoubtedly have learnt from them.

The earliest record of ship building in Jersey that we do have for certain dates from the eleventh century. A certain Wace of Trinity (who is believed by some scholars to be the father or grandfather of Wace, the Jersey poet) is described as *ingenieur charpentier marine*, a shipwright, and this is a term only used in the construction of large vessels, not boats. It is feasible, though unproven, that Wace the shipwright helped to build some of the ships used by William, Duke of Normandy, on his voyage to conquer England – maybe just one or two – for after the conquest William granted him a small fiefdom on the north coast in the parish of St. John, which must have been a reward for services rendered.

In October 1241, and again in May 1244, the Warden of the Isles was ordered to build galleys out of the income of the Channel Islands, which clearly implies that experienced shipwrights were to hand. Galleys, using oarsmen as well as sails, were common in the Mediterranean, where the sea was normally fairly calm, but the much rougher seas in northern waters meant that they were of little use except to carry troops across the short distance of the Channel in a hurry, when the weather allowed. They were therefore uncommon, and usually built to order when required.

Harbours

In medieval times built harbours were generally unnecessary, as most vessels were small enough to come close inshore at high tide, drop anchor, and as the tide receded they were left high and dry on the beach, where their cargo was unloaded into carts. This was still common practice in out-of-the-way places right up to the end of the nineteenth century, and even in the 1930s I can remember seeing vessels using their own spars and winches for unloading, though in harbour. In this case it was simply to save the cost of hiring a crane with its crew.

Any bay with a gently-sloping beach made a suitable harbour unless the approach was too rocky, while others still acquired the name of 'port', 'portelet', or 'havre' because they were sheltered anchorages, though they may not always have been satisfactory for beaching.

The population has been reliably estimated at about 11,000 at the beginning of the thirteenth century, which is, of course, the period under review. This was roughly 200 to the square mile; more than double the ratio of 90 to the square mile at that time in England, and the ratio has not changed much since! About 3,000 of these earned their living either fishing or in the fish trade, gutting, salting and packing, with very substantial quantities exported annually. There must have been hundreds of small boats using the various bays around the island, while larger vessels were used to keep contact with England, though most of these were not locally owned.

There is strong circumstantial evidence that St. Helier was a port by the year 1200, and probably well before then, as an abbey had been built on l'Islet in the mid-12th century. This was at first an important foundation, with strong connections outside of the island, and it would have created a fair amount of trade in the small town. In addition, St. Helier had the right to a weekly market, which would not have been the case unless it was a town of some importance, and this can only have come about by it being a trading centre, which of necessity involved it being a port.

King John is said to have instituted two taxes in the Channel Islands, and as this statement was made shortly after his reign there is no reason to doubt it.

The first was a tax on every vessel mooring or anchoring within the limits of the island, known as the 'Great Custom'. In 1331 this was 27/- for vessels over 40 tons, 22/6 under 40 tons, and it was estimated at that time at 9 livres per annum, which would imply 6 or 7 large vessels, while Guernsey, with far better harbour facilities and fewer offshore reefs, had over a hundred vessels a year, the great majority of these being involved in the Gascony wine-trade.

There was also the 'Little Custom', an export tax on livestock, except on animals going to England, and which again, in 1331, was 12d per horse, ox or cow; 2d per pig or sheep; 1d per lamb or piglet.

This was giving an annual return by the end of the century of around £11, (240d. = £1) showing a reasonably large export trade of animals, presumably to Normandy and Brittany rather than elsewhere.

Fisheries

The seas around the islands were abundant in fish, particularly mackerel and conger, and gave rise during this period to a flourishing fishing industry. The evidence of the Close Rolls seems to suggest that the men of the islands caught the fish, and Gascony and English vessels visited the islands to supply the salt necessary for curing purposes, and to buy the dried fish. King John, on the 6th September 1199, granted to one Vitalis de Villa the sum of fifty pounds of the money of Anjou taken from the revenue of two *baleinae* (whalers) in the port of Biarritz, rather than the *eperquerie* revenue taken from a drying place of fish in the islands of Guernsey and Jersey. *Eperquerie* was a universal tax, peculiar to the Channel Islands, being the right of the seigneur owning a creek or port. The Crown therefore only received tax through its own fiefs and the Demesne.

A check on the map of the boundaries of the fiefs (which can be found on the back end-pages of *Old Jersey Houses*, Vol. II) shows that the Fief Le Roi held about one-third of the coastline of Jersey, almost all of this being on the south and east. Tying this in with the statement of the king's evaluation of the *eperquerie*, which relates to a part-year income only (Easter to Michaelmas), it is clear that the fisheries were very extensive.

According to Falle, writing centuries later, 'The seas about these islands might be called the Kingdom of Congers, so great is the quantity taken at all seasons, some weighing from 30 to 40lbs.'

In 1247 strict regulations were enforced relating to the fisheries. Absolute freedom of trade was granted to the islanders to sell their goods, alive or dead, in Normandy or elsewhere, (though, of course, this was now a foreign country) except in congers during the time of *eperqueries*, which extended from Easter to Michaelmas. (Congers were then considered a Royal delicacy.) At the time of *eperqueries* the owners, namely the seigneurs (but in the case of the Royal fiefs the 'farmers' of the tax), had the right to purchase all catches except enough for one day's food for the fisherman's family, and those considered too small, at an agreed price. If the price was disputed, 'market inspectors' were brought in to settle the matter. At other times the fishermen pleased themselves as to the disposal of their catch, retailing it personally or selling to a merchant.

But you will notice from this that they were completely free to do what they wished with regard to the sale of mackerel, which were also caught in very large quantities.

Pilgrims

There may not have been annual holidays for workers in medieval times, though there were numerous Saints' Days which were treated as 'Holy Days', but that did not debar anyone who could collect together enough money from going on a pilgrimage. That could be anything from one to three months for a local journey, to far more than a year for a pilgrimage to the Holy Land, and with the Church having so much power even grasping lords of the manor could not easily refuse permission.

From *Lettres Close* (the Close Rolls), dated 8th June 1213:

> The King at Rochester orders Adam du Port to allow to go in liberty whither they will the pilgrims on a ship from the Isles which has docked at Portsmouth, and hand the ship over to Nicholas, a man of Philip d'Aubigny [Warden of the Isles] at whose request it has been re-routed to the Isles.

These folk were almost certainly on their way to Canterbury, to the tomb of Thomas à Becket, who had been murdered during their lifetime, it being the centre of pilgrimage in England during that century. On board would most probably have been one or two of the richer locals, with an offering of an ounce of gold or a jewel, in the hope that it would be added to the tomb, already ablaze enough for a king's ransom. There would also be a number of peasant farmers/fishermen and their wives, who had saved enough to have the journey of a lifetime – for money was not in quite such short supply as many school books would have us believe – and combining religious and holiday experiences in one. Even today pilgrims to Lourdes and other places are likely to include one or two local coach trips in their visit. Lastly, often through the combined generosity of neighbours, the church, and the master of the vessel, the blind, the crippled, the infertile, any who thought that the Lord would solve their problems if they could pray at such a holy place, might be found a place on board.

On the other hand, but a few years later, most Channel Islanders went on pilgrimage to the tomb of St. James at Santiago de Compostella in northern Spain, and whilst a few would have gone the whole way by sea this was unusual, as that journey involved crossing the notorious Bay of Biscay. Consequently they usually went to St. Malo, and from there walked the rest of the journey. Pilgrims had a scallop shell in their hat-band, to show that they were not merely beggars, for this allowed them to beg if necessary without being arrested – and the shell came in useful as a dinner-plate as well!

Pirates

Norse and other pirates were still around, though less frequent than they had been in the 9th and 10th centuries, but Eustache le Moine, acting for the French but considered a pirate, held Sark for some months in 1214, causing much trouble.

The Minquiers in particular were the haunt of pirates throughout the centuries. It is known that there were five separate gangs hiding there as late as the time of Elizabeth I, though they were not the Spanish Main variety, but petty criminals in small boats, who, with a generous supply of weapons, would be able to rob any boat of about their own size.

Conclusion
De Gruchy suggests:

> That the islanders should combine as they did [towards the end of the 13th century] in order to increase or maintain their ancient rights and customs, may result from their previous training in co-operation and association. They were for the most part fisher-farmers. In their dependence on the sea, co-operation was necessary not only in the ownership of the boat and the taking of the catch, but also in the regulations for the sale of the surplus to the merchants. A certain organisation was bound to evolve amidst this fishing community; and their subsequent independent constitutional government may have had its foundations laid in the domestic organisation of a fishing race.

Farmer/fishermen throughout Europe were much less dependent on manorial control than were inland villagers, and it seems that life around the island at that time was not that dissimilar from that of two or three generations ago. They were poorer and lacked our medical knowledge, but in Jersey boats were being built, while harbour dues were probably as much of an irritation then as they always will be. Fishing was on a substantial scale, to the point that both merchants and market inspectors were necessary, and the processes involved in that trade were still familiar to the 19th century Newfoundland and Gaspé fishermen. Even a form of tourism was in existence, though in a reverse direction to the present day. They did not have boats with engines – we do not have piracy – but it is nevertheless surprising that after eight hundred years the differences that most of us were led to believe existed were not so greatly different after all!

* * *

I am indebted to the work of two former members of the Société Jersiaise, namely GFB de Gruchy and Charles Stevens. De Gruchy wrote *Medieval Land Tenures in Jersey*, and Charles Stevens translated the ancient records *Lettres Close* from Latin to English, without which I would have been stumped.

Société Jersiaise Lunchtime Lecture, 2004

2

Pirates around the Channel Islands

Piracy is simply any substantial act done at sea which would be illegal if done on land, such as robbery and/or murder, and in international areas, where no individual nation has control.

It was common in western Europe from about the 5th century (if not before) right through until the late 17th century, when it was almost completely eliminated in that area. It then moved to those areas where European ships would be more vulnerable, such as the West Indies, where Haiti was a pirate republic for over forty years at that time, and to Madagascar in the Indian Ocean.

Nowadays it is largely the China Seas and the Philippines that are still troubled in this manner.

In Europe, during the 11th to 16th centuries in particular, it was quite common for local lords, and sometimes great lords also, to be the actual financiers behind pirate vessels, while the crew frequently consisted of ordinary sailors who had found themselves unemployed, with no income, and who returned to such employment when opportunity arose. Many were simply ignorant and uneducated, as spectacularly illustrated by the 16th century crew of an English ship, who, upon capturing a prize, found that it was only carrying a cargo of tin. They were so incensed that they threw the lot overboard. It was not tin, it was solid silver!

What about the Channel Islands?

Probably the best way to tell this particular story is in the form of a chronology:

c.1100 'Multitudes of pirates around these coasts.'

1200 Sark was captured by French pirates led by Eustache le Moine, who was a famous sailor at that time. It was recaptured the next year, after Eustache had been defeated in a sea-battle by Philip d'Aubigny, Warden of the Isles, who had him beheaded on his own deck.

1371, June A Portuguese ship called the *Sainte Marie*, with 120 barrels of wine on board was captured at sea near the Channel Islands by John Cosynet and others of the said isles, and they sold seventy-one of the barrels, and also the ship, to John Le Clerk at Southampton. The owners, when they found out a long time afterwards, complained to the king, who ordered an enquiry. By then there was no wine left, and the ship had sunk at sea in a storm. All that was left were a few bits and pieces of the rigging.

So Jersey and Guernsey men were not always innocent either!

1409, November An order from the king to the bailiffs of Southampton and other south coast towns,

> ... to arrest Sir John Trevele and all goods stolen by him, and to hold him in custody. He lately robbed Jersey and Guernsey merchants at sea, despite the king's safe conduct [a special document which they were carrying], and took some of their goods to Southampton.

1412, August Richard Duneville, a Normandy fisherman, was pardoned by the king of France, Charles VI. He had been on a boat which was captured by Jerseymen, the rest of the crew had been ransomed, but he had no money. He was detained in various prisons and tormented for six years, after which he was compelled to put to sea on a Jersey vessel as one of the crew, but they were captured by Guillemin Sequin of Harfleur and his crew and taken to St. Malo, where Richard was in danger of being charged with treasonable conduct until he obtained the pardon.

1480, February 'On a petition from the inhabitants King Edward [IV] has obtained confirmation from the Pope that all pirates in the area of the Channel Islands, whether captured or at large, shall be forthwith excommunicated, and subject to anathemisation, eternal malediction, confiscation, etc., etc.'

This was published in all the important towns on both sides of the Channel, in England and in France.

Three pirates were hanged in Jersey at about this time.

From 1483 to 1689 the Channel Islands were officially neutral, even in time of war, so that the amount of shipping trade increased substantially, and so too did piracy.

1455-1485 During this period of disorder (the Wars of the Roses) most of the principal seigneurs of the islands openly practised piracy.

1549 Henry Cornish, Lieut.-Governor, was dismissed from his post for aiding and abetting local pirates, and the next year Barnabé Le Quesne was hanged in chains at Noirmont while his English accomplice was hanged at Rozel.

1556-1603 During the reign of Elizabeth there were no less than five pirate ships using the Chausey Islands as their headquarters, and pirates also occupied Sark, which was uninhabited, on more than one occasion. It has steep cliffs on all sides, and so it was very difficult for anyone to recapture. But in the end Helier De Carteret, Seigneur of Saint Ouen, got permission from Queen Elizabeth to take over the island, and landed forty Jersey families there, so that it was no longer uninhabited, and could defend itself.

Very sadly, one ship that was carrying children to join their parents, who were now safely in Sark, struck on the reef of rocks between Jersey and Sark, and all of the children were drowned. From then on sailors began to say the Lord's Prayer as they passed that reef, which is why the name Paternosters has stuck to it ever since.

1556-1660 Some time during this period, though I cannot remember the dates, an English ship anchored off St. Aubin (St. Aubin's harbour was not built at that time). The crew got friendly with the crew of a foreign ship alongside, and then one day they threw all the foreigners overboard, cut the rigging of the ship so that it could not sail, stole its cargo and sailed away.

1562, August The Governor, Sir Hugh Paulet, and some other officials waiting in the Isle of Wight, had to have a navy ship to bring them to

Jersey, 'they being delayed because of great numbers of pirates around the Channel Islands.' The captain of the ship was ordered to take more than the usual fourteen days provisions, and capture as many as he could without going out of his way.

1599, May 'A Jerseyman' (meaning a Jersey ship) 'and a Dutchman' captured by four small Spanish ships lying off the south coast of England, and flying the English flag.

1625 'Trade has almost completely stopped due to the numbers of pirates.'

1625, October The Lieut.-Governor, Sir Philip de Carteret, sent a letter to the Lord Admiral of England asking for an anti-piracy patrol to be stationed in the Channel Islands, '... as the waters are infested with pirates.' He received a reply nine months later, (May, 1626) saying that they were getting a ship ready for this job. Sir Philip then wrote in December 1626 to say that it had still not arrived!

Two ships finally arrived in July 1627, nearly two years after the first request!

1631-1632 Ten 'Lion's Whelps' (naval ships specially built to chase and capture pirates roaming in the English Channel), reported that no pirates had been seen for the past year. They had been scared off! But a couple of months later they captured a French pirate ship, captained by an Englishman, which was roaming around the Channel Islands. They also reported that there were three others, only small vessels, 'which go so extraordinarily well with sails and oars that they cannot be caught', especially as they could dodge in amongst the rocks which were too unsafe for the naval ships to follow.

1632, June The pirates were again so dangerous that Sir Philip Carteret, Lieut-Governor, and Sir Peter Osborne, Lieut-Governor of Guernsey, had to ask for a Lion's Whelp to take them from Portsmouth to the islands. They finally got to Jersey on the 26th August!

1635, September A Jersey ship on its way home from Newfoundland was captured by six 'Turkish' pirate ships (at that time all Arab races were called Turks) as it was nearing the English Channel, but the master of the ship pretended that it was a French ship (Jerseymen normally spoke both Jersey-French and French) so the pirates took a few things but let the ship go, saying that they were friends with France, and that they had twenty ships waiting for the English ships coming from Newfoundland. In fact they later captured nearly all the English ships, and took their crews to Morocco in North Africa to be sold as slaves, or ransomed if they could pay enough to get free.

1639, June   Nicolle Effard returned from his voyage to 'Turkey' (Morocco) at the request of the States to rescue those poor seamen who had been taken slaves by the Turks. He left 4th August 1636 and rescued seventeen, including his brother Pierre.

1639   Petition of Marie Le Ruez, wife of Nathaniel Vibert, to the King. Her husband, being on board a boat bound from Jersey to St. Malo, was captured by a French pirate, which then roved about the coast of Jersey, and landed some men ashore, when they forced her husband to go with them to plunder the house of Heliary Le Mountais, near the shore. They then left him on another island (one of the reefs?) after much cruel and barbarous treatment. Her husband then coming back into Jersey was arrested by the Saint Brelade's police, and put in prison, where he remains in danger to lose his life, the law being such, if His Majesty's pardon be not extended to him.

★ ★ ★

1905   Captain Morrison, a Jerseyman, was master of a ship which was searching for pirate treasure on Cocos Island, about 300 miles west of Panama. Mr. G Carter, also a Jerseyman, was third officer on the ship. They had to give up after an accident on the island, when a quantity of dynamite blew up, and many men were injured. Another ship continued the search, and this was commanded by Captain Mallet, still another Jerseyman! To the best of my knowledge no-one ever found anything.

3

St. Peter's Marsh (Goose Green Marsh)

Laying-up harbour and battleground?

This marsh, at the seaward end of St. Peter's Valley, is largely hidden from view by the ribbon development of houses along the coast road between Bel Royal and Beaumont. There is, however, a good view of it from the public footpath known as *Le Perquage* which crosses it from the coast road to the inner end of Rue du Craslin, or Sandybrook Lane. Nowadays, though it floods occasionally, it looks much like green fields anywhere, except for a large area covered by stacks of scaffold poles and girders, on the site rented by the Jersey Steel Company. It is hardly worth the name of a marsh any longer.

Three centuries ago it was very different. John Speed published an atlas in 1631, which includes a map of Jersey dated 1610, though it is not known who drew it up (see map overleaf). This was the first to show a truly recognisable outline to the Island as we now know it, but it also shows a large tidal inlet where the marsh now stands. Inlets are also shown at Le Dicq and at Samarès, both in St. Clement, and both well documented as areas subject to flood at high spring tides. It is likely that the lack of documentation for this marsh is simply because the area was relatively uninhabited when compared with the St. Clement areas.

These details, incidentally, suggests that whoever drew this map was in the island at a time of flood tide, for though previous maps were much more rudimentary none had shown any hint of these areas in such a fashion. The earliest maps (14th and 15th centuries) show the island as no more than a round or oval, which later became more like a holly leaf, but it is not until Popinjay's 'Platte' of 1563 that we find any vague semblance to the outline as of today.

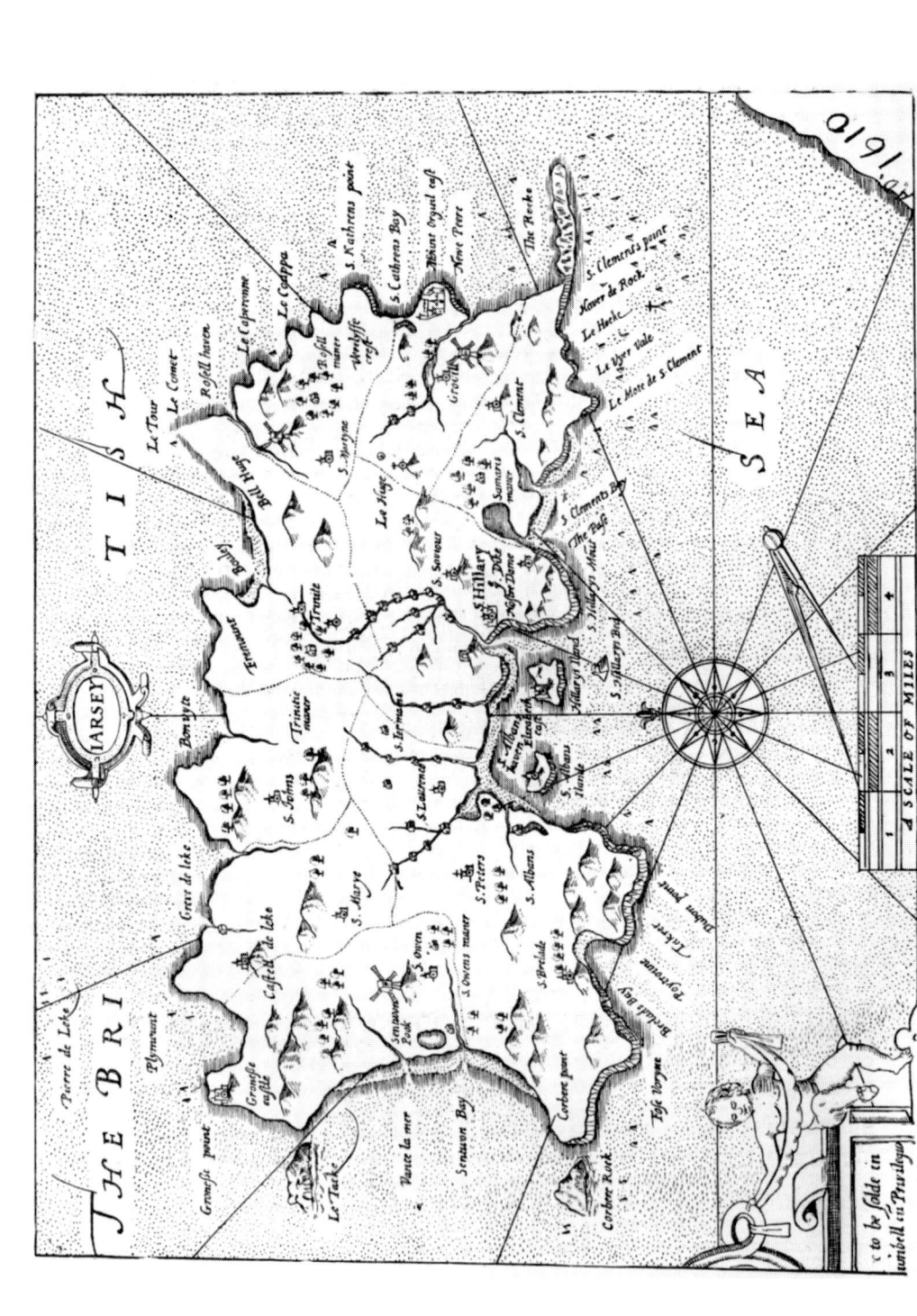

St Peter's Marsh (Goose Green Marsh)

Roger de Carteret, who has had considerable experience in sailing small boats around the coasts of Europe, has allowed me to put forward a theory of his in relation to this marsh, of which he is one of the Tenants. In his view the area has been gradually silting up over the centuries with soil brought down the stream through the valley, and would have been a muddy creek subject to flooding at high spring tides in medieval times, though not normally open to the sea. He therefore believes that it was probably used by fishermen to haul their boats up on to the mud-flats there as a lying-up place during winter, where they would have been well sheltered.

Another pointer to the fact that this was a semi-tidal area in earlier times is in the name 'Sandybrook', which covers the western side of the marsh. This can only imply that the brook ran for a considerable way through a sandy area, which would be the case if the region was frequently tidal, but not otherwise.

This led me to wonder about the medieval chapel of St. Nicholas, which is reputed to have existed in the vingtaine of that name on the high land above the marsh, and to have been a leper-house. There was another chapel of St. Nicholas on the heights above Gorey, which was also a leper-house, and which, from evidence of its finances would appear to have acted as a lighthouse, since the amount of money for candles seems very excessive unless they were used for this purpose.[1] Might not the St. Peter's leper-house have also been a lighthouse, to guide ships safely into the creek? Roger disputes this, on the basis that it is improbable that the creek would have been sufficiently tidal to classify as a harbour. On the other hand St. Nicholas is the patron saint of children and of sailors. He is not, as far as I can trace, the patron saint of lepers, so this problem remains unsolved.

An anonymous map shows a straight line leading inland across the marsh area, but ending before it reaches the stream running down St. Peter's Valley, which is the boundary between the parishes of St. Lawrence and St. Peter. This map can be dated at the late 1600s, for the straight line is the 'Canal Sir Edward', as named on subsequent maps. Sir Edward de Carteret was granted all of the perquages and waste lands in 1663 by Charles II in recognition of the loyalty and

Opposite: Map of Jersey, 1610, showing clear tidal haven at Goose Green Marsh (John Speed)

help of the de Carteret family both to him and to his father during the Civil War. The stream here, and therefore the perquage also, ran around the west side of the marsh, but Sir Edward exchanged this land for land in the centre of the marsh, and presumably then had the canal dug in order to drain the marsh. There was a spate of canal building for drainage in England during the reigns of Charles II and James II, while in Jersey the canal at Samarès was also dug at this time.

The map also shows the Havre des Pas pier, and no other in St. Helier. This was the only pier in use at St. Helier for large vessels in the 1600s, but it is mentioned as 'decayed' by 1698, and Meade's map of 1737 shows the new harbour at the south-western corner of the Mont de la Ville, the Havre Neuf, (which was still under construction) but does not show the Havre des Pas pier at all. Consequently our map can be dated at later than 1663 and not later than about 1700.

Dumaresq's map of 1685 (see opposite) also shows this canal, but with its northern end joined to the stream. It also shows the northern end of the western section of the stream joined to the canal, but as though originating from the canal. This seems incorrect, as this section, flowing around the west side of the marsh, then has both ends in water, the other end finishing in the sea, unless the intention was that it would dry up, but act as an overflow in times of heavy rainfall.

The marsh is nowadays known as St. Peter's Marsh, but when the stream ran around the western side the whole of it would have been in St. Lawrence, and it is therefore reasonable to suggest that it was originally St. Lawrence Marsh.

Assuming this, the story of the marsh now takes a new twist, for it is mentioned in the well-known legend of La Hougue Bie. A dragon was haunting St. Lawrence Marsh, and the local inhabitants sent to Normandy for help. A knight by the name of Paisnel, from Hambye, came to fight the dragon and succeeded in killing it, but was himself seriously wounded. His manservant seized the opportunity to kill him where he lay, went back to Hambye and told the knight's lady that her husband had been slain in the conflict, but that it was his dying wish that she should marry the servant who had been so dear to him. Somewhat unwillingly she felt obliged to obey her husband's last wish, and did so, but soon discovered the deception when the man cried out

Opposite: Dumaresq's Map of Jersey, 1685

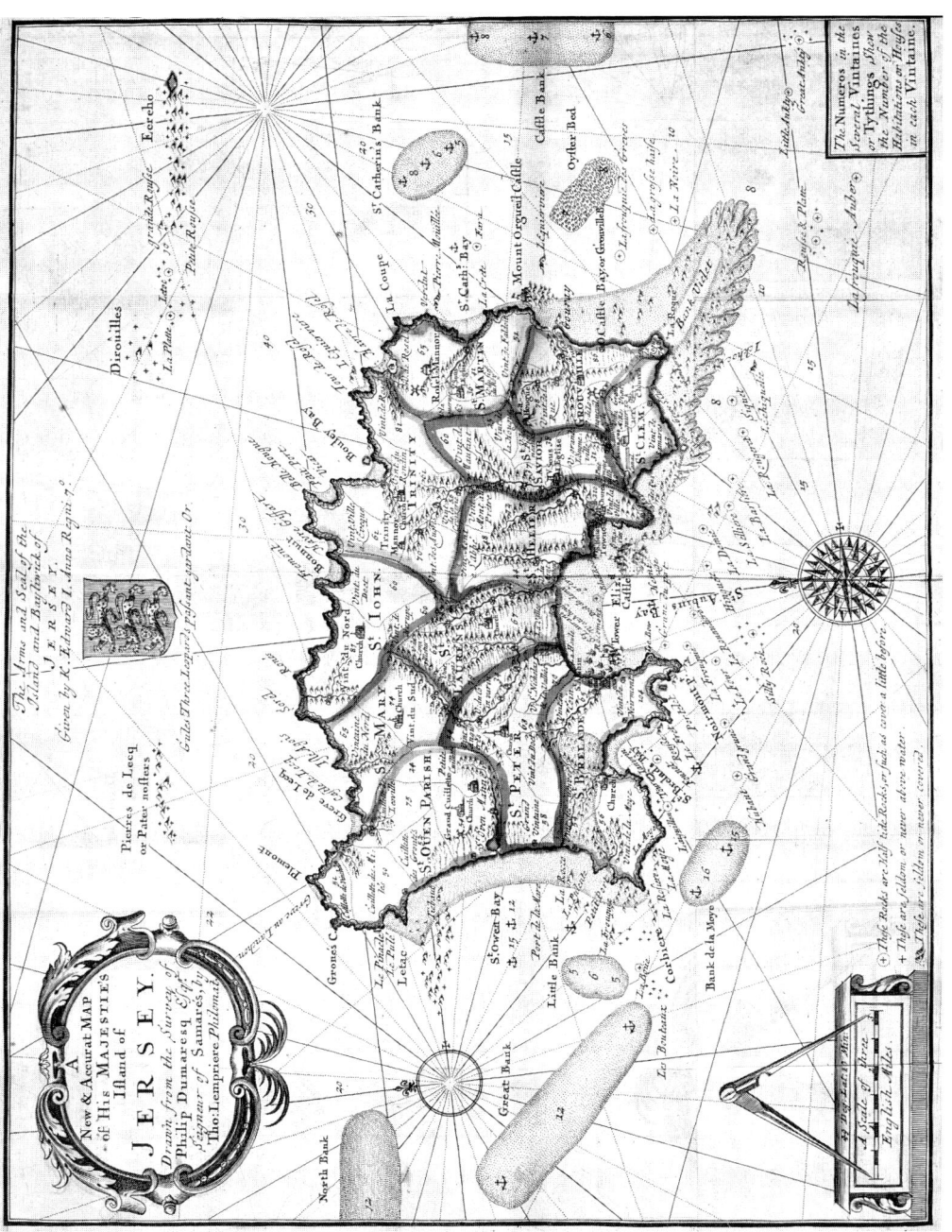

in his sleep. He was tried, confessed, and was hanged. Subsequently she had a great mound built over her husband's grave in Jersey, so that she could see it from her home in Normandy.

Such is the legend of La Hougue Bie. The mound is known to pre-date the age of knights by many centuries, but it is generally accepted by scholars that the numerous tales in Europe of dragons being fought by knights has an historical basis, the dragon being in fact a pagan chief. The word 'knight', though very ancient, does not seem to have been in common use until the late 10th or early 11th century. Viking raids in the western end of the English Channel were particularly serious between the years 980 and 1000AD, an era of Christianity versus paganism. It is known that a Paisnel was one of the knights accompanying William when he invaded England in 1066, so it is not improbable that the action referred to in this story, if it has an historical basis, could belong to this time.

The legend had puzzled me for many years. The majority of these stories tell of dragons 'roaming the countryside', but this one, which can be traced back as far as the early Tudor period, specifically mentions St. Lawrence Marsh. Why? Roger's theory appears to have answered the question for me, for if this was an occasional tidal creek in medieval times it could well have been even more tidal the further back in time we go. A Viking ship looking for a suitable landing-site would have headed for just such a creek, where it would have quickly been hidden from view, and safe from storms. A dragon-headed ship, it would not take many generations for the tale of 'the chief of the dragon-ship' to be abbreviated to 'the dragon-chief', and so to 'the dragon'.

If this story has any basis in truth, (and why should it not have?) then what may remain under the present-day marsh-land? It seems very probable that some small remains of medieval boats may be there, but as for a Viking ship, that would be a different matter. Viking chiefs were often buried in their ship, but these were, so to speak, 'state funerals', not the result of a raid in foreign territory. If the chief was killed some of his men may have escaped in their boat, for although the legends only talk of knights killing dragons they would clearly have been the leaders of small bands of men who attacked groups of Vikings. If they were all killed it is much more likely that the boat was dismantled and its planks re-used by local inhabitants, unless they set fire to it on the spot. Under that soil there may still be, perhaps, some signs of an early battle. A Viking sword or two, maybe a helmet or a shield?

If anything of this nature is ever found the legend of La Hougue Bie may be turned from legend into history, but even so, it will never lose its fascination as a tale worth the telling.

NOTE: This article was prepared for publication, but there were still one or two points needing discussion, including whether this area or the entrance to Waterworks Valley was the St. Lawrence Marsh mentioned in the legend, when Roger died, in early middle age. As you will see, he had a great love of Jersey and its history, as well as of life, and his death was a great blow to everyone who knew him.

It was therefore not published, but I think it not unreasonable to do so now, unchanged, but with his draft comments attached, thus giving the two points of view. His widow, Mary de Carteret, was pleased to agree to its publication:

Vale Farm
St. Peter

Thank you for your draft on the Marais de St. Pierre, which I found of great interest. I want to offer a series of suggestions, mainly to change the emphasis of what you have written, and perhaps the easiest way of doing so is by offering comments paragraph by paragraph, for if I try to redraft sections of your text I suspect that the different styles will be too obvious. Recently I had the opportunity of walking the boundaries with our lawyers, and large sections of the ancient perimeter wall can still be seen. The Germans did much damage, and traces of their structures still remain.

First paragraph: I think that it is worth mentioning that the marsh is the commune or marais for the tenants of the Fief de la Reine in the Vingtaine of St. Nicolas, and some eighty houses share the rights in it. Unusually, the Bailiff by virtue of his office is a Tenant, and is paid his 'bonus' each year. This present Bailiff chairs the assemblies of the Tenants.

Second paragraph: I cannot help but wonder if 'the lack of documentation' relative to the other areas does not follow on from the fact that the marsh is part of the royal fief, more firmly managed perhaps than the lesser fiefs. The special position of the Bailiff might point this way.

Third paragraph: I would suggest 'spring' rather than 'flood' tides.
Fourth paragraph: I would prefer to be described simply as an experienced small-boat sailor - I am horribly conscious that much of the coast of Europe remains unvisited by me – and much of the rest I have seen only hazily on the horizon! I want to suggest a different text following 'In his view…':

…the streams draining from the valleys will have always gullied through the low rim of dunes to reach the sea. Nowadays, of course, the main road and its ribbon of houses occupy and obscure that ridge, whilst the streams are hidden in culverts underneath. Roger suggests that in earlier times the situation may have been quite mobile, with spring tides flooding through the gap in the coastal dunes to inundate the marsh, whilst sometimes storms and the sweep of tide round the Bay might have closed it off, causing the stream water to back up over the marsh until there was enough pressure to scour out a new outlet, perhaps in a slightly different position. Often it must have been possible on a spring tide to float quite a large vessel into this creek. The practical effect of all this might well have been to provide a vital winter refuge for those boats which were too large to drag above the tide line with a couple of horses, not a harbour in the modern sense, but rather in the manner of the mud-berths among saltings that are such a feature of many English estuaries.

Sorry, Alec, despite my best intention I've offered you a chunk of text. Needs honing, though.

Fifth paragraph: I had never given a second thought to the name Sandybrook. But why in English? Would that suggest the area taking it's name from a house, itself perhaps a product of the Victorian fashion for English names [like 'Vale Farm'!]. By then the 'sandy' description might well have owed more to romance than fact. [We know, incidentally, that the Marsh was extensively drained in late Victorian times – Frances le Sueur in her 'Flora' mentions plants that were recorded before those drainage improvements, but not afterwards.]. Note also how far inland 'Sandybrook' is.

Sixth paragraph: My other doubt about the chapel is one of location. *Jersey Place-Names (JPN)* offers a possible site in a field which I own, Clos Laurens (p.742), based I think on a suggestion made by my late father to Joan Stevens. I have heard a site just to the north of this field, the property now called Manleys, also suggested, more on instinctive than learned grounds. It does seem reasonable to suggest that the site may have been within a stone's throw of La Croix de Nicolas, the junction better known now as 'Oak Walk.' [I have another field, p 731, Clos de Devant in *JPN*, which is in part more correctly called Clos de Nicolas.] This area is well back from the brow of the high land overlooking the Marais, and a 'lighted chapel window', indeed the chapel itself, would be quite invisible from the foreshore or the sea. Nor, as you say, would there have been a 'harbour' as such to require the facility. But do you remember the quotation that I produced? It is from *The Encircled Sea*, by Sarah Arenson, the book of the Channel Four series. 'Before lighthouses were built, most ports were marked by an elevated area, topped by a statue or temple, dedicated first to Astarte or Poseidon, then later to Mary, Aghios Elias or St Nicholas.'[p.170]. Again, [p.172], 'St. Nicholas is another guardian St. of marine fishermen [as well as thieves and children]. The vicissitudes of his transformation from a martyred bishop to Santa Claus are a fascinating theme to follow.'

Roger de Carteret

Written but publication witheld, 2002

Drawing of Mont Orgueil in the 14th century (NV L Rybot)

4

Living in precarious times: Jersey, 1300-1456 AD

Introduction
Those of you who are familiar with Jersey history will not find any new facts in this work, but I felt that maybe looking at things through a different window might at least stimulate some extra thought on how and why we have acquired the status which we enjoy today in the Channel Islands.

At the time that we are going to hear about the map of France was quite different to that of today. It was much smaller. Normandy had earlier been taken from the kings of England and added to the French Crown possessions, but the kings of England still ruled Aquitaine and Gascony, a very large region in the south around Bordeaux which had been acquired by judicious marriages, and the finest wine-producing area of Europe. Brittany also was not French but ruled by its own dukes, who were relatively rich and powerful. Sometimes they were allied to the King of England, at other times they were antagonists.

Therefore, when Normandy was lost, it became imperative that the kings of England hung on to the Channel Islands, since without them there was often nowhere safe for the merchant ships to shelter between Bordeaux and Southampton or London, and the wine trade from Bordeaux was one of the two principal sources of the king's wealth, the other being the export of wool to northern Europe. Guernsey had the better harbour, in that it had deep water and was sheltered from the prevailing winds, and so St. Peter Port was far more important as a harbour than anywhere in Jersey for hundreds of years, but its security depended on Jersey not being in French hands. Gorey Castle and Castle Cornet were built to ensure that these islands would remain as safe refuges for the vessels carrying that profitable trade, not for the protection of the islands' inhabitants. They were given some freedom to rule their own lives in order to keep them loyal, but in any case this was something which could not easily be done from England at that time.

The French realised the value of the possession of the islands as a naval base. They knew that their failure to bring the islands under subjection, unlike the rest of Normandy, was due to lack of naval strength, and it is not surprising if they clung to the hope that some day they might be able to capture them. Once taken, it would not only be easier to attack English ships, or maybe England itself, it would also be much easier to conquer the wine regions, as the English would have no base to work from except in England itself, too far away.

The Story

From now on quite a few dates will have to be given, but don't think in terms of school learning, or even of normal adult reading. Think instead in terms of three generations of one imaginary family, grandfather, father and son. If each lived to about sixty, which was more common than we may think, (it was the death rate among infants that brought the average age down to about forty) and they each had offspring born when they were about fifty, which although unusual is also quite possible, then what happened to them will cover the period of this talk. You should at the same time think in terms of grandmother, mother and daughter, but you then have to overlook the possibility of births at fifty. But for reasons which will become obvious, and with no sexual bias, I shall in general be referring to 'he' rather than 'she'.

Population

We know the approximate size of the population of Jersey in 1331, for in that year every house had to pay a shilling hearth tax, and 1,865 shillings were collected. Some people were exempt from this tax, so that there must have been at least 2,000 houses in the Island, and if one allows an average of six persons to a house the population cannot have been less than 12,000.

So what did happen during the lives of these three generations? Although the title of the work gives 1300-1450 as the period covered, both ends are in fact a bit flexible. Grandfather, for instance, had been born at the end of the 13th century, in 1290.

1295

We know very little about French attempts to take the islands during the 13th century, after John's loss of Normandy in 1204, but it seems probable that there were several. We do know of one. In a petition sent to King Edward I the islanders say that in 1295 'The body of our Lord was hacked down and spat upon. The images were smashed with swords and given to the flames. The chalices were destroyed and taken away. The women and girls were taken by force from the Churches. The men and women were killed 1,500 in number. The houses were burnt and the corn; whereby we have nothing to eat. Our money and all our other chattels were carried off. Of the chasubles and the vestments, trappings for horses were made, and when the horses had served their purpose they were hamstrung' (in terms of the present population that would be about 11,000 men and women killed within only one or two days.)

And in another petition:

Sir, you had mills in the said island which were burnt and destroyed during this war, together with all our goods; your bailiffs wish to make us rebuild them, but Sir, we have nothing to do it with. Wherefore we pray you that you will command the said bailiffs that they rebuild the same and we will do the services as we did before.

1335 Bruce

In 1335 there was another attack by David Bruce, the young Scots king, who had been driven by the English from his throne. He fled to France and collected a fleet, with French help. A proclamation of Edward III says that 'David Bruce, with other Scots and their adherents, has attacked Jersey and Guernsey, inhumanly committing arson, murder and divers other atrocities' – and this was to become only too frequent in the immediate future, for two years later (1337) saw the start of the Hundred Years' War. In that same year another document from King Edward III states that '... the French have often lately attacked the isles.' Note the use of the word 'often'.

Militia

The king also ordered 'all his faithful peoples of the islands' to be levied for war. There is some argument as to whether there was already a militia in being or whether this began it, but every man from 16 to 60 was bound to serve. This confirms that 60 was not an uncommon age to achieve. If, as we have said, the population was somewhere around 12,000, then we can assume that the number of men available for this duty was about 3,000, but it must be obvious that at least initially a considerable proportion of these would be armed with nothing much more than whatever farming implement they could bring from home. So what did our grandfather and his neighbours have to face?

1338 Behuchet

Less than twelve months after the declaration of war there began a series of attempts by the French to capture the island, the first being in 1338, when an Admiral of France by the name of Béhuchet, '... on the morrow after the Annunciation, invaded the Island with a great host, and burnt every blade of corn and all the houses.' (At that period corn was the principal crop). He then besieged Gorey castle for at least six months, but failed to capture it, so instead went and captured Guernsey, including Castle Cornet, and also Alderney and Sark. (Gorey castle was not known as Mont Orgueil until the mid-15th century). We know that there was some military resistance, but it sounds as though the number of French – who would have been mainly professional soldiers – was far too great for serious opposition.

1339 Bertrand

The next year, 1339, Robert Bertrand, Marshal of France 'with a multitude of barons and notables to the number of about 8,000, arrived in 17 Genoese galleys and 35 ships of Normandy.' (An army of 8,000 then would be about equivalent to an invading force of 60,000 today, or roughly twice as many soldiers per head of population as were here during the German Occupation):

> They landed and summoned us to parley. We made answer that while ten men were alive in it, the Castle would not surrender. Whereupon they returned to their ships. On the Monday following they made a foray and burnt many houses and mills,

carrying off much plunder. But some of our men sallied forth from the Castle and slew forty or more. On the Tuesday Bertrand and his fleet sailed for Normandy.

It seems that with such overwhelming numbers they must have discovered that the previous year's attack had depleted the food stocks so seriously that there would be insufficient to last them for a siege, otherwise why did they give up so quickly?

Another petition declared 'The island hath been destroyed and burnt three times this year.'

Guernsey had also suffered similar raids and burnings. It would have been of more value to the French at that period, but they could never have held it while the English could use Jersey as a base. Jersey had to be captured first.

1348 Plague

Then in 1348 came an even worse event to top this string of disastrous happenings: the arrival of the Great Plague, commonly known as the Black Death. In Normandy the ravages of the plague were exceptionally deadly. 'No taxes could be gathered because there has fallen on the land so great a mortality.' Being so close, and with the great fairs there acting as the islands' medieval supermarkets, the Channel Islands could not escape, and thousands died. In ten parishes in Jersey, whose records go back to that date, only two Rectors survived, and 'by reason of the mortality among the fishing folk, which has been so great, our fishing rents cannot be obtained.' It is also accepted by most English historians that the plague in England began in Melcombe Regis, on the opposite bank of the river Wey to Weymouth, carried by a vessel from the Channel Islands, while maybe it also arrived at about the same time in London, with a vessel from the continent.

The principal effect of this massive drop in the population, not only here but throughout Europe, was a labour shortage so severe that large areas of land were left uncultivated, while prices rocketed, as those labourers who were not tied by serfdom were able to demand greatly increased wages, or go elsewhere to get what they wanted.

(Grandparent died in 1349)

1372 Owen

The old problem flared up again in 1372, when Owen, or Ifan, of Wales, son of a Welsh princeling whom Edward had slain, with 600 French men-at-arms, after '... burning and wasting Guernsey, with much slaughter, entered Jersey and burnt and wasted there also.' He was not out to capture the castle, so that it was a quick raid, merely to 'get his own back' for being dispossessed. (I should explain here that a 'man-at-arms' was normally two or three persons, for it included a groom and sometimes an extra hand, who, though not proper fighting men, would have been armed for self-defence.) So there were probably well over 1,000 men with Owen. If a 'man-at-arms' was two or three people sounds odd, we used to talk about a 'fork' for potato digging, and that was three people. The first went ahead with a fork, loosening each plant in the soil, the second lifted the plant and shook the potatoes free, the third collected them into a basket. In the same manner a 'knight' was expected to include at least six others.

1373 Du Guesclin

It was different in the following year, when Bertrand du Guesclin, Constable of France, attacked Jersey, together with the Duke of Bourbon, 2,000 men-at-arms and 600 crossbowmen. He had risen rapidly to become Constable of France, and in five years stripped England of almost all of her Continental possessions. On landing the Duke of Bourbon marched against Grosnez Castle, which he captured without difficulty, while du Guesclin approached Gorey Castle, which he attacked many times, until eventually a section of the walls collapsed, but he was unable to take the Keep. He may have had the walls undermined, but it is more probable that he was using one or more mangonels, which catapulted boulders at the walls to weaken them. Finally the defenders paid a ransom with a guarantee that they would surrender if not released by Michaelmas, which, fortunately, they were.

Though he had been only partially successful in his attack on the Castle King Edward complained to the Pope's representatives in 1376 that

> Du Guesclin, with whom our liege men agreed to pay ransom for one year only, which ransom was paid in full, and later to pay another fixed ransom for one year only, has again compelled them

by harsh imprisonments, burning to death, to pledge themselves to pay yet a further year's ransom.

So it would seem probable that he had left some of his men behind to act as an occupying force. He died four years later, in 1380.

1380 De Vienne
In that same year another French Admiral arrived, Jean de Vienne, and occupied Jersey and Guernsey for two years. France and Spain had jointly agreed to depopulate the islands, to destroy all crops, houses, trees and everything, making them completely uninhabitable, but the Admiral ignored these orders. We do not know why, but we thank him.

On top of all this there were numerous occasions during the 1300s when the islanders petitioned the king that the Warden or his officials were robbing them, falsely imprisoning them, and even burning their houses! It seems a wonder that there was anything left to make rebuilding possible! (**Father died about the year 1400**)

1403 De Penhouet
Almost thirty years were to pass after du Guesclin's attack before there was major trouble again. Then, in 1403, Jean de Penhouët, Admiral of Brittany, raided Jersey, and again a petition says, 'fired the houses, took prisoners and booty, and laid the Island under a contribution of great and intolerable sums of money as acts of reprisal, thus punishing the innocent for the guilty.' This last phrase is explained by the fact that English pirates had been plundering merchant vessels off the coast of Brittany. The Admiral had already captured forty of them, but seemed to think that that was not enough. Or did he maybe have a suspicion that 'the innocent' of Jersey were not quite that innocent!

1405 De Pontbriand
Only three years later Pierre de Pontbriand, a distinguished Breton knight, with Pero Niño, a Spaniard, as tactical commander, landed with 1,000 French and Spanish armed mercenaries. Their reason for doing so was that 'many rich merchantmen had feared to enter the port of St. Malo, being unarmed, and Jersey pirates swarming the roadstead.' Jean de Penhouet was right! They occupied l'Islet overnight, and next morning advanced along the 'Bridge'. (L'Islet is an island at

high tide, but the causeway locally called the 'Bridge' allows access on foot before the tide has fully receded.)

The local forces of four to five thousand men were drawn up on the sand dunes which are now West Park and the Esplanade. Diaz de Games, who travelled with Nino everywhere and acted as his biographer, says of the battle:

> The invaders advanced slowly under cover of a wall of linked shields.... The Jerseymen opened battle with a charge of 200 horse, but a deadly volley from the French archers threw them into confusion. The first line (of Jerseymen) then charged: the Jerseymen fought right sturdily, but they were reluctantly forced to retire.

The charge of the second Jersey line broke the ranks of the invaders:

> They joined in a fierce rough-and-tumble. Then you could see helm severed from breastplate, and arm-plates and greaves hacked off [leg-armour which a man on foot could cut from a man on horseback] ... blood flowed in torrents.

Such steadfast courage did both sides show that all would have been slain, but the Receiver-General, bearing the white flag with St. George's Cross, and guarded by doughty knights, was slain,

> 'Then the Jersey troops withdrew to Castel Sedement, a fortified area at Trinity, but the French were so fatigued that they could not pursue.'

Some prisoners that they had taken told them that

> ... most of the survivors of the battle, together with non-combatant civilians, labourers and fishermen were taking refuge in this fortified area, surrounded by palisades and good wet ditches, whither their wives with their children and goods had already fled. Rather than surrender this fortification to an enemy, it had ever been a law amongst them that they should all first die in its defence.

The next morning they marched inland, with a view to attacking Gorey Castle, and the country en route 'was covered with houses, gardens, harvests and flocks; and all the country was burning, which was a most pitious thing to behold, for the inhabitants were Christians.' When they got to the heights of Grouville they found their way blocked, and another indecisive battle took place. The site of that battle is marked to this day with an ancient cross, La Croix de La Bataille, at the top of Grouville Hill. Now seeing the castle from its landward side, they realised that they did not have the force to capture it, and both sides being exhausted, a truce was made, in which Jersey agreed to pay a ransom of 10,000 gold crowns, to release all French prisoners, and to pay for the next 10 years a tribute of 12 lances, 12 axes, 12 bows and 12 trumpets, which they much resented and found humiliating. (But this was, in fact, only paid for one year.)

1461 Maulevrier
In fact, there was one more event of this nature, but it was somewhat different to all the others, and just outside the period that we are supposed to be discussing. (**The junior member of our imaginary family had died in 1450**).

It was only eleven years after his death. The island was occupied by the French for seven years, but this period of occupation was relatively peaceful, for it seems to have been occupied on behalf of King Henry VI of England and his French queen, who were at that time losing the Wars of the Roses. Men of the Queen's cousin, the Count of Maulevrier, captured Mont Orgueil with the help of a Lancastrian supporter, the Attorney-General, who got the guards drunk and left a small door open. It was re-taken by the Yorkist navy in 1468, with the help of the Militia, when it was surrounded by sea and by land, and the occupants were forced to give in after a twenty-seven week siege.

To conclude, I think we should just remind ourselves of the lives led by those of our family, whether it was grandfather, father and son, or grandmother, mother and daughter, and though they are imaginary, this really was life in Jersey (and to a slightly lesser extent, Guernsey) at that time, for everyone.

Grandparent's death

The weather, which for several centuries had been of a warm and mild Mediterranean-type, changed dramatically during the lifetime of our imaginary grandparent to frequent powerful gales, which produced massive sand-storms. On the nearby coast of Normandy one parish is recorded as having lost a fifth of its arable land, and in Jersey houses on the west of the town, where Old Street now lies, were abandoned because of the invasion of sand. What did these storms do to grandfather's small crop of corn, his livelihood?

He died at the age of 59. At the age of five his village had been destroyed by fire, and hiding terrified in bushes he had seen and heard his mother and older sisters dragged from the church, raped and then slashed to death with swords, together with many others.

Then, in his forties and fifties he had been called out at least four times to face overwhelming invading forces. (Relative to today's population, these four armies would have ranged from about 20,000 to 60,000 men, impossible to oppose seriously). As far as we know there were few major battles, but skirmishes with smaller groups were undoubtedly commonplace, and the chances of getting killed were just as likely in a small battle as a large one. He had to answer many call-outs when unrecognised vessels were seen near by, and his house was burnt several times. Finally, knowing that hundreds of islanders had already died of the plague, he also developed the great purple-black boils in the armpits and in the groin, and died in the same agony. Thousands more followed him that year.

If it was grandmother's generation that was more in your thoughts, with so many major attacks during this period she would have been fortunate not to have been raped more than once, for that was simply one of the spoils of war, and remained so for several centuries.

Parent's death

Our imaginary parent died about the year 1400. As a child he had also been through terrible fear, the trauma of the Black Death. How did a nine-year old cope with the fact that not only his father and mother, but most of his friends as well had died in such hideous circumstances?

The countryside now seemed all desolation, with empty houses, crops rotting in the fields, and the bodies of sheep and cattle, which, with no one to milk them, had died of milk-fever. He had probably had to help fill in many graves, which even a small boy could do, for labour was desperately scarce, and there was so much to try and rescue.

Some time in the mid-1400s almost two square miles of St. Ouen's parish was flooded, the land and manor house of La Brequette was destroyed, and St. Ouen's Bay as we know it today was created. If this shattering event did occur in 1356, as one document suggests, its impact would have been vastly reduced due to the massive loss of population by plague only seven years earlier, but it must still have had disastrous consequences for many. He was among those who heard and experienced this great storm, and like his father, lived through many others.

He had to face three enemy invasions in early middle-age, the first of which, by Owen of Wales, was a bloody affair which did much damage, but with a comparatively small army was basically a raid rather than an invasion. The second, in the following year, saw du Guesclin's attempt to capture Gorey Castle. This army was in the island for almost three months, taking whatever they needed from the land to feed some 3,000 men. The third, by Jean de Vienne, seems to have been a relatively peaceful occupation, since there do not appear to be any petitions or strong complaints to the king about this period.

He was lucky enough to die at home, at age sixty, in peace.

Death of the last of our family

He had been much luckier than either his grandfather or father. At the age of thirteen he had experienced the usual burning of the countryside when Jean de Penhouet 'punished' the islanders for alleged piracy, and again at sixteen, after the battle of the 'Bridge', in which, even though only 16, he had been involved as one of the 3,000 men. He may also have been at the battle above Grouville Hill the next day, or, because of his youth, he may have been transferred to guard-duty at le Chatel-Sedement. If, as was likely, he had a boat (for most Jerseymen did), then he was greatly inconvenienced at the age of 28 when King Henry V ordered all Jersey boat owners to join the blockade of Cherbourg (at their own expense, of course) but for the remainder of his life he was left in peace.

An artist's reconstruction of Le Chatel-Sedement (Les Câtiaux) and extensive square enclosure at Trinity, designed as a shelter from enemy raids for the population and their cattle, and which men were sworn never to surrender. (N V L Rybot)

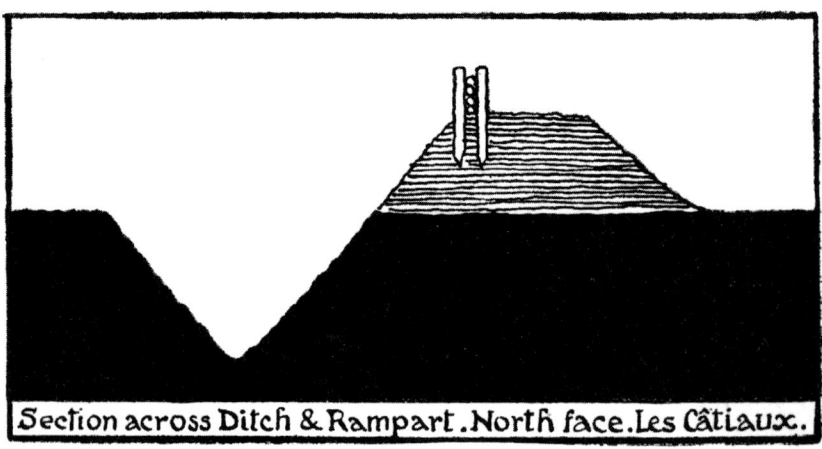

Section across the ditch and rampart at Les Câtiaux. The ditch is about ten feet deep and twenty feet wide. (N V L Rybot)

Our forebears

His ancestors (our forebears, if not, in most cases, our direct ancestors) paid a very heavy price indeed so that the English kings did not lose their profit from the loss of trade with Gascony and Aquitaine. We have benefited since from the reward given them by those kings, that of some relative freedom of self-government which is now ours, but how many today know how it was achieved? There is a city on the borders of France and Germany – I cannot remember which one – which has been attacked so many times that it has erected a tablet showing the dates on which these events occurred. Maybe a large block of granite with a flat face showing how many times this island has been attacked would help others to understand our history. The number of attacks would exceed those shown on that city's memorial!

Société Jersiaise Lunchtime Lecture, 2000

5

Two cases of Deodand

The Ship

'En 1619, le 4 Novembre, le navire appélé la Fleur, appartenant à Jean Bailhache, tombé sur deux hommes, les tua; la moitié fut confisquée comme deodandum. Bailhache appela, et fut le tout confisqué et l'Appelant condamné a 30 ls. sterl. de depens.'

In translation:

'In 1619, the 4th November, the ship called the Fleur, belonging to Jean Bailhache, fell on two men, and killed them; half the value of the ship was confiscated according to the law of Deodandum. Bailhache appealed, had the whole confiscated, and the Appelant was condemned to pay £30 sterling costs.'
(Quoted in *Les Manuscrits de Philippe Le Geyt, Ecuyer, Lieutenant-Bailli de l'Ile de Jersey, sur la Constitution, les Lois, & les Usages de cette Ile,* Tome IV, p. 343)

Deodand: 'A personal chattel which, having been the immediate occasion of the death of a person, was forfeited to the Crown to be applied to pious uses.' (Medieval law, abolished in England in 1846)
(*Shorter Oxford English Dictionary*)

It is still today the vehicle that is insured – the driver is secondary!

Grouville windmill

The second case involves Grouville windmill, which was ordered to have its sails removed, which came very close to ground level, because a man was struck and killed by them as they revolved.

At first glance these decisions seem childishly primitive, but that is not at all correct. The Oxford Dictionary definition says '... forfeited to the Crown...' and it seems that this was clearly a method of evaluating the amount of damages which should be paid to the dependants of the victim. It was not intended that a ship should be sawn in half, or a windmill left sail-less, but that the owner would have to pay that value into the Court, hopefully for transmission to the dependants.

Extract from a talk to University of the Third Age, 2004

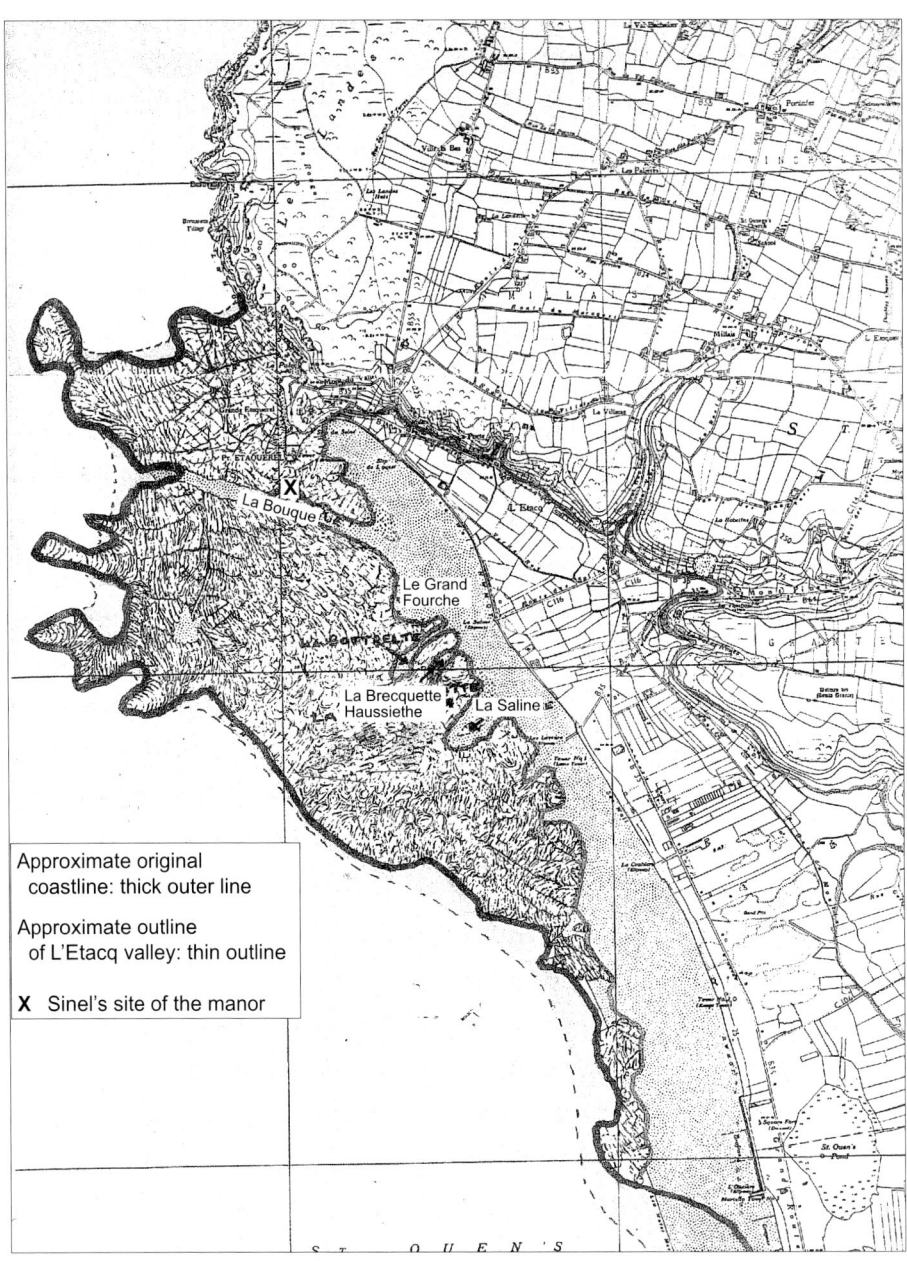

The northern end of St Ouen's Bay as it is today, with some names added (Ordnance Survey for the States of Jersey, 1935)

6

Disaster at St Ouen

A Discussion on the problem of La Brequette Manor

This is an historical 'detective story' in that La Brequette Manor is said to have disappeared and all sorts of people have been trying for over a hundred years to work out where it must have been sited, so I decided that I would have a go as well. If you want to join in it will mean taking careful note of the first two pages, because nearly all of the clues will be found there. It's a challenge!

[a] Lawsuit dated 1669 between the lord of the manor of St. Ouen and the lord of the manor of Vinchelez de Haut, regarding the limits of their possessions in the Bay of St. Ouen. (Translation)

Philip Mahaut (aged about 80) declared upon oath that when he was a boy, he had been in the company of old people fishing at low tide, and had seen a quantity of stones belonging to Wallis: he had been informed by these people that they were the ruins of the former castle of La Brequette. He had also seen trees along the sea shore which separated the two fiefs in question.

Elie du Heaume (aged about 70) deposed that he had heard that the Manor of La Brequette lay to the north of a stream which went through a field called "La Haussiere".

[b] MS of c.1680s (Translation)

The fiefs of Morville and Robillard were part of the fief St.Germain in Jersey formerly belonging to John (Jean) Wallis, Gent. His manor house was situated in this same fief, in the valley of l'Etacq, close to the sea shore, known as the Manor of La Brequette, near which is a forest of oak trees both on the east and north sides of that manor which is now below the level of the high tide. The above valley and manor have, for several years, been lowered by the sea; nevertheless at low tides the remains of the manor can be seen, and after stormy weather, a quantity of oak tree stumps, which at one time flourished in the valley, are visible.

[c] ANCIENT MS. (said to be known to Poingdestre) published in *"Almanach de la Chronique de Jersey"*, 1849.
In 1356, the sea engulfed a large area of fertile land in the Parish of St. Ouen. The accounts of the Exchequer mention the names of people who inhabited that locality. The forest of La Brequette was overwhelmed and swallowed up by a terrible hurricane. In that year Jean Mathurin (Maltravers) was the Warden of the Island and William Hastein the Bailiff.

In 1495, a great sandbank was flung at high tide which completely covered up and swallowed a large area of land at the western end of the Island, whereby it resembles a desert. And following all these happenings the strong west winds which blow here at all seasons and for a part of the year have further lifted the sand which caused this disaster. [This is the traditional explanation of the origin of Les Quennevais.].

It is about 1131 years since the little island on which Elizabeth Castle was built was detached from the land, about the year 687.

N.B. "According to an old tradition, it is said that the house of M. de St. Germain was buried under the sea at the west of the Island, after which, having measured the length and breadth of the Island, he built a house in the middle thereof in the Parish of St. Lawrence, which goes by the name of St. Germain today — but I have never seen the authority for this tradition."

(Extract from an ancient manuscript)

These documents are a good introduction to the problem of La Brequette manor-house, namely that as far back as the late 1600s the site on which it had once stood was a matter of argument, though at that time its actual existence was not doubted. Many folk have set their minds to solve the problem, both by studying documents and by physical searches of the area involved. Following in their footsteps, I intend to use these various proposals as a stepping-stone to my own findings. Consequently, before discussing various theories as to where the house stood, it is essential to achieve a good picture of the general topography of the west coast of Jersey as it would have appeared many hundreds of years ago.

[d] Study of 14th century sand invasions in the Normandy area, by Dr. John Renouf, writing in 1980. Dr. Renouf states that, about the year 1000 A.D.,

"If you'd been standing where La Rocco Tower was to be built centuries later, (at low tide level in the middle of the bay), looking inland you really would have had a surprise — a view of fields and trees with not a sand dune in sight!"

[e] Excavations at Old Street, St. Helier. Margaret Finlaison, writing after having been in charge of the above, says

".... Climate conditions generally are known to have been at an optimum between AD 400 and 1200, ...

"It was not until the middle or end of the thirteenth century that the weather is thought to have gradually begun to deteriorate again, and this seems to be reflected in the blown sands found in the later levels (referring to the Old Street dig) and the total abandonnment of the area to the dunes after the thirteenth century."

Clearly if the weather had this effect in St. Aubin's Bay it must have done so also in the St. Ouen's area, and the weather from then on, for a century or so, began to create quite drastic changes:

[f] John Renouf also quotes (From University of Caen, Dept. of History). Diocese of Coutances, 1332. Parish of Les Moitiers d'Allonne, on the western coast of the Cotentin. (Translation)

Notre Dame d'Allonne. This parish is diminished, because of the sands which covered the lands around the Sea, and caused many parishioners to flee, almost to the number of one sixth .....

Saint-Pierre d'Allonne. One fifth part of the produce of the said parish is consumed by the sand of the sea and is abandonned. ..... [Another document says 'one fourth part']

It is certainly true that from the late thirteenth century there were many decades of very violent storms. These are recorded throughout NW Europe, and Jersey did not escape. Western coasts in particular in the Cotentin, and presumably in the Channel Islands too, were liable to inundations of blown sand. It is not at all unlikely that the land extended out and over what is at present tidal areas, especially in the west, and that the sea reclaimed quite extensive zones for its own during the later medieval period.

[g] Records at the National Meteorological Society

The National Meteorological Library have one, and only one record for the English Channel area in the 1300s, and that was 1334, 23rd November, when major flooding occurred all along the south coast of England. As it is known that storms were fairly frequent in the 1300s this very specific date suggests that it was extra special enough to stick in people's memory.

Old Jersey Houses (**Vol.1**) Joan Stevens, p.60:
> The distribution of our older houses is instructive, and the map shows, as far as it is possible, all those dating before 1700. ..... It will be seen that they are fairly evenly scattered over the Island, with the exception of Les Mielles de St. Ouen. There are fewer in St. Clement and St. Brelade, particularly the former, than in other parishes, and this is explained by the fear of raids from France. ..... Very few old houses have a sea view, and only one or two, such as Portelet Inn, can be seen from the sea. This again is understandable, from the point of view of protection both from raids and weather. The oldest centres of habitation were definitely inland, and near water, and were most often in or near a valley, not in the main valleys where the vital water-mills operated, but in tributary valleys.

"Recueil des Matieres Historiques, touchant les envahissements de la mer dans les parages de la baie de St. Ouen." (*Bulletin of the Société Jersiaise*, 1883, Col. C.P.Le Cornu.):
> p. 391. "Commencant au-dessous de la Mare de St.Ouen, ou "Mare au Seigneur", nous sommes a la partie appelée L'Ousiere; ensuite, allant vers l'Ouest, viennent La Crabiere, La Pierre, Les

Laveurs, La Fenêtre, La Guette, Les vieux-Douets, La Haussiere, Les Quiesses, La Brequette, La Botterel, La Verte, Les Fourchiaux, Les Bancs tocques, Le gris-pays, La grise, La Rocque, La Mare Alexandre, Le Havre, La Hurette, La Bouque, Les Havres de dehors, La Pulec. Au bas de la Bouque et a droite sont les Noires Roches, plus bas La Moulliere. Au sud de la Bouque sont les Maraines et plus bas Le Houmet et au sud du Houmet est un ecueil que l'on appelle L'Espe. Le Banc du Rigdon qui est a l'Ouest parait être en continuation de cet ecueil. Plus au Sud est le rocher appelé Coupadan, haut elevé, et bien connu. En continuant vers l'Est on vient a une partie platte, appelée Le Laggie, au bas de laquelle est Le Pont, un rond Rocher."

"La Brequette est la partie elevée des rochers, au-dessous et un peu a l'Ouest, du Douet de ce nom. Entre La Brequette et les banques, la Greve fait un col par l'amoncellement du sable. La même chose ce voit a la Rocque près du Havre."

p. 394. (He continues by pointing out that there is virtually no sand covering the land on the northern end of the bay, while the southern half is covered to a considerable depth right up to the high land at Les Quenvais [his spelling]. Consequently, it is evident that while the northern half was the subject of a flood, the southern half was the result of a great sand-storm, but the Quenvais area itself apparently remained usable land until the 1600s).

"The Relative Ages of the Channel Islands"
Bulletin of the Société Jersiaise, 1909, Joseph Sinel.

p.442 et seq. "In September, 1902, there occurred in St. Ouen's Bay, Jersey, what must be a record exposure of the old forest bed.

I was spending, as is my frequent custom, a weekend at the home of my friend, Mr. Dancaster, which is situated about a couple of hundred yards from the shore in this bay, when one morning my host summoned me to the beach to witness an unusual scene. I was amazed, for the fine white sand which usually lies throughout this bay from five to ten feet thick had disappeared, and in its place there stretched, as far as the eye could see - North, South, and seaward, an expanse of firm, brownish-black peaty soil, which was studded with innumerable tree stumps, most of them just level with the soil, but many hundreds of them projecting above it for two or three feet. Between these stumps were prostrate trees and large branches, with acorns, seeds of telia, and hazel nuts in abundance.

The trees were close set. In one spot I roughly counted over four hundred large ones within a space of one acre ..... Very grand indeed, and quite unlike anything we have today, must have been this vast forest, through which the Neolithic people roamed."

He states that this forest died through gradual subsidence of the area, until it was under sea-level, though the presence of large branches as well as prostrate trunks does at least suggest that this forest was severely damaged by violent storm prior to its submergence, though no date can be attributed to this occurrence. Radio-carbon tests which have been carried out date this forest at late-Neolithic or early Bronze Age, {Dr. John Renouf}.

p445. "Between the two extensions of the sea wall at Lea Laveurs, for a length of about three hundred yards, the sand bank at tide margin rises eight feet above the shore level, and usually (I say "usually," because it is sometimes hidden by a bank of pebble) presents a vertical and clear section of the soil. At the foot, and level with the shore is the forest bed peat, with tree stumps protruding, — part of the inland extension of the submerged forest without. In this portion, between the sea walls, I have located the stumps of eight trees, just beyond tide margin, and Mr. Dancaster, who lives close by, tells me that he has located over two hundred such beneath the present inland soil. Over this there lies three to four feet thick of blown sand, blackened by infiltration from dead vegetable matter. Over this again another layer of peaty soil, brown in colour, five to ten inches thick Then comes from two to four feet in thickness of recently blown sand, clad with growing plants, — the edge of thr present district of Les Mielles.

The upper layer of peaty soil, formerly extending seawards, and sloping downwards, marks the land surface of a few centuries ago; marks the land, which together with the flat rocky reefs beyond, at the same elevation, was that upon which stood the "Manoir de la Brequette", and on which grew its "Forêt."

At this point, although a matter of history rather than of physical geography, it may not be out of place to locate, if we can, the actual site of this ancient Manor, the property of a certain Jean Wallis, which is said to have been inundated by the sea about the year 1350 ....

On the northern side of St.Ouen's Bay, at L'Etacq, we note a reef of flat low-lying rocks extending seawards for about three-quarters of a mile. The greater portion (in fact all but a few heads, which rise ten to twenty feet above the tide), is submerged at high tide by about ten feet of water. To the North of this reef, — that is, towards the Pinnacle Rock, — the water suddenly deepens to 20, 50 and 80 feet at low tide, which means that at high water, there, is, just off the reef a depth of from 60 to 120 feet of water. On the West (seaward) side, it also deepens rapidly, so that just beyond the reef there is at high tide a depth of 50 to 60 feet of water. These points must be borne in mind.

Near Mont Thiebault, running direct west to the sea, is the stream, known as La Haussiere. Now, ... Elie du Heaume states that the manor stood a little to the North of the stream known as La Haussiere. ...We also read that the house stood near the sea ("au bord de la mer") and that there was on the North of it a "forest of trees" – "as also to the East."

We are now brought within narrow limits. Three-quarters of a mile from the shore the water is of such depth, that whatever subsidence or other factors may have accomplished, it is certain that there was no dry land there six centuries ago. An examination of the locality shows that if a forest, however small, ever existed it could not have existed to the north of the manor; for north of L'Etacq point is deep water.

Now, between parallel lines drawn east and west, at L'Etacq point and at the stream of La Haussiere, there is a strip of but four hundred to five hundred yards, and within this strip and within three quarters of a mile of the present shore line the manor must have stood."

He goes on to say that he and Mr. Dancaster spent some time

exploring the reef]

"Our search on our two first visits was unsuccessful. Only here and there could we find a bit of stone foreign to the locality,, but on the third morning our attention was arrested by a considerable number of fair sized granite stones, — stones measuring from about six inches to a foot in diameter. These were scattered over an area of about a hundred yards wide; and, furthermore, sunk in the sand in a gully close at hand, we discovered what is unmistakably a building block measuring thirty inches in length by about a foot in each other dimension. Some of the granite is of the La Moye type; there is also some from Mont Mado, whilst a block of diorite is to all appearances from St.John. These stones were certainly not brought heere by the sea, nor would they by such agency have been selectively grouped in one place. Here then, we thought, was the site of the historical manor, but the finding of only one large building block was disconcerting. Within a hundred yards or so of this spot, however, there is a fisherman's jetty, erected there some seventy years ago. It occurred to me to examine this jetty, and here I believe we have found the missing link. Nearly all of the seaward end of this jetty is constructed of large granite blocks, of the same type as that to which I have referred as being imbedded in the gully, and all bearing evidence of having been sea-worn before having been used in the construction of the jetty. The shoreward part of the jetty is built of stones of the locality. Here then undoubtedly is the site of the "Manoir de la Brequette." It lies about three hundred and fifty yards from the present shore line, and from one hundred to one hundred and twenty, due south of L'Etacq Tower."

He then goes on to say that no trees worthy of the name cooould grow on this low land at sea margin. ["... au bord de la mer"] But he may have forgotten that the weather was mild up to about 1300.

Neither is he quite accurate at one point, where he says "Elie du Heaume states that the manor stood a little to the North of the stream known as La Haussiere". The actual statement says "to the north of a stream which went through a field called La Haussiere". This, as we shall see, could make quite a difference.

Letter in response to the above from Ralph Mollet, *Evening Post*,. 20 Aug. 1955. Mollet here picks him up on his point that no trees were likely to grow in that area.

"... Over 50 years ago I was with the late Mr. George Piquet, a learned local topographist, on the reef of rocks between "Les Laveurs" and "l'Etacq." It was after a storm: he pointed out a quantity of stones in the vicinity which he claimed as the ruins of 'La Brequette'.

Some 25 years ago a large surface of the 'Foret de la Brequette' was exposed after a storm. I examined the root stumps with the late Mr. G.S. Knocker and we found that they had been planted in rows forming avenues; we assumed that they were the remains of the oak trees which we read about growing at La Brequette. Further, I have found an Act of the Royal Court dated 17th June 1749, referring to a lawsuit claiming a piece of land at St. Ouen for drying vraic bordering on the west on the sea and on the north by '... le Chemin Public de la Brequette'."

MORE ABOUT LA BREQUETTE: Does the Chemin still exist today?" (F.Le Maistre, *Evening Post*,. 8-9-1955.)
...I am quite convinced that the now famed Chemin de la Brequette still exists, either in part or as a whole, and can be seen to this day....

He goes on to state that he has two theories as to the origin of this road.

"(1) Some 100 yards to the west of the slipway known as La Saline and several dozen yards inland of the sea-wall is to be seen the well-defined remnants of a 'way' leading to a 'field'. On the left side or 'bank' of this 'way' (facing the sea) grows Atriplex ('Argentinne') and immediately before that, landwards, is the 'certaine place ou mielle' (for drying vraic) in question. This 'way' leads to a field as already mentioned, known as Les Hurieaux. The latter is at present worked by Mr. J. Vibert, of Millais, and until recently appertained to the farm which he tenants from Mr. E.F. Selous, the land in question now belonging to another member of the Selous family.

The 'chemin public' would have apparently long since fallen 'en desuetude' beyond the entrance to the field 'Les Hurieaux' and have been swallowed up in cultivation.

(2) It is equally possible ..... that the present Route de la Saline was made on the site of the Chemin de la Brequette. ..... What is still known to hundreds of St. Ouennais as 'la Bretchette' is the little sandy 'bay' immediately below la Saline slipway, some 150 yards away, as also the elevated portion of rocks below this 'bay' and a little to the west, including 'le Douet de la Bretchette' ..... The Route de la Saline is in direct line with 'la baie de la Bretchette' and an interesting and supporting feature in favour would be the fact that this road is still public.

As regards the meaning of the term 'Brequette', it has the same etymology as the English words 'breach' and 'break', and would appear to signify a small gap or opening, a depression maybe, and thus an opening between higher portions of land where the Manoir de La Brequette was situated."

In other words, as referred to in *Old Jersey Houses*, a small valley.

"... the legend has always been handed down orally and traditionally in St. Ouen that 'when the Great Bank of Le Port broke, Les Mielles was invaded with sand'."

Le Cornu

p.394. Le Cornu, in his account, continues by pointing out that there is virtually no sand covering the land on the northern end of the bay, while the southern half is covered to a considerable depth right up to the high land at les Quenvais. Consequently, it is evident that while the northern half was the subject of a flood, the southern half was the result of a great sandstorm.

DO NOT OPEN THIS PAGE
UNLESS YOU ARE READY TO
COMPARE YOUR FINDINGS
WITH MINE. I AM NOT
CLAMING THAT MINE IS
THE DEFINITIVE ONE

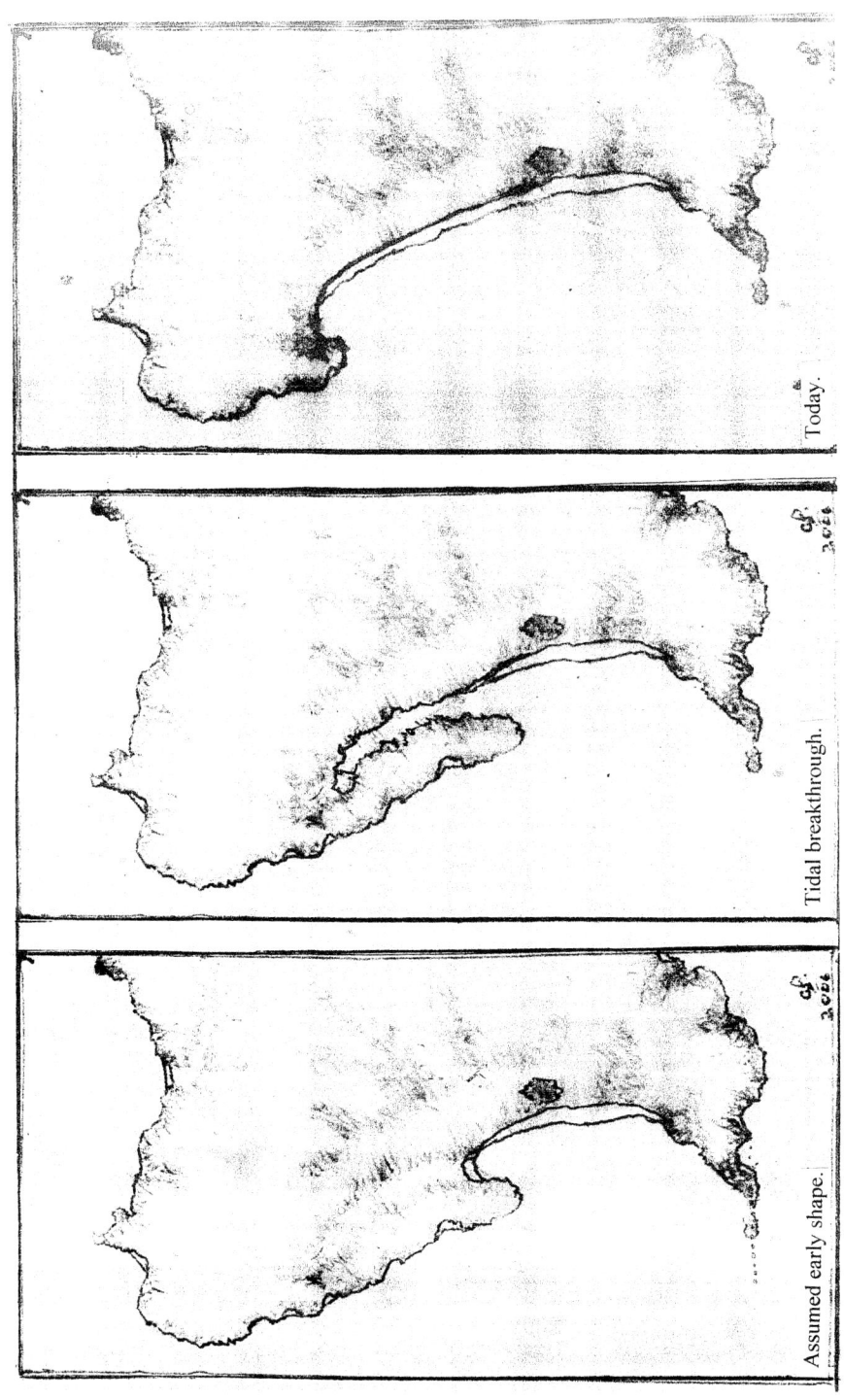

Criticism

So now let us complete this story by taking a careful check of the evidences that have been given. It was at this stage that the 'ancient MS' first began to worry me. The first, the witnesses in the lawsuit, were stating on oath what they knew. The second, the MS of c.1680, suggests that there was a forest, or wood, though it has been questioned in the other sense that Jean Wallis cannot be traced.

The third, of 1685, attributed to Poingdestre, merely describes the l'Etacq valley, and states that the sea has encroached "during the past 350 years."

Sinel was quite wrong in his assumption that the manor was so near to l'Etacq tower, and that there was no forest or wood, for several reasons. He took it for granted that the stream known as 'La Haussiere' was the stream mentioned at the trial, and he does not seem to have checked with Le Cornu's account, or with the local inhabitants, the names of any parts of the reef. Had he done so, he would have discovered that one part of the reef is called La Haussiere. In Jersey-French *la haussiere* means the tow-rope, but Mr. François Le Maistre accepted that it might well be the normal French meaning, 'a rise', in which case more than one Jersey field might well have this name.

In the law-suit it was stated that the manor was north of a stream 'which ran through a field called La Haussiere'. The present stream called La Haussiere (which he took to be the one referred to) cannot have originated in earlier times on the reef area as it flows down the other side of l'Etacq valley, and no stream can have existed on both sides of a valley at once! There is no reason why there could not have been another small stream where the reef is now, which ran through *that* field called la Haussiere, and la Magni *would* have been just to the north of this stream, all as stated in the law-suit. With the manor in this situation there was plenty of room for a forêt, or wood, both to the north of the manor and to the east of it, as was stated in the MS of the 1680s. So, will anything else help us with this problem?

[c] ANCIENT MS. (said to be known to Poingdestre) published in *Almanach de la Chronique de Jersey*, 1849.

This document puzzled me right from the start. How is it that it has not been seen by anyone else? All of the writers on this subject from 1880 onwards quote it, but always from the Almanach! Why did

Poingdestre not say "1356" if he had seen this document, or at least "One document says 1356"

Furthermore, the Exchequer accounts said to contain the names of the people involved have been searched for, but cannot be traced.

And also, according to the *Shorter Oxford English Dictionary*, the first known use of N.B. was in 1721, well after the death of Poingdestre.

These combined facts made this 'Ancient MS' seem very suspect!

So far I have been referring to it solely from the various accounts in my own Bulletins and scrapbooks, but decided that it was time to check the Almanach itself, and Hey Presto!, *the answer is there*! How previous writers have not picked up on this most damaging statement of all, the bit about Elizabeth Castle, I do not understand. "It is about 1131 years since the little island on which Elizabeth Castle was built was detached from the land, about the year 687."

This quite clearly dates this "ancient manuscript" at about 1818. (c1131 + 687 = c1818).

Would any other events which might have influenced the loss of this manor help us to date it?

A History of Jersey, G.R.Balleine.

This book lists major attacks on Jersey.

In 1336 David Bruce, the young Scots king, had been driven by the English from his throne

"...[he] has attacked Jersey and Guernsey, inhumanly committing arson, murder and divers other atrocities".

In 1338 Admiral Behuchet, of France, ".... invaded the island with a great host, and burnt every blade of corn and all the houses". He then remained here for six months, besieging Mont Orgueil Castle, though unsuccessfully.

Less than a year later, in March 1339, Sir Robert Bertrand, Marshal of France, "... with a multitude of barons and notables to the number of about 8,000,..." [Jersey population about 12,000!] "... arrived in 17 Genoese galleys and 35 ships of Normandy. They burnt many houses and mills, carrying off much plunder,...but seeing that the Island, and especially Mont Orgueil, was so well guarded, they returned to Normandy." And yet another petition declared 'The island hath been destroyed and burnt three times this year'"!

Then, in 1348, the Black Death swept the Island. Two-thirds of the Diocese of Coutanche (which included the Channel Islands) died, and it is recorded that deaths in Jersey were so great that the King's taxes could not be collected. [Probably about two-thirds of the population, as it was in nearby Normandy].

Remembering that Poingdestre wrote in 1685 that the event we are talking about took place during the past 350 years, i.e. from about 1335, there is little doubt in my mind that the 23rd November 1334 is the most likely date when the tide first broke through to overwhelm the l'Etacq valley, probably after some damage two years earlier, in the 1332 storm. It is also almost certain that what is now just a reef remained a peninsular for some time.

With the severe damage done by the attackers only three, five and six years after this great storm, followed by such heavy loss of life during the Black Death, land recovery took second place to mere survival. As a result, subsequent gales, which we know were fairly frequent during this century, would have eroded the soil covering of this peninsular, now from both sides, while vegetation would have rapidly decayed as the soil became more impregnated with salt. So, within a few more years, (by that mysterious 1356?) the Manoir de la Brequette, with its "forêt", and no doubt other small houses as well, would have had to be abandoned, and at some time later disappeared for ever.

François and Jean Le Maistre, sons of Dr. Frank Le Maistre, were very helpful, and later confirmed my thoughts, but which I could not put on the map within giving you more advantage than I had, and that is that the area immediately to the north of La Haussiere on the reef is called La Magni (the manor)!

One puzzle remains. On maps is a mention of "le Port", which, according to the book *Jersey Place-Names* is "... an old name for part of St. Ouen's Bay and beach from the S. end of La Mare au Seigneur (St. Ouen's pond) to Le Braye; mentioned by La Cloche, 1651, as "le Port de la Mare de St.Ouen." Just what was the shape of the land, and when, that part of the bay which is now most exposed to the full force of the seas was at that time fit to be called a harbour? That's a *real* puzzle.

Société Jersiaise Lunchtime Lecture, 1991

Gorey Harbour at low tide, showing the large number of small vessels that can be contained in these apparently tiny harbours.

7
A Brief Glimpse at the Maritime History of Jersey

The inhabitants of an island, and especially a small island, are bound to be sailors of some sort, even if only as local fishermen. The Channel Islands, and especially Jersey and Guernsey, provide plenty of evidence of this fact.

We can go right back into the mists of time, 4,000 years ago to the New Stone Age, to find that seal-hunting took place in this area, in skin canoes or kayaks, just as the Esquimaux do to this day. By the time of the Roman occupation of Britain oysters were being dredged off the shores of Jersey, and conger fishing was established, though the extent of these operations remains conjectural. However, as the time of the Roman Empire was one of comparative peace and considerable trading in most of Europe it is probable that these fisheries enjoyed a fair amount of prosperity.

As the Empire fell the Saxons came, but they appear to have left the inhabitants in peace. Two centuries later came the Vikings, and their warlike raids all along the coasts of the English Channel took in the Channel Islands on more than one occasion. At last Normandy was settled by these Vikings, and Rollo, the Viking chief, became Duke of Normandy, but it was his son, William Longsword, who annexed the islands to the Duchy. The conger fishery expanded, and by the time of King John it had become Jersey's main industry, with an annual export of about 30,000 fish, each of 10 lbs. or more in weight, or at least 150 tons, yielding a tax of 140 livres Tournois yearly. These figures do not take into consideration those fish which could be spanned by the hand round the middle, and which, although not subject to the tax were still allowed to be exported.

Newfoundland cod

In 1497 John Cabot sailed from Bristol into the unknown North Atlantic, and 'discovered' the cod fishing grounds off the coast of Newfoundland. A fleet of several dozen Breton fishing-boats were already there when he arrived! He also 'discovered' the land itself, though it is uncertain whether he arrived at Newfoundland or Cape Breton Island. He was rewarded by Henry VII of England with a sum of £10, and a pension of £20 a year, but it was the fishermen of Normandy and Brittany, and not the English, who were crossing the Atlantic regularly on fishing trips within a few years of Cabot's great find. It seems a reasonable certainty that the Channel Islands fishermen would be among them, because relations were friendly, and maybe in that fleet when Cabot arrived, but the first proof we have of Jerseymen taking this journey seems to be a Will of 1582, by which Pierre de la Rocque left to his sons equal shares in his ship 'now unloading after her voyage to Newfoundland.' In 1618 the Governor of Jersey received an Order from the Privy Council that stores from the Castles could only be sold to the inhabitants in times of stress, for they had been receiving complaints that these stores were being sold and used to provision ships sailing for Newfoundland.

Privateering

During the 17th century this trade continued to increase, but became subject to violent fluctuations as the medieval status of neutrality which the Islands had enjoyed for over two hundred years became a dead letter. Every war now led these ships into the hands of enemy privateers, and pirates were still to be found in the Channel, so that local ship owners began to see that privateering might be more profitable to them than risking their ships on peaceful missions.

The Civil War had led to extensive operations in this field, and the vast profits thus made by some ships became a subject of envy among many, who obviously determined that they would join in when the next war came along. Each time after this more and more ships fitted out as privateers, until their number reached its peak in the mid-18th century, when we are informed that at one time about one hundred and fifty captured vessels, ranging in size from fishing-smacks to full-rigged ships, were lying at anchor in St. Aubin's Bay waiting to be sold by auction. It would therefore seem that there was here a much greater chance of getting your money back than in most modern forms of gambling, for with so many ships to choose from they must have been sold at very low prices, and they could then be cheaply equipped with captured guns. Several Jersey fortunes were made this way, but the number of dead or captured Islanders must not be overlooked, for they too were considerable. We have no time to stay with these dashing ancestors of ours, however, and must return to the greatest of all maritime ventures in Jersey's history, the cod-fisheries of North America.

Cod

In the 17th century the harbour facilities in Jersey were certainly not big enough for the larger ships which had now begun to appear in this trade, and in consequence these ships used to lay up for the winter in St. Malo. They used to gather offshore at St. Aubin as the time for sailing approached, for we read in G R Balleine's *A History of the Island of Jersey:*

> By 1611 this fishing fleet had become so important that St. Brelade's was allowed to hold its Spring Communion earlier than other churches, that the fishermen might all communicate before sailing from St. Aubin's.

At this time Communion was held only four times in a year, and there was no church at St. Aubin itself.

Settlements in Gaspé

As a result of the French ownership of Canada Jerseymen were unable to gain a foothold in the extensive fishing-grounds off the coasts of Gaspé and Labrador, but they were keeping their eyes open for such a chance, which came with the capture of Canada in the 1760s. John Clarke, in his *Sketches of Gaspé*, published in 1908 in the USA, has a great deal to say about this, as the following extracts prove.

> It was not till after the fall of Quebec that capitalists from the Channel Islands became interested in this Gaspé fishery, and among the first of these were members of the Robin family of Jersey. The Robins were established in Bay Chaleur in 1764, and

probably on Cape Breton as early, doing business in the latter place under the firm name of Philip Robin & Co., and in the former at Paspébiac, as Charles Robin & Co., Philip and Charles being brothers.

When Charles Robin came to Gaspé the fishing was scattered in small establishments and without organisation. Though his purpose was to seek locations for new establishments on the capital he represented, yet the outcome was the development of a concern with interests so wide upon the coast and influences so commanding upon the greater part of the fishing industry as to practically consolidate and control the entire business without serious competition for nearly a century, and to set the pace for all future undertakings along this line.

These notes, written as far back as the early 1900s, do not tell the end of the tale. The firm of Charles Robin & Co. was controlled from Jersey right up to the year 1904, although it was virtually driven to bankruptcy in 1886 by the failure of the Jersey Banking Company, as were several other companies, all of which were already suffering from an economic depression. It was only saved by selling off a large number of its ships, and floating a Limited Liability Company called Charles Robin & Co. Ltd. This failure of a Jersey bank had far-reaching effects, for troops had to be sent to restore order in Paspébiac when the fishermen stormed the food stores on finding that there was no money to pay for their fish, which was in almost all cases their sole livelihood. In 1904 the company combined with the Canadian firm of Collas & Whitman (later Robin, Jones & Whitman Ltd.), and transferred its headquarters to Halifax, from whence it is still operating today, not in fishing, but as owners of several large retail stores. (The firm finally ceased trading in December 2005, when its creditors filed for bankruptcy.)

Several other Jersey firms operated on the eastern seaboard of Canada from the end of the 18th century onwards. The most important of these were Janvrin & Co., whose establishments were later taken over by William Fruing & Co., De Quetteville & Co., and the firm of Valpy & Le Bas, while Guernseymen were also prominent. In the year 1837 no less than seventy-nine Jersey ships were operating on the Banks and coastal regions of Canada. They were of 8,485 total tonnage, or an average of about one hundred tons each, though it is interesting to note that the large ships were nearly all found off the coast of Lower Canada and Labrador, while quite small schooners of sixty tons or less were usual off the coasts of Newfoundland and Cape Breton Island. The schooner crews did the fishing, the larger vessels did the ocean-going carrier trade. Over twelve hundred Jerseymen were employed on these boats, while nearly three thousand natives and settlers were employed at the shore establishments in drying, salting and packing.

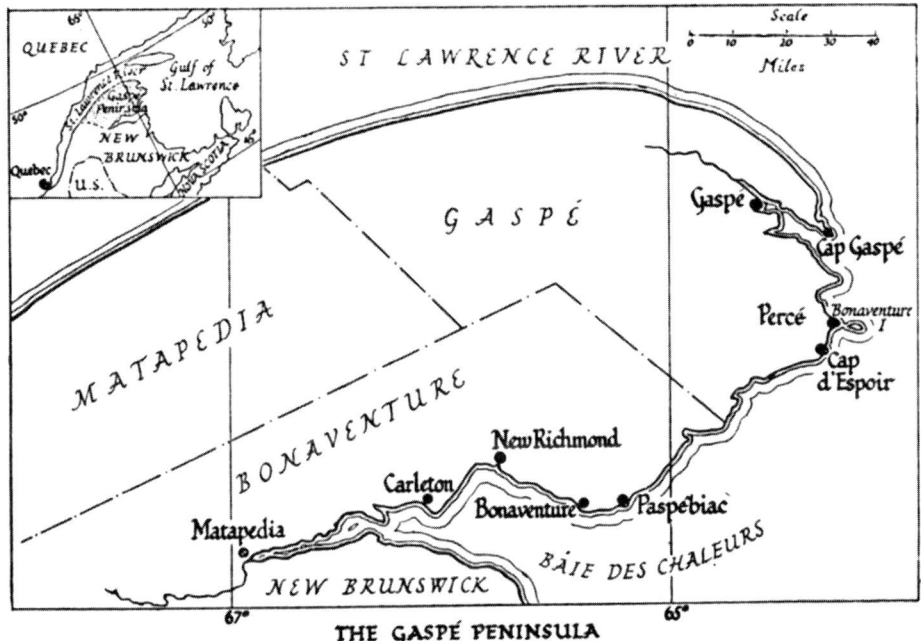

Map of 17th-18th century Jersey settlements in Gaspé, Canada (Marguerite Syvret, BA)

Two years previously, the Jersey Merchant Seamen's Benefit Society had been set up by an Act of the States to collect $7\frac{1}{2}$ d. per month commencing 1st July, 1835, from the wages of every seaman sailing from Jersey, and with this money to pay out pensions to sailors, and allowances for widows and orphans of sailors. Thus Jersey can be ranked among the first places in the world to have a compulsory Social Security Scheme of any sort, and it is interesting to note that this Society is still in existence today.

Wide-ranging trading

It was, of course, quite impossible to sell all this fish locally, and very rapidly an extensive trade was built up to special markets. These were mainly Roman Catholic countries, where frequent fast days caused a constant and extensive demand for fish. The cod were packed in tubs and drums of one 'quintal' (128lbs.) for the Brazil market, and about 16,000 quintals were shipped there yearly. Barques and Brigs were mostly used for this run, as it was too dangerous for the small schooners, and the crews were paid a form of danger money owing to the ever prevalent possibility of yellow fever. These ships would then load coffee and sugar, and return to Jersey, from whence their cargo would be re-exported as required. Occasionally they would call instead at Honduras, where other Jersey companies had forestry rights and saw-mills, and return with a cargo of mahogany, but this trade was usually carried out by other locally-owned vessels. Most of the mahogany was sold in England, but enough was imported into the Island to fill the better houses with some fine furniture.

The remainder of the fish were packed in casks of 448lbs., and taken mainly by the schooners, some to the West Indies, where they would load sugar and molasses before returning to Jersey, but mostly to the countries on the northern shores of the Mediterranean, where the demand for salted fish was insatiable. From these countries they would bring wines and brandies, oranges, lemons, dried fruit and salt, selling most of this in England before returning to Jersey. Occasional bulk shipments of the poorer qualities of cod were also made, and these were usually sold in Portugal, from where figs and lemons were shipped.

In addition to this trade, which can be considered as being directly related to the Newfoundland trade, there was a large amount of coastal traffic between Jersey and most of the countries of northern Europe. Coffee and sugar imported from Brazil was re-exported to Norway and Sweden, in exchange for timber for masts and spars, as there was naturally a constant and heavy demand for these among the local shipbuilders. (It is perhaps not generally realised that the life of masts and spars on a hard-driven ship was usually not more than three or four years, so that the demand was even greater for refitting than for ships newly launched). Wine was exported to Russia, in exchange for hemp and cordage (mainly required for rigging), linen, and tallow. On the return journey from these countries ships would frequently call in at Prussia and Denmark for wheat and barley, and there was a very considerable traffic with Holland for brandy, cheese, barrel-hoops and roofing tiles. In addition to these a large number of ships, mainly cutters and other small craft, carried out a constant trade with France, bringing back still more wines and brandies, fruit, linen and cotton, and a good amount of pottery, which was mainly for use in the farm dairies, while huge quantities of French leather were imported.

The main imports into Jersey from English ports were meat, wheat, and coal, and exports to England were dairy cattle, potatoes, butter, apples and cider, bricks, and oysters. Huge quantities of goods were taken to North America each year by the fishing fleet, and indeed almost the whole of the requirements for the resident populations of the fishing establishments were sent from Jersey. In the early part of the 19th century tremendous quantities of biscuits were made in the island for this purpose, and boots and shoes were taken in abundance. By 1840 no less than five tanneries were processing leather, and up to 12,000 pairs of shoes and 1,000 pairs of boots were being exported there annually, also about 1,000 pairs of woollen stockings. Most of the barrels and tubs for packing the fish were made in Jersey, and whole shiploads of salt were taken for processing the fish.

Building the ships

Among all this hustle of trade through the centuries it is strange that we find virtually no references to building ships. It is very probable that this craft commenced locally with the conger fisheries of Norman times, and we know that the Channel Islands had quite large ships at the end of the 13th century, for King Edward I ordered them to send ten ships to Berwick for his attempted invasion of Scotland.

Apart from a reference made by Jean Chevalier in his famous Diary to the building of a fairly small boat, the first real comment appears to be one referred to by Falle, in his second edition of *Caesarea, or an Account of Jersey*. In this book, which was published in 1734, Falle mentions that 'Most wood (in Jersey) is knotty, but here and there sticks are found fit for the building of good ships.' From this we can deduce that ships were being built in the island at that time. (We now know that there was a man named Wace building ships – not just boats – at St. John or Trinity at the time of the battle of Hastings.)

It is very probable, however, that there were no shipyards as such, but that Jerseymen would have followed the same method of shipbuilding as was commonly in use right up to the beginning of the twentieth century in all except a few recognised shipbuilding centres. When a merchant wanted a new ship he simply hired a team of shipwrights, who would set up stocks anywhere convenient, build the ship, and then go off to the next job, in the same manner as a modern building contractor will hire himself and his men to build a house on your own site.

During the 18th century there was probably little need to build ships in the island, for the privateers were so successful, as we have seen earlier, that there must have been good second-hand ships available at almost any time. By 1821, however, George Deslandes had an established shipyard, and in 1832 we get some further insight into the development of this industry in a guide-book entitled *A Brief Description of the Island of Jersey*, published in the island by C Le Lièvre. He remarks that '...two or three ships are annually built in Jersey, and principally of the native oak: some have lately been launched of the size of 400 tons.' It is obvious from the size mentioned that the local shipwrights already had considerable experience in their craft, and in the next two decades we find five more firms setting up in this business, including that of F C Clarke, which was to become by far the largest shipyard in the Island. There is, however, a statement made in *The Channel Islands*, by HD Inglis, which seems to contradict Le Lièvre's comment, for Inglis, writing only a year afterwards, states that '... more ships were built in Jersey in 1833 than in the whole of Ireland.' If the number built in Jersey was only two or three then Irish shipyards must have been in a sorry state indeed, but so far I have been unable to gain sufficient proof to judge which statement is correct. (Since writing the above I have found thirteen built in that year in Jersey.)

By 1850 there were permanent shipyards spread extensively around the coast of Jersey. There were two at St. Aubin's harbour, six large firms between Gloucester Street and First Tower, two near the La Folie Inn in St. Helier's harbour, four between Green Street and Roseville Street at Havre des Pas, five in Grouville Bay, and two in St. Catherine's Bay. The yards in the east concentrated almost entirely on cutters and smacks for the oyster fisheries of that area, but in St. Aubin's Bay the output was both larger and more varied, ranging from schooners, brigs and barques up to full-rigged ships of about 900 tons. By 1865 the trade had reached its peak, and in the previous year the firm of Daniel Le Vesconte & Co. at First Tower, had no less than eight vessels on the stocks at one time, including three 900-ton ships.

Defeated by iron and steam

From then on, however, building declined rapidly as iron ships came more into demand, for while it was possible to import vast quantities of wood, and also to grow it in the island, it became economically impossible to work with iron against the great yards near the iron and coal fields of England. By the end of the 19th century the yards were derelict, except for one or two whose work consisted entirely of repairs.

The economics of the iron ship killed not only the shipbuilding industry of this island, but the whole shipping trade. It was, of course, not so much the iron ship itself as its engines which had such devastating effects on the sailing craft of most of the world. In a matter of fifty years or so a whole way of life was changed, and only now and again would a ghost of the old times come up over the horizon and sail proudly into oblivion. There were two main factors which made the steamboats a better proposition. It was possible to build them larger and larger, until ten thousand tons was quite customary, and yet they required very few men extra to crew them. Sailing craft had reached their most useful maximum at about two thousand tons, but even this size required a larger crew than the much bigger steamships. The second reason was, of course, reliability: one could set a specific date on which a steamboat would arrive, and only the most abnormal weather would affect this. A sailing-ship which took two weeks to make a journey might well take the best part of two months the next time, for too much wind or not enough wind were both adversities which only engines could conquer.

A tradition lingers

All through the centuries the sailing-ship has been an essential, and often a dominating part of Jersey's economic life. Many an Island family today still owe their sound prosperity to those ancestors who made small fortunes, in the first instance by privateering, and later by fisheries and commerce. Wealth in some way or other has always flowed into the island pattern of life; most of the money remained in a few families only, but in the 19th century in particular the vast amount of commerce ensured the security of everyone. So many subsidiary trades were necessary to keep the shipping supplied with its own requirements, as well as the requirements of the many small colonies of Jerseymen in North America, that unemployment as a social problem has not been known in the island for nearly two centuries. The working man of the 19th century was poorly paid, but he was assured of a job at any time, while the money amassed by his masters kept taxation at a very low level. The fact that the ships came from all over the world to this port also ensured a constant supply of small luxuries such as fruits and spices, wines, and clothing, at a price which was not excessive for most of the population. The Jerseyman enjoyed a reasonable state of comfort, of security, and was in consequence satisfied; but this was all based on a challenge to Nature. His grandsons are found today on the farms that he bought; they, too, are prosperous, and they, too, challenge Nature. Maybe that is where the inborn strength of the real Islander lies, the reason for his quiet happiness.

★ ★ ★

In such a short chapter as this it has been impossible to mention everything connected with the sea. The harbours played an important part in the history of the shipping, and a study of this subject alone would be most interesting. There was the extensive oyster fishery at Grouville in the 19th century, which is now being revived; this once led to a battle against the French, and on another occasion was the cause of the death of a Lieutenant-Governor. There are intriguing stories to be told of smuggling and even of piracy, of shipwrecks and castaways, of spy-boats and galley slaves.

Today hundreds of little boats designed mainly for pleasure show that the Jerseyman has not forgotten the sea, and small boat yards have come back into their own. The day of the sailing ship has gone, but the spirit of their crews remains always with us.

Jersey Society in London Bulletin, 1961

8
Privateering: a General History

What is the difference between a pirate and a privateer, since both attack other shipping and help themselves to their cargo, and often to the ship as well?

It all depends!
In the late 15th century all sorts of things were happening at sea. The Portuguese, for the first time, sailed around the Cape of Good Hope into the Indian Ocean. Columbus, working for Spain, was the first to leave a certain record of crossing the Atlantic, but not the first to cross, and discovered land on the other side. Then the Portuguese discovered Brazil, as we now know it. It was obviously not going to be long before the mariners and merchants of both countries headed for the same area, and trouble would arise, so the two countries appealed to the Pope to sort out the problem. In 1493 he got a map which was naturally showing the little that was known at that time, and drew a line from the north pole to the south pole, roughly down the middle of the Atlantic. He then decreed that everything discovered west of that line would belong to Spain, and everything east to Portugal. Easy! Because the line just chops off a little tip of Brazil that is why Portugal 'owned' Brazil, but Spain 'owned' everything else in America.

There was trouble, of course. Was the Pope just being cynical – sort it out for yourselves – or did he still have the medieval belief of a flat earth, in which case his answer would have been logical for that period. He was a Borgia – one of a cunning family – so either answer could be right. But the trouble didn't come from there, but from France, Britain and Holland, all budding maritime nations, who all said 'What about us?' Not many years later Britain and Holland became Protestant countries, so they felt that they could now ignore the Pope, and later still, in the reign of Elizabeth, Drake was attacking Spanish ships in American waters. The Spanish said that he was a pirate, the English that he was a privateer defending the right of the Protestants, and because he had the blessing of the queen, (though the Spanish weren't supposed to know that). So that's why the meaning all depends which side you are on!

Letter of Marque for the Revenge (1756)

So let's talk about privateering, or Letter of Marque ships, as they were officially known.

According to dictionaries a Letter of Marque was 'a commission formerly granted by the Lords of the Admiralty to a merchant-ship or privateer, to cruise against and make prizes of the enemy's ships or goods belonging to or destined for the enemy, but on neutral ships.' The Act of Parliament requires that on granting letters of marque and reprisal, the captain and two sureties shall appear and give security.

What is of particular interest to us is that the system of privateering seems to have been instituted by Edward I, during one of the many wars of that period, though in this instance the enemy vessels were not French, but Portuguese. It is referred to in the State Papers known as the *Lettres Close*, or *Close Rolls*, of 26th August 1295.

Calendar of Close Rolls
26 August 1295 The King (Edward I) at Westminster, to Henry de Cobham, Warden of the Isles of Guernsey and Jersey.

> We desire that all goods which our islanders are able to capture at sea from the enemy should remain in the possession of those who capture them, unchallenged, and order you, if the facts are as stated, to give immediate satisfaction to Thomas for the 57 casks, and to permit all our men in those parts who in future acquire enemy property in this way, to retain it without hindrance and make profit therefrom, until we order otherwise.

Thomas Distelfeld, Esq., of Guernsey, had captured a wine ship, but the Warden of the Isles had confiscated the cargo.

23 November 1296 The King, at St. Edmunds, to Henric de Cobham, Warden of the Isles of Jersey and Guernsey.

> Having granted as a gift to Reginald de Carteret for the good service he has given us in Jersey those 7 casks of wine which he confiscated for his own use from our wines lately taken and seized in those parts from our enemies; we order you to suspend absolutely the claim you make on him for £35 sterling [!] payable to you for us for this wine, and leave him henceforth in peace.

It is notable that these two orders refer only to ships of the Channel Islands. Edward apparently got the idea from sheer necessity. He could send soldiers to garrison the castles at St. Peter-Port and Gorey, but this was of no use in preventing damaging raids on the islands. The castles remained safe, but the people suffered greatly. The idea was therefore quite in keeping with those days, in which kings licensed lesser lords to keep the peace in their area by having their own armies, as long as they were made available to the king if required. The only difference here being that the licences were granted to individual ship owners, who would be able to help protect the islands, at least against small marauding forces.

Over the centuries it gradually became customary for most of the maritime nations to use this system. As far as the kings were concerned it was a cheap method of having a navy, and even those nations that did have a navy found it a useful additional tool. Ultimately it was recognised and organised under international treaties, but in the late 18th and the 19th centuries, as navies became more powerful, there developed a school of thought that this was not warfare, but piracy. The interesting thing is that most of the noise came from naval men – that well-known matter of professionals versus amateurs, with which we are so familiar in many fields. And, of course, it cut down on the prize-money that the naval men could get, 'amateurs' taking some of their 'justified' bonuses – to which, by the way, they were still entitled during the Second World War, and so, probably, still would be in future as well.

But why were the islands so important to both England and France in the 13th and 14th centuries? Gascony and Aquitaine were both ruled by the kings of England, not of France, which at that time was militarily very weak, and these are the two very rich wine-producing provinces around Bordeaux, just north of Spain. Every year large numbers of ships passed up Channel from Bordeaux, laden with wine, on their way to London and Southampton, and returned with varied cargoes. This wine made up by far the greatest portion of English imports at that period, and so of the king's income also. By 1300 around 200 ships of about a hundred tons each were paying Customs dues at St. Peter-Port, which not only had the good fortune to have deep water sheltered from the prevailing winds, and so had the finest harbour in the islands, but was also found to have an excellent climate to store and to mature the wine in massive great cellars. Jersey had little share of this trade, for its rock-bound approaches made it a much more dangerous port to visit.

When Normandy was lost to the French, in 1204, it became imperative that the Channel Islands should remain in English hands, to protect these vessels from attack and to act as shelter to run to in stormy weather. Without modern navigation instruments crossing the

Channel was a risky business, except in fairly calm weather, for they could not absolutely guarantee where they would finally land.

The loss of the islands would have been a very serious blow to this trade, and to the economy of England. On the other hand, if France could gain them it would make it not only more difficult for English kings to receive their income from the wine, it would become extremely difficult for them to keep control of Gascony and Aquitaine. The ships going needed a secure harbour on the French side of the Channel, and heading for the islands meant that even with inaccurate seamanship they were almost bound to find the islands and security. This is not to denigrate the seamanship of that time – it was much better than has generally been accepted until now – but Channel waters have always been subject to tidal and weather changes, which ships without a proper keel, as most were then, could not easily overcome.

Going back to the *Close Rolls* in Edward's reign, there is some other useful information. The previous entries were in 1295 and '96.

3 December 1297 A ship chartered by Malcolm de Cheney, Keeper of the Isles, to spy on the French and 'aggrieve' them took a ship loaded with salt, etc., from a port in Brittany, against orders not to annoy Brittany, and sold it at Southampton to some merchants from Bayonne. Orders to the bailiffs of Southampton to send one or two of the sailors to Westminster for questioning, etc.

Brittany was at that time a separate Dukedom, so it was made clear that even someone as important as the Keeper of the Isles could not use this new ruling as an excuse for piracy!

Between 1294 and 1406 the islands suffered at least eight major attacks by the French, two of them led by the greatest generals of their time, and one of them landing 8,000 men – more than the entire male population of Jersey – as well as numerous piratical raids, but at length both sides found the cost too much.

We read in the *Register of Papal Letters* in 1480 that:

> ... on a petition from the inhabitants King Edward has obtained confirmation from the Pope that all pirates in the area of the Channel Islands, whether captured or at large, shall be forthwith excommunicated, and subject to anathemisation, eternal malediction, confiscation, etc., etc.

This was published by order in the churches of Canterbury, London, Salisbury, Nantes, Tréguier, St. Pol-de-Leon, and St. Peter-Port. Jersey was not specifically mentioned, as its trade was comparatively small.

Neutrality: 1484-1689

Finally, in 1483, Edward IV and Louis XI agreed that in future the Channel Islands should be considered neutral, and this was confirmed by a Papal Bull in 1484, which declared that all ships, of any nationality, were safe while they were in sight of the islands, and this remained in force until 1689, when William III ordered its cancellation. In consequence it was possible to see English, French and Spanish ships trading goods quite legally during war-time, in the harbours of the Channel Islands. This gave the islands considerable profit for 200 years, though the French temporarily repudiated it in the 1620s.

Acts of the Privy Council

31 March 1628 Sir Philip de Carteret, Bailiff, was captured by Dunkirk privateers while returning to Jersey with munitions, and taken prisoner to that port. There was fear of a French invasion at this time, and the king in person ordered that a similar supply be forwarded immediately, and sent under naval convoy.

15 April 1628 James Ginot and Peter Wethereall, appointed military instructors for Jersey, were captured with Sir Philip, when they were robbed of all belongings and left ashore at Calais. The Council allowed them £30 in recompense, and they continued on their way to Jersey.

31 May 1628 A letter from Peter Bor, engineer appointed to modernise Elizabeth Castle, to say that he also was taken with Sir Philip, robbed and stripped, and that a shot in his arm has caused it to be lame for life, but he is ready to continue to Jersey. £50 granted.

31 May 1628 A letter to Sir John Peyton, Lieut-Governor:

> A complaint has been received from merchants of London, Humphrey Slany, Arthur Shares, William Even, Emmanuell Finch and Jonas James, that Sir John sent for the captain of a pinnace of theirs which was off the Island on pretence of sending

letters to the King, detained him ashore 14 days, and after, while he was waiting in the Castle, the rest of the crew put to sea and captured a French barque laden with canvas, etc., and then returned to pick up the captain. Instead, Sir John sent out a shallop full of soldiers and took both pinnace and prize 'Into your protection', when they obviously needed no such thing.

Orders to deliver up both ships to petitioners or explain why not, because this was a breach of neutrality.

Calendar of State Papers (Domestic)

12 July 1628   Letters of Marque granted to Sir John Peyton [Governor] for *Elizabeth* (20 tons) of Jersey, and *Alezan* (25 tons). [Should this have been written 'Alison'?]
On 28 Sept. John Fantris & Co., of Guernsey, were also granted Letters of Marque for the *Pilgrim*, (50 tons)
[Still during the period of neutrality, but France had closed its ports, not only to English vessels, but to Channel Islanders also.]

Civil war

Sir George Carteret equipped about a dozen small Frigates or Privateers, which did so much damage to Parliamentary shipping that convoys had to be resorted to. Much of the money from the prizes was used to provide for the garrisoning of the Island.
History of Guernsey: Duncan
1689-1714   During the reigns of William III and then Queen Anne, Jersey & Guernsey took 1,500 prizes between them.

Letters of Marque (Jersey)
William Snow & his brother-in-law John Maugier took out a Letter-of-Marque for the *Jersey Sloop*, of 30 tons, in 1692, and this is the oldest known document of this type still in existence in Jersey.

Daniel Messervy (papers)
1739-1748   Jersey ships took prizes worth £60,000, (several million today) and 600 prisoners-of-war.

1756-1763 Jersey had about twenty-four privateers during this war, and Daniel Messervy owned or had a major share in 10 of them. He also kept careful records of each vessel, which still exist. He says that in the first year the Jersey privateers took £95,000 worth of prizes, against a cost of about £20,000. *Charming Nancy*, (Capt. Ph. Winter), *Charming Betty* (Capt. Fiott), and *La Défiance* (Capt. Le Cronier) were the three most successful of these.

During this period most of these ships used St. Aubin's harbour, as most of the merchants had their homes there, and in many cases their own private quay for their ship. This was before Le Boulevard was turned into the public road that it now is. As a result the harbour was sometimes so crowded that ships were often laid up four vessels alongside each other – and Messervy says: 'The *Phoenix* has bruised her side by kissing a Dutchman so hard in the night', and he then goes on to say, 'The other privateers have again sailed, but the *Phoenix* has had to stay behind because of her condition'!

Spying
Calendar of Home Office Papers
29 July 1761 Affidavit of John Kerby, of the privateer *Lively*, which met with a French sloop on the 27th inst. coming out of St. Malo, which he took and ransomed. The master informed him that there were 12,000 troops and 60 flat-bottomed boats in the river Dinan; also at St. Malo and St. Servan 2 row-galleys, 11 very large flat-bottomed boats, and several privateers.

4 August 1761 Affidavit of Charles Gallienne, of Guernsey, and of Matthew Guerin, jun., who were taken by a French privateer and released on a cartel-ship, that they heard information similar to the above, except that they saw 20 flat-bottomed boats at St. Malo, and were told that there were 150. They were also hard at work fitting-out 50 sail, and also 2 privateers of over 20 guns.

Journal of the Commissioners for Trade and Plantations
10 October 1777 Permission granted to Le Cras and Le Masurier, on the ship *Jersey*, to export military stores for use as a privateer fitting out.

10 September 1778 Permission granted to George Lemprière, on the ship *Mars*, sailing from Dover, to export military stores to fit out privateers in Guernsey and Jersey.

13 November 1778 Permission granted to De Gruchy and Fiott, on the *London Packet*, to export military stores for arming trading vessels and privateers.

Some vessels took out Letters of Marque to chance their luck, carrying on normal trade unless they saw a prospective prize. General Dumouriez, Governor of Cherbourg:

> These two islands make the despair of France at the beginning of every war by their very active privateering, which at once proceeds to seize a large number of vessels and cut all communications and destroy all traffic between the Channel ports, ere France has had time to take the necessary steps to ensure due naval protection for coasting traders.... During war this coastwise trade can only be carried on by convoys that are always hampered and often attacked and captured by guardships of the Islands.... Inured as they are to braving the dangers of the sea, the island population are very hardy and bold. Good neighbours in time of peace, they become most dangerous foes as soon as war breaks out. Or rather they are always in a state of war, now with the Customs Officers of both kingdoms, and then with the French navy. During the winter of 1777-78, on the outbreak of war, there were in St. Helier's roads more than 150 French prizes, and over 1,500 seamen prisoners belonging to these vessels.

Memorial to the Lords Commissioners of the Treasury:
(Jurats Dumaresq & Le Masurier – appealing on behalf of the islanders against new Customs Dues.)

> In 1779 there were 71 ships owned or registered in Jersey, with a total crew number of 3,454, and armed with 696 guns' [an average crew of 50, with 10 guns.] 'Most of these were privateers or dispatch-boats.'

'Only two years after this war many Jerseymen were again signing on as crew of French ships at St. Malo, as they have customarily done in the past, but unless these Dues are relaxed Jersey will lose even more of its sailors, to the detriment of its economy.

Napoleonic Wars 1793-1814

During the 18th century French naval & military experts put forward to their Government no less than fifty schemes to capture the Channel Islands, showing just how much trouble the islanders were causing them – the Battle of Jersey in 1781 was the only one of these plans that nearly succeeded. For the Napoleonic wars, commencing in 1793, the French – joined by the Spanish – had clearly made careful preparations, for they captured two-thirds of Jersey's shipping during the first two years of the war, taking 900 sailors prisoner. By 1798 Jersey had recovered its shipping tonnage, and for the next three years had great success with its privateers, but it was becoming difficult to keep up the pressure, and from 1802 onward only spasmodic gains were made. Nevertheless, they had done so much that Edmund Burke, one of England's leading politicians, declared that the Channel Islands alone might rank as among the naval powers of Europe.

The more successful privateers of this period were *Alligator* (Ph. Hamon), the *Aigle* (James Torre), the *Hope* (Elie l'Amy), the *Lotterie* (several masters), and the *Phoenix* (Daniel Hamon). The *Hope* was the only one of these not owned by the Janvrin family. Then there was the *Vautour*, or *Vulture*, and amongst its captures was the vessel with the extravagant name of *Nostra Señora La Virgin Del Carmen Dolores Y Providad*. Try painting that on your skiff!

Prisoners of war (from *Mourant's Gazette*)

22 January 1814 Capt. Dolbel and Ph. Mourant, two natives of this Island, together with an Alderneyman and an Englishman, broke prison in France and arrived here Sunday last. They left their depot at Longwy [right on the bend in the French border between Belgium and Luxembourg, about 250 miles from Calais], and when they left the under-mentioned were all in perfect health.

Capt. P. Le Vesconte & Son.	Messervy
Capt. Le Gresley	Romeril

Slous	Alexander
Becquet	Amy
Montbrun	Le Brun
Asplet	Clem. Laffoley
Le Geyt	Bechervaise
Benest	Hacquoil

Capt. Dolbel has been a prisoner nine years.

12 March 1814 Escaped from prison in France after nine years, M. Richard Roissier, and has arrived in Jersey. He has studied for five years the art of surgery, under the direction of a chief surgeon at the Hospital where he was prisoner in France, and he is now setting up as a surgeon, etc.

In April and early May, 1814, about 1,300 prisoners of war arrived from St. Malo and Granville, of which over 200 were Jerseymen.

The international system allowing for the issue of Letters of Marque was abolished by the Council of Paris in 1856. No more privateering!

Conclusion

The Channel Islands were of such importance to both England and France during the medieval period that the whole international system of privateering grew out of this quarrel.

The system of neutrality, in which ships were safe from enemy action while within sight of the land may have initiated the internationally recognised system of territorial waters, which for centuries became fixed at three miles from the shore.

During the Civil War Sir George Carteret's privateers were such a serious nuisance to the English that Cromwell sent his greatest general – Blake – with a fleet to capture Jersey, which they achieved after three days' effort. On hearing the news Cromwell ordered all the church bells in London to be rung in thanksgiving.

During the Napoleonic Wars Edmund Blake said that the Channel Islands' ships alone could rank among the naval powers of Europe. In other words, he was saying that if they were not there to guard the Channel the English navy would have had to be even larger, or have to forego some of its activities elsewhere.

Sketch of French woman smuggling clothes from Jersey to Granville in the 18th century.

9
Smuggling by Channel Islanders

All quotations in the first half of this article have been taken from Smuggling Days and Smuggling Ways, *by HN Shore, retired Chief Officer of HM Customs, England, published in 1892.*

The background to smuggling by Channel Islanders can be directly attributed to their original status as a Free Trade zone. In 1394 King Richard II granted them a Charter to the effect that they were to be free of all tolls and customs within the realm of England, on goods 'the growth, produce or manufacture of the islands', and this was confirmed by subsequent sovereigns for several centuries. In fact it still applies today, though the qualifications have been tightened as times change, especially since the entry of Britain into the Common Market, now the European Union.

Additionally, in 1483, Edward IV and Louis XI of France had agreed that the Islands should be neutral in times of war, for both kings had found the costs of trying to attack or defend them too great, and this was strengthened when confirmed by a Papal Bull in 1484. They were thus now a Free Trade zone, and made the most of it, until two hundred years later, in 1689, when the Bill of Neutrality was ordered to be discontinued by the Privy Council, on the instructions of England's new Dutch king, William III.

The attitude of the officials of the Island to smuggling was therefore 'Anyone can come and buy anything, but what they do with it afterwards ... well...'

Tobacco
The first clear evidence comes from 1628, with the smuggling of tobacco, both into England and France.

Large quantities of tobacco are planted in Jersey and Guernsey, to the detriment of corn crops, and against proclamations. Recommends John Blanch [an English Customs officer, based – I believe – in Southampton. AP] to see it is destroyed.

Sir Philip de Carteret, however, complained when an English naval commander arrested two ships in the harbour, for trading with France:

He has almost undone us. Contraband trade carries on despite the French king's edict. [He had closed all French ports to English and Channel Islands ships, despite the Treaty of Neutrality]. If redress be not obtained all trade and intelligence will be stopped.

So, in other words, smuggling and spying went hand in hand, even in times of peace, due to the constant fear of a French invasion.
Nevertheless, the Privy Council ordered that:

All tobacco planted in the C.I. to be destroyed, and no more to be planted. All tobacco brought to England from the C.I. in future to be landed at the Port of London, and nowhere else.

This local trade then stopped, though the smuggling of imported tobacco continued on a lesser scale. Then, in the 1680s, the English Customs awoke to the fact that Jersey was importing far more tobacco than it could possibly smoke! Enterprising merchants were buying it in Southampton, getting a rebate on duty, bringing it to the islands and then landing it on moonless nights in remote Devonshire coves.

A Customs House officer, William Hely, was sent to keep an eye on things in 1685, but he complained that everyone in the island was against him, including the Jurats and Constables. He finally gave up and joined the smugglers!

It was not until 1837 that it was stated to be no longer a major activity!

Spirits

The most common image of smugglers is almost certainly that of them carrying barrels of brandy or other spirits ashore in small coves on dark nights. This was in fact a vast trade in the 18th century, and the south coast from Southampton westwards was serviced from the Channel Islands and Brittany, but mainly from Guernsey.

> Up to the period of the first American War, in 1775, the trade of the island (Guernsey) was chiefly confined to the import of spirits and tobacco to supply the wants of the English smugglers.

After four unsuccessful attempts in the 18th century to force Custom House officers on the C.I., the British Government finally succeeded in 1767, with a schooner of 14 guns, a cutter, four or five boats, and 40 men under the command of a Mr. Major. They were only in the Islands for two years before being withdrawn, but much damage had been done, for within a very few months of their arrival the French King Louis XIV issued an edict to the effect that the port of Roscoff in Brittany (a tiny fishing port) was to be a free-trade port. The smugglers moved there, and instead of Channel Islanders being paid by Bills on London, payment in Roscoff had to be in gold, causing a severe drain on the English gold reserve, instead of the improvement through increased tax that they had anticipated.

Another attempt was made to stop the 'trade' in 1801, with the appointment of a new Customs Officer. The islanders appealed officially to the British Government to the effect that '… unless they were allowed to continue the smuggling trade they would be ruined', and pointed out that it would simply go elsewhere, but their appeal was in vain.

Nevertheless, it continued.

17 March 1819 or 1823 (according to two different sources) 'A Cawsand Bay boat of 15 tons took in at St. Brelade's Bay upwards of 300 ankers (10-gallon barrels) of brandy and several bales of tobacco.'

31 March 'A cutter of 25 tons from near Plymouth took in at the same place upwards of 600 tubs of brandy and geneva, besides a quantity of other goods.'

10 June 'A cutter of 25 tons from East Looe in Cornwall took in at the same place 690 casks of brandy, and during the same month a

Cawsand Bay boat took away a large cargo of spirits.'

A lot of men must have been involved to load those cargoes in one night!

And early in 1826 a thirty-foot galley to row ten oars was reported to be building at Jersey for the purpose of smuggling between that island and England.

I can remember a large shed, known as the Black Shed, in the centre of St. Brelade's Bay, which was used as a cafe in the 1920s and '30s. It has long ago been demolished. The bay at that time still retained some of the 'lonely wild feeling' with which it was described in early 19th century guide books. The hut was clearly very old, tarred inside and out, hence its name, and was reputed to have been where barrels of spirits had been stored ready for the smuggling ships to collect.

There are a few other items of interest that were also smuggled at various times.

Rebels

In 1641, a few months before the start of the English Civil War, Jersey was already split into two camps, some in favour of the King, some for Parliament, as was commonplace almost everywhere throughout Britain. The Privy Council sent a note to the Governors of Guernsey & Jersey.

> The Board are informed that some inhabitants of the C.I., under the colour of trade, transport soldiers and munitions of war into Ireland, whereby the rebels (against the king) are strengthened. You are to prohibit transport of men, money or munitions to Ireland, either from the Islands or from France.

These smugglers were clearly Parliamentary supporters, but whether from Guernsey or Jersey, or both, has not been established.

Ammunition

In 1690 the Privy Council complained to the Lieut-Governor, Edward Harris, that inhabitants were smuggling ammunition to St. Malo, via the Ecréhous. 'Upon the lighting of a fire on the Ecréhous, small vessels belonging to Normandy and Jersey make for that place and drive a

trade for lead (which was cheap in Jersey), powder and other things.'
The Lieut-Governor did nothing, as he was making money by granting passes to these boats, while the Crown Officers declared that whoever tried to stop the trade would have his ears cut off!

This may seem distinctly unpatriotic, but the Channel Islanders were in fact trying to protect, however illogically, the Free Trade status which they had enjoyed for over 200 years, and which had been cancelled by William III only a few months earlier. It may also have been to supply the many Jersey ships sailing to Newfoundland, which at that time had to winter in St. Malo, as there was insufficient harbour room for them here.

Salt

In the 1700s salt, mainly from Spain, was smuggled to Cornwall via the Channel Islands for the pilchard fisheries, and the English Revenue was reported to be suffering a loss of at least £10,000 per annum.

Cattle

Before the specific breed of Jersey cattle was created there had been a considerable trade in cattle between the island and England. French cattle was subjected to a heavy duty in England, and in the late 1700s the Normans and Bretons began to send their cows to Jersey, pasture them for a few weeks in the fields, and then Jersey boats shipped them to England as Jersey cattle, thus making a good profit and evading duty.

This trade became so large that the price of English beef was lowered due to the glut, and Jersey farmers had to export their own cattle in order to meet the competition from the French, forcing up the price of beef in Jersey. The States therefore passed a law that no cattle should be imported at all, on pain of the confiscation of the ship and cattle, the latter to be immediately slaughtered, plus a fine for each animal imported. From this law originates the separate Jersey breed.

Drugs

In 1931, quoted from *The People:*

> 'The Channel Islands, and Jersey in particular, is the centre for a flourishing industry of whisky and drug smuggling into England.

> The smuggling is carried out with an auxiliary motor ketch. After calling at Dutch ports to collect cocaine it calls at Jersey, where whisky is taken on board. It then creeps up the Thames, the ship's papers faked to pass the Customs, the cargo is unloaded and taken by motor lorry to the town it is destined for. The headquarters in Jersey is a ramshackle hut some miles in the country.'

The People loved to dramatise its news, and this may be more rumour than fact, but maybe not!

In 1992, the *Evening Post* reported that a motor-launch had been chased into Grouville Bay by the new local Customs launch, drugs seized, and two men arrested. And, of course, there have been many postal packets of drugs seized in the last few years.

Ormers: a type of shellfish

Then, finally, again quoting from the *Evening Post*, but this time from 1958:

> 'A certain townsman is wondering what happened to a quantity of ormers consigned to him last week. I understand that he made arrangements with a fisherman in Guernsey to land several bags of ormers at Grosnez, where he would collect them. The Guernsey fisherman, under certain difficulties, landed the ormers on the jetty at Ronez, and quickly sailed away. The ormers also quickly vanished – where it is not known.
>
> By law, ormers can only be landed at Jersey through the ports of St. Helier and Gorey.'

Ronez is a busy quarry with many staff.

People will smuggle anything, if there might be some small profit!

10
Was your ancestor a Smuggler?

Hope　　　　　　　　Schooner　　　　　　25 tons
Owner/s Frs.de St. Croix & J Newman Reg.No.9/1804
Was a prize taken from Spain
1804: Seized at Dartmouth

Active　　　　　　　　Sloop　　　　　　　21 tons
Owner/s Jacob Voisin　　　　　　　　　　Reg.No.14/1806
Built 1778, Southampton
1807: Seized in Jersey

Dapper　　　　　　　　Schooner　　　　　　45 tons
Owner/s Richard Aubert　　　　　　　　Reg.No. 6/1807
Built Newfoundland
1807: Seized at Scarborough

Queen Charlotte　　　　Smack　　　　　　　28 tons
Owner/s Philip Simon　　　　　　　　　　Reg.No. 1/1807
Built 1797, Isle of Wight
1807: Seized at Dartmouth

Duke of Argyle　　　　Brigantine　　　　　43 tons
Owner/s   John Mahé　　　　　　　　　　Reg.No. 8/1805
Built 1794, Saint John, Newfoundland
1808: Seized at Plymouth for smuggling and re-registered there

Mars　　　　　　　　Brig'tine　　　　　104 tons
Owner/s James Hemery sen. & Co.　　　　Reg.No. 9/1807
Built 1799, Fowey, Cornwall
1808: Seized at Jamaica for trading in Montevideo, Argentina, without a license.

Papillion   Sloop   42 tons
Owner/s John Bruton   Reg.No.17/1807
Built ? Foreign
1808: Seized in Guernsey and sold at Plymouth.

Rover   Cutter   124 tons
Owner/s Ph.Janvrin & Co.   Reg.No. 4/1814
Built 1806 Looe, Cornwall
1815: Seized by Spanish

Mars   Ship   272 tons
Owner/s John P. Collas & Co.   Reg.No.11/1815
Built ? USA?
1818: Seized & condemned at Saint John, Newfoundland for a breach in the laws of trade, but reverted to same owners 1819

Kitty   Sloop   44 tons
Owner/s Ph. Durell   Reg.No. 2/1818
Built ? Foreign?
1819: Seized in Ireland

Nancy   Schooner   22 tons
Owner/s Ph. Le Caux & Co.   Reg. No. 4/1818
Built ? Foreign
1820: Seized in Spain

Mary & Ann   Sloop   22 tons
Owner/s Wm.Anson & Co.   Reg.No.13/1820
Built 1790, Cowes, Isle of Wight
1820: Seized at Southampton and sold

Olive Branch   Sloop   63 tons
Owner/s John Dorward   Reg.No. 9/1821
Built 1812, Plymouth
1820: Seized for smuggling at Plymouth, sold by public auction, bought back by owner John Dorward

Mary   Cutter   21 tons
Owner/s Amice Dolbel & Co.   Reg.No.14/1816
Built 1816 by John Valpy Jersey 1821
Seized: at Plymouth and sold there

Hope   Cutter   63 tons
Owner/s John Benest   Reg.No.21/1819
Built 1813, Fowey, Cornwall
1821: Seized, condemned and sold at Plymouth

Nelson   Schooner   75 tons
Owner/s Ph J Le Feuvre & Co.   Reg.No.25/1825
Built 1806, Nova Scotia
1824: Seized and condemned at Waterford, Ireland, and sold by auction, bought back by owner/master (Francis Le Feuvre)

Le Heraux   Smack   15 tons
Owner/s J Le Feuvre & J Prouings   Reg.No.39/1825
Built 1813 by Ph.Heraux, Jersey
1826: Seized at Padstow

Integrity   Smack   35 tons
Owner/s Edward Purchase   Reg.No.71/1826
Built 1802, Weymouth
1828: Seized at Poole and broken up

Spright   Cutter   26 tons
Owner/s James Harnett   Reg.No.48/1825
Built 1805, Southampton
1830 or '31: Seized, condemned and sold at Exeter

Dolphin   Smack   14 tons
Owner/s Ph Perrée jun.   Reg.No.45/1826
Built 1825 by Ph.Hacquoil, St. Ouen, Jersey.
1831: Seized in Jersey for smuggling, condemned and sold

Duke of Wellington　　　　Smack　　　　19 tons
Owner/s Ph.Mourant & Ph.Asplet　　　Reg.No. 7/1832
Built 1821 by Ph.Nicolle, Jersey
1833: Seized at Penzance & ordered to be broken up

Rambler　　　　　　　　Smack　　　　30 tons
Owner/s Richard Butt　　　　　　　Reg.No.26/1832
Built 1800, Cowes, Isle of Wight
1834: Seized and broken up at Portsmouth

Sea-gull　　　　　　　　Cutter　　　　21 tons
Owner/s John Le Quesne　　　　　　Reg.No.21/1834
Built 1824 Guernsey
1835: Seized and destroyed at Dartmouth

Joseph & Benjamin　　　　Cutter　　　　14 tons
Owner/s James Jackson　　　　　　Reg.No.23/1833
Built 1798, Southampton
1835: Seized at Bembridge, Isle of Wight, and broken up

Diana　　　　　　　　　Cutter　　　　35 tons
Owner/s Thos. Mahy　　　　　　　Reg.No.9/1837
Built 1817, Guernsey
1836: Seized in Jersey & condemned by Royal Court for smuggling

May Flower　　　　　　Schooner　　　60 tons
Owner/s Fr.Misson & Ph.Perchard　　Reg.No 46/1835
Built 1828, Cape Breton
1836: Seized & broken-up at Falmouth.

Liberty　　　　　　　　Cutter/Yawl　　24 tons
Owner/s George Martin　　　　　　Reg.No.14/1833
Built 1820, Faversham
1837: Seized for smuggling (no port mentioned)

Spartan Schooner 37 tons
Owner/s Frcs Perrot & Logan J Finnie Reg.No.55/1836
Built 1827, Chaleur Bay, Canada
1838: Condemned and broken up for smuggling (no port given)

New Eagle Smack 23 tons
Owner/s John Chiverton Reg.No. 3/1828
Built 1807, Cowes, Isle of Wight
1841: Seized for smuggling

Dart Packet Cutter 42 tons
Owner/s Chas. Bisson Reg.No. 4/1836
Built 1835 by Geo Hampton, Jersey
1844: Seized and condemned for smuggling at Plymouth

Courier Cutter 8 tons
Owner/s George Noel Reg.No.35/1843
Built 1818, Trinity, Jersey
1846: Seized off Portbail for smuggling

Sylla Cutter 18 tons
Owner/s John Journeaux Reg.No.31/1847
Built 1842 by John Gray, Jersey
1847: Seized at Cork, Ireland

Lion Cutter 5 tons
Owner/s Elias Coutanche Reg.No.13/1850
Built 1836, Guernsey
1849: Condemned and sold by public sale at Jersey

Zeus Cutter 12 tons
Owner/s Jos.Matthews & Frcs.Picot Reg.No.33/1849
Built 1838, Exeter
1850: Seized and condemned at Plymouth, having cleared for Looe

Fly   Cutter   11 tons
Owner/s Philip Baudains   Reg.No.25/1860
Built ?, Wooden Bridge, Isle of Wight
1860: Seized for smuggling and sold by public sale

Mary   Cutter   15 tons
Owner/s Albert W. Sherlock   Reg.No.29/1864
Built 1841, Guernsey
1871: Seized for smuggling and sold at Guernsey

Lively   Cutter   15 tons
Owner/s Geo. Allix jun. & Co.   Reg.No.54/1863
Built 1842 by Clem Richardson, Saint Martin, Jersey
1881: Confiscated by French Government for smuggling and sold to a French subject

11
The Social Ladder in the 17th Century

The 'Upper Class'

No-one has ever given a guide to the population of Jersey such as Gregory King gave for England in 1688, and only a number of rather generalised comments are to hand regarding the different classes in society in the 17th century. Nevertheless it may be worth making an attempt to organise these comments into some semblance of order, however rough and ready it may prove.

At the top of the tree were the Seigneurs, lords of the manors, who numbered between 100 and 130 as fiefs became divided or amalgamated by marriage or by death, and with their families this class totalled about 600 persons. Many of these manors were little more than 100-225 vergées (44-100 acres) in size. Balleine, in his *History of the Island of Jersey*, states that they considered themselves as the Noblesse, following the French pattern of nobility commencing with the Esquire, rather than the English, where it commenced only with the Baron. But this is perhaps a rather sweeping generalisation, applying only to the upper level of Seigneurs. The comparison between Jersey Seigneuries and French aristocracy has been made by other local historians also, pointing to the frequent squabbles about precedence between the various manors, to much time spent in leisure pursuits such as hawking and falconry, reading (for many of them were University-educated), and vying with each other in dress and in the novelty of their gardens. There was even a tennis-court at Rozel Manor at this time.

There is a disputed will of the Seigneur of Trinity, as to who should inherit his two collars of pearls (one with a rose of diamonds), whether the heir who received his clothes was entitled to the gold buttons, and who should have the gold chain and the silver-hilted sword, while the young Seigneur of La Haule, who had only recently inherited the property, spend £220 on new suits, as well as buying a quantity of books and furniture, most of this in London, and there were several manors which ranked higher than these two. It is clear that a very high standard of living obtained at this level of society.

But unlike the French, and like the English Gentry, they also spent much time in local government as officials or as members of the Royal Court and of the States, and neither did they scorn to act as merchants, or to run their own manorial farms, and indeed many of the lesser Seigneurs were full-time farmers.

There were both similarities and differences with the English class structure of the 17th century. Beneath the Barons this consisted of Baronets (a new rank created by King James I in 1611), Knights, Esquires and Gentlemen. From these ranks came the Members of Parliament, judges, sheriffs, mayors, etc., so that they could in reality be called the ruling classes. Beneath them the Yeomen and the Husbandmen, but especially the former, were likely to be involved in Parish administration, and lower still came the vast bulk of the population. In towns the Aldermen and Burgesses were roughly on a par with the Gentry and the Yeomen respectively, though the Aldermen did not have quite the same status as the Gentry.

Jersey records make no mention whatever of Yeomen, and I only found two of Husbandmen,[1] but the *Extente* of 1668 lists the ruling classes strictly according to the English system, though the earlier Extente of 1607 does not. In 1668 we find one Baronet, one Knight, four Esquires, and 22 Gentlemen. The list is not entirely complete, as at least two other Esquires are recorded elsewhere.[2] As might be expected, all of these were Seigneurs. According to Gregory King's figures of 1688 we would expect to find in England, to every 15,000 or so people (the estimated population of Jersey at this time), two Knights, eight Esquires, and 32 Gentlemen. As a fairly important but somewhat isolated trading centre, a place with numerous very small estates and few of any substantial size, the figures for Jersey appear to be quite in keeping with those of England.

It seems that the local officials who drew up the Extente had a very clear distinction in their own minds as to what constituted an Esquire, a Gentleman, or a lesser person, and that this was in line with a nationally accepted standard. This is somewhat of a surprise, for English historians tend to accept that there was no exact measure, even annual income being very widely variable in each class. King does give annual income figures for the various classes, which are referred to later in this article, but specifies that they are only averages. In Jersey historians have tended to assume that these titles were taken on by the Seigneurs themselves, but if this was so we should expect to find many more of the hundred or so Seigneurs referring to themselves as 'Gentleman', or being called this by their relations and friends who were responsible for drawing up the Extente. Neither would we expect to find the ratio between Knights, Esquires and Gentlemen so closely comparable to that of England. It would therefore seem that there are reasonable grounds for a closer study of the whole subject of these titles, quite beyond the scope of this present work, but the following gives us a fascinating glimpse, nevertheless.

On 15th November 1684 Jean de la Cloche instituted three cases before the Jersey Royal Court, describing himself as *Ecuier* (Esquire). The Crown Officers intervened in all these cases to dispute his right to the title, thereby implying that in their view there was either a legal distinction between Gentleman and Esquire, or that he was not a fit person to classify as Esquire. The case was adjourned to the 29th November, in order that he might have time to prepare a justification for the use of the title, but then unfortunately disappears from the records. However, only eight months later, in an Acte of 7th July 1685 he is reported as stating that he would not attend the Court, of which he was a member, (he was a Jurat) unless he was given the title *Ecuier*. On 21st October 1689 he is sued by the Attorney-General as 'Jean de la Cloche, Esqr.' so that it would seem that he won his point, but after his death an action about his estate describes him as '*Gentilhomme*'! (For this information I am indebted to S W Bisson, Esq., past Judicial Greffier of the Royal Court of Jersey).

But there is a further twist, connected with the religious dissention in England, which caused James II to flee the country in that year, and which would also seem to be the reason for de la Cloche's demotion back to Gentilhomme. According to Balleine, both of the castles in Jersey had Catholic Irish troops and chaplains, installed at the instigation of James, and a very unpopular move in a strongly Protestant community. Sir Edouard de Carteret, now back in Jersey, had been King James' Cup-Bearer. Jean de la Cloche not only asserted that he was a Papist, but that he was inciting the militia officers not to resist if the French attacked Jersey. He was accused of libel, found guilty and deprived of his Juratship.[3]

From these somewhat involved circumstances it would seem that the title of Gentleman was based on the financial situation of the person involved, but Esquire was in effect a reward for someone of high standing within the community who was of not less than the status of a Gentleman. In any case, it would seem that both had much more definite limits than have been previously envisaged.

Farmers

Reverting to our description of society at that time we now come to those beneath the Seigneurs. Next down were the Farmers, living on small farms of about 10-25 vergées (4-11 acres), which they and their families cultivated. Like the Yeomen it was from this class that most of the Parish officials were drawn. Only the very big farmers employed paid help, but whenever there was a substantial job to be done, such as ploughing, neighbouring families teamed up in traditional units, and worked each farm in turn. This not only made the heavy work easier and more economical, as each farmer brought his own horse or oxen to make up the large team of animals necessary for the deep ploughing, but turned it into a festive occasion, the host farm for each day entertaining the other families after sunset. These gatherings of families, called *Vielles*, took place two or three times a week throughout the winter, with songs and yarns (ghost stories were always popular), while the younger children amused themselves with such toys as they had – home-made dolls in particular, unless they had been spoilt by the present of a toy bought at Guibray Fair in Normandy, which their parents probably visited at least once in the year.

The homes of these Farmers were massively built of local granite, the doors of which were usually topped with a semi-circular arch, while the stones making up the sides of both doorways and windows were chamfered, and the lintels of the windows were often carved. Gable-stones, too, were sometimes carved with faces. All this was done in granite, a stone expensive to work due to its extreme hardness, and the fact that it was commonplace to have some bit of carving on a house suggests a fairly high level of income. They were two-storeyed, with separate outbuildings.

The Social Ladder in the 17th Century

Very few farms were rented, the vast majority being held in a form of freehold which probably owed some small service to the Seigneur, in the feudal manner, but often not even this, so that the farmer's income was his own. The means of finance available made it possible for even a relatively poor man to buy a property, or for the heirs of an estate to raise sufficient money to divide the estate but keep the property in the hands of the family. This was a system known as *rentes*, by which a sum of money could be borrowed on the security of a house or of land, and annual interest paid. It was thus a form of mortgage, but with the peculiar advantage that the *rentes* themselves were saleable, and in the 18th and 19th centuries, if not earlier, were known to change hands almost with the frequency of stocks and shares, which they thus also much resembled.

This meant in effect that the capital sum was rarely called in, as the *rentier*, (the owner of the *rente*) would normally regain his capital simply by selling the *rente*. This system, though not without its faults, had the overriding advantage that in general the farmer could only pay back capital when he had it available, wished to do so, and the *rentier* was agreeable. At other times he was liable to pay the interest only, usually in kind, not in cash, and he was thus less liable to bankruptcy by a series of bad harvests than his English counterpart. As in every period of history, there were inadequate farmers as well as good ones, and it was quite possible for these to over-borrow and ultimately find themselves dispossessed due to inability to meet even this commitment.

In 1673 the States forbade the building of further new houses, except in the towns of St. Helier and St. Aubin, unless they had at least 20 vergées of land attached, apparently in response to a boom in building at that time. The population of the Island in 1625 had been given as about 25,000,[4] but twelve years after the States' decree, i.e. in 1685, Dumaresq's Survey lists '3,069 houses in ye whole Island',[5] based on hearth tax returns. He suggests that the population is a little over 15,000, and both Falle and Poingdestre, writing at about this same time, put the figure at 15,000-20,000. It therefore appears to have dropped no less than 20-40% in a mere sixty years. The figure for 1625 has been questioned as possibly a deliberate exaggeration, as it was being used in an application to the Government for assistance for the Island, but it can hardly have been exaggerated by as much as 10,000. During this century the population of England rose from 4

Typical peasant-farmer's house – one or two storeys; Le Rât, St Laurence

17th century double arched gateway common to more prosperous farms; Morel Farm, St Laurence

million to 5 million.

Why there should be this difference in the movement of the population in Jersey as compared with England and most other European countries is not clear. Possibly the thousands of Huguenots who had fled to Jersey in the late 1500s had a bulge effect for a few generations. Some had moved on to England or elsewhere, others had gradually drifted back to France, but many stayed for decades, until they felt completely safe to return to their own country, while a comparative few never returned at all. It is possible, too, that the abortive Huguenot rising of 1622 may have led to a further gradual drift of more refugees to the island over the next few years, as measures against them were tightened in France. There is no record of another wave of refugees at this time, but there may have been a steady trickle, which would account for the seemingly large estimate made by De Carteret. It is also a possibility that the Civil War and the Commonwealth gave rise to sufficient uncertainty for there to be a temporary reduction in the size of families, but it is impossible to check this without a major study of contemporary records.

Dumaresq lists the number of houses in each vingtaine (sub-division of a Parish) as well as quoting the island total. The only two towns of any size were St. Helier and St. Aubin, but these are not treated as separate entities. St. Helier lay mostly in the Vingtaine de la Ville (210 houses), and St. Aubin in the Vingtaine de Noirmont (104 houses). As the average number of houses in any vingtaine lay between 50 and 70, the town of St. Helier must have been somewhere in the region of 150-180 houses, (230 less about 50-70) and the town of St. Aubin about 40-60 houses, (104 less 50-70). The Extente of 1607 lists 25 new buildings 'edifyed within the Towne of St. Helliers'[6] (i.e. since the previous Extente of 1528) and the *Extente* of 1668 lists a further twenty.[7]

The inhabitants of St. Helier were fairly mixed, while St. Aubin consisted almost entirely of substantial merchants and their families, and although the island as a whole was heavily populated the towns were still quite small. Neither were they at any time before or since incorporated, as were so many English towns, and hence there were no Burgesses as such.

The farmers and their families made up a substantial proportion of the total population, and we can gain an approximate estimate of their number. By the end of the 16th century almost all arable land was enclosed, so that little but sand-dunes remained open. Consequently the amount of 51,000 vergées enclosed land given in 1795[8] cannot be much more than the figure which already prevailed at the end of the 16th century. Taking the size of an average holding at 20-23 vergées (and we know that many were smaller than this) the number of farms must have been around 2,000 to 2,500. We can therefore say with reasonable certainty that there were about 2,000 Farmers, who with their families made a total of 10,000-12,000 people. (In very recent years there has been a marked change in the size of holdings, but as late as 1950 there were still 1,371 farms of under 25 vergées [11 acres] in a total of 2,132.[9])

If we now relate these figures to Dumaresq's Survey, allowing five persons to a household, a picture begins to emerge, as below:

	Houses	Inhabitants
	3,069	(x5) = 15,345
Manors, about	120	= 600
Farms	2,000	= 10,000
Town Houses, about	230	= 1,150
Very poor	300	= 1,500
	2,650	13,250
Balance	419 houses	2,095

As we have numerous comments that a substantial number of full-time fishermen also existed, but no clue whatever as to what a 'substantial number' might mean, we can only say that the balance shown above is likely to consist of these fishermen and the relatively small number of paid farm-hands and servants of other types who did not live in with their employers.

This can only be viewed as a crude estimate indeed; the evidence is too scanty, but nevertheless the attempt has probably been worth making, and suggests a relatively sounder economy than that of England, in that a very high proportion of the population were self-employed, and property-owning in addition. There may have been many who were comparatively poor, but the distribution of wealth was more evenly spread.

The Social Ladder in the 17th Century

Yeomen and Husbandmen?

It must already be clear that wealth had a great deal to do with social class, and it is now worth looking at Gregory King's estimates. The following is quoted in *A History of the Cost of Living*:

> Gregory King estimated knights at 600 (average income £650 per family), esquires at 3,000 (average income £450), and gentlemen – the loosest of all categories – at 12,000 (average income £280).... The total possessions of knights and esquires accorded quite closely with the annual value of their estates, those of the former amounting to some £150 on average and of the latter to about £75. By contrast, the wealth of the gentlemen was often measured in chattels rather than in real estate. As a class their average possessions perhaps totalled £30-£40, but individuals having a connection with a trade or a profession might be as rich in personal property as a knight.... Robert Ashbrooke, mercer of Chipping Wycombe, Bucks., was one of 'the richest men in the county with £240.'[10] He estimates elsewhere that the number of yeomen was about 40,000 with an average income of over £100, and a further 120,000 with from £40-£100 per annum.

There was no clear dividing-line between a yeoman and a husbandman, though in general terms the yeoman was likely to be a land-owner while the husbandman rented his land. A farmer with more than 100 acres was almost certainly a yeoman, under this he was probably a husbandman, but under about 10 acres (the size of a high proportion of Jersey farms) he was not considered a farmer at all. Although Jersey farms were therefore minute by English standards, the Jersey houses were solid and substantial and almost without exception of two stories, while most farmers were producing cash crops, or at least a surplus to their own requirements. It would therefore seem that their position lay somewhere in the region of the husbandrnen or lesser yeomen, for although they owned good houses like those of the yeomen their income was more that of the husbandmen. But in character they again tended to resemble the yeomen.

The characteristics of the (yeoman) class were supposed to be their industry, frugality, patriotism and solid worth. Although some aspired to, and achieved, gentility, most were content to farm their lands quietly, to invest wisely, to educate their sons and pass on a better Inheritance than they had acquired.[11]

The typical Jersey farmer could not be more accurately described than by this picture of the English yeoman, though he was more like the French small-holding peasant in that he was liable to a surly depression at times, uncharacteristic in the yeoman.

The next picture we have is of 'ten poor mercers' (as they styled themselves) petitioning the Privy Council in 1624. Sir Philippe de Carteret had obtained a Royal Warrant giving licence to import a specified quantity of mercery goods, worth £600-£1,000 according to qualities, as an annual extra to the amount already allowed, and he was now demanding from them £334 as their part of the costs of obtaining the patent. They had already paid him £80, and petitioned to the effect that they considered the additional £254 should come from the islanders in general, with which the Council agreed.[12] The amount already being imported is not stated, but Jersey was a very sound trading community, and it cannot have been less than the amount newly granted, thus making a minimum annual import in this field of £1,500-£2,000. These 'ten poor mercers', then, had an average annual turnover of at least £150-£200, a very substantial amount indeed. In England a trader who died would normally be expected to leave an estate about equal to one year's turnover, and yet as late as the end of the 17th century a tailor in Wiltshire who died and left £150, and a miller in Cornwall who left the same amount 'were merchants with a thriving trade ... in the same category as a substantial husbandman or small yeoman.'[13]

Our mercers, then, were hardly as poor as they claimed!

Even among the farmers we find mention of silver in wills, while books and pewter were commonplace. The amount of furniture is small, but so it was among all except the more well-to-do Yeomen and those above them. This too shows a very much better standard of living for the Jersey farmer per acre than for his English counterpart, possibly as much as four to six times more.

So we have an overall picture of Jersey as a fairly wealthy community, and though it was more evenly distributed than in England the gap between the rich and the poor was still enormous. As in England, maximum wages were fixed (in England by the Justices of the Peace, in Jersey by the States), but as in England it seems that this type of order was never capable of being fully enforced. In the first half of the century maximum daily wages were 3 sous for expert Woolcombers and Tailors, 3 for Thatchers, 5 for Masons, and 6 for Carpenters.[14] (5 sous was almost exactly equivalent to 6d.)

The Castles, being Royal, were outside the jurisdiction of the States, but Governors were not likely to pay more wages than they were forced to when making repairs, as they were customarily having to pay out of their own pockets and then having to reclaim the amount from Sovereigns, who were themselves notoriously short of cash. In repairs to the castles in 1617-1619 we find Halliards, Masons, Masons' labourers, and Carpenters all paid 6 sous, and Halliard's labourers paid 5 sous.[15] In 1634 Halliards had jumped to 8-10 sous, though their labourers still received 5-6, Masons 6-10, Carpenters and Thatchers 10.[16] In England at this period Masons and Carpenters were receiving 12d, (the same as the 10 sous of those in Jersey) but labourers were much better paid at 8d, or 3d plus food. Jersey wages were therefore on average a little lower than English. The price of food was roughly the same, except for fish, and the poor must have lived very largely on fish, which was normally plentiful.

One peculiar local law designed to aid the poor was that every shipmaster arriving in the harbour with coal, salt, or other essential commodities such as foodstuffs (and most ships in those days had a very mixed cargo which would include these items) had to sell his cargo by retail for four days before he was allowed to offer it wholesale. No modern government is ever likely to emulate this method of poor relief!

Their houses

The houses of the Farmers have already been described as solid and substantial, and this is corroborated by the fact that about two hundred dating from the 17th century are still in use today, and nearly all in excellent condition. The majority have a dower-wing attached, and some of these are almost as large as the main house, though generally they are about half the size. It was customary for the eldest son to take over the farmhouse on the death of his father, and mother moved into the dower-wing, with her own kitchen, but close enough to be looked after if necessary in her old age.

Considering the size and strength of these houses a surprising number appear to have been built in the 17th century, and especially in the latter half of that period. There appear to be two reasons for this, the steady economic improvement during much of the century, which does not appear to have been seriously affected by variations in world trade in general, and an increase in the amount of lime available for building. Prior to this, as very little wood was available, houses were built of stone with clay packing, lime being virtually unobtainable. The fault in this type of building is clearly shown in a mention in the La Cloche Memoirs, which state that in 1650 '...many houses fell down from the abundance of rainfall, which was more than there has ever been in living memory.'[17] Many more, of course, were severely damaged, and a great deal of replacement was necessary.

It was a common practice to put carved date-stones on domestic buildings, but Joan Stevens suggests that these dates can be misleading. Individually this may well be true, but taken as a whole there appears to be no reason to doubt the evidence which they offer. Of the houses still in existence today 84 known to have been built in the 17th century have no date-stones, and so cannot be attributed to any specific year, 61 do have dates and there is an upsurge of building and of major additions (usually a new dower-wing, and also dated) in the second half of the century. This is in line with the pattern of building in England.

The complete lack of building of any sort during the period of the Commonwealth is very noticeable. No doubt it was largely due to the insecurity of the time, the Royalists being unable to build due to the possibility of having their estates confiscated, or of having to pay a heavy fine to avoid this, and the Parliamentarians (who, in general terms, were not quite so well-to-do) feeling insufficiently secure in their newly-acquired estates to risk any great expenditure on them. But with the Restoration comes a great upsurge in building, some no doubt being replacements for those houses fallen down in 1650, and some new buildings which, in the ordinary course of events, would have been built during the preceding ten years. In 1673 the States became so alarmed that they passed the Ordinance referred to earlier, stopping indiscriminate building.

It is also logical that many new buildings in the 18th and 19th centuries replaced those of the earlier part of the 17th century. It may well be, therefore, that there was rather more building then than can now be traced.[18] This does, however, confirm the steady economic expansion throughout the century, as there is no clear evidence of periods of prosperity or decline in the building industry, apart from the artificial boom after the Commonwealth period, but only a fairly steady upwards trend until right at the end of the century. The decline in building in the last decade can be explained by the fact of the war with France, which was affecting the Island economy to a much greater degree than usual, due to the end of the privilege of Neutrality in 1689. This resulted in a manpower shortage due to the rush to man the numerous privateers which the island provided in this war.

From an essay, 1971

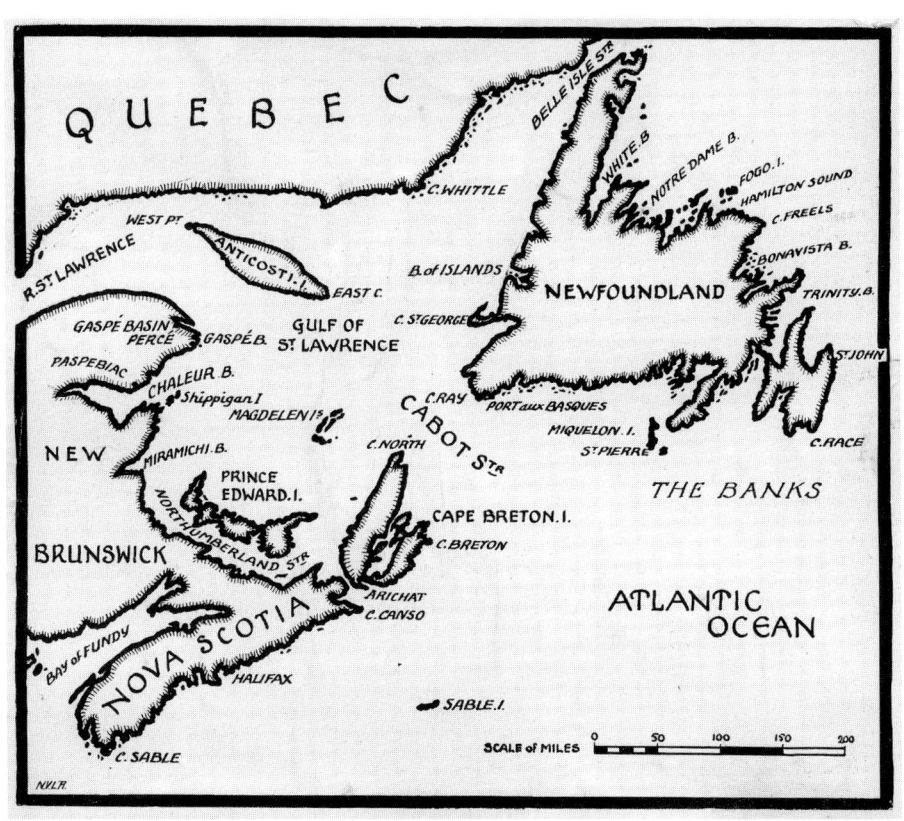

Jerseymen were among several other nationalities who fished around the coast of Newfoundland in the 17th century

12

Fishing and Agriculture in the 17th Century

Export experience

When the Channel Islands first come into the full spotlight of history, at the commencement of the 13th century (when John lost his mainland Duchy of Normandy to the French, and nearly lost the Islands as well), they are found already to be centres of considerable prosperity. Guernsey had gained its reputation as a safe anchorage for ships en route from Aquitaine and Gascony to England, while Jersey was exporting conger-eels on a large scale. The shallow waters around the Island teemed with this fish, and with 3,000 men and women engaged in catching and salting, the income from this source was substantial. Although John owned about one third of the Island he received more income from the *esperquerie* (tax on congers) than he did from his lands. Guernsey had a similar trade, but smaller, as its waters are deeper and thus less suitable as breeding-grounds.

The export of congers continued through the centuries, the salt fish going to England and Normandy, and the trade was still considerable in the 17th century, though on a smaller scale than earlier times. It gradually declined, but did not finally disappear until the early 19th century, although the *esperquerie* had depreciated to such an extent that it had not been collected for some decades.[1]

Thus from the earliest times Jersey was fortunate in having the support of a substantial export trade, but by the beginning of the 17th century there were also other promising exports coming to the fore. At a very early period (certainly before the 16th century) Jersey farmers were in the habit of taking their surplus wheat to Carteret on the nearby coast of Normandy, or to the great Guibray Fair held twice a year at Falaise, the early capital city of that province. They brought back in exchange pottery, pewter, 'Sunday-best' clothes for their wives, and all those little extras which only the great fairs provided for the countryman of the period. By the commencement of the 17th century it was no longer small surpluses but a full commercial enterprise, for the English government in assessing the value of the Islands in 1595 had a note before them to the effect that 'wheat is super-abundant, for both islands do utter great quantities of it.'[2]

In view of the very large populations, about 13,000 in Guernsey and 20,000 in .Jersey (or 450 to the square mile), this is quite astonishing. England was unable to rely on an annual wheat surplus until the beginning of the 18th century, and yet her population at this time was only around one hundred per square mile. There are two factors that contributed to this: the islanders had never had to slaughter their animals in winter in any numbers, as the milder climate than much of England meant that there was a certain amount of grassland all the year round. This in turn led to more animal manure being available, which was not to be the case in most of England until root-crops became available as winter feed for cattle in the 18th century.

The second factor was the sea, which was providing still another rich harvest, for in the past centuries islanders had discovered the high fertilising value of the *vraic*, or seaweed, which grows so prolifically around the coasts, and especially on the outlying reefs. Either spread straight on the fields and ploughed in, or burnt and distributed as ash, it was the universal provider, and its collection from the shores had been regulated by law from very ancient times. So, in effect, the sea gave the farmers their livelihood, as well as the fishers.

Much of this 'super-abundance' of wheat was taken up by Spanish merchants at St. Malo in Brittany in the early 1600s, and, according to Falle, barter was still the principal method of payment. If such large quantities were involved one would have expected this to be a cash trade, and it is difficult to explain why this had not happened. Channel Islands' ships (and especially those from Jersey) traded constantly with St. Malo, but for much of the 16th and 17th centuries the route was infested with petty pirates. It may be that the shippers would have stood in jeopardy of their lives through an increase of these robbers if they were frequently carrying gold or silver bullion. But this is mere guess-work. It may just as well be that money was not trusted, for many currencies had suffered depreciation more than once during the 16th century.

Fishing and Agriculture in the 17th Century

Vraic (seaweed) drying in the sun

Though some of the farmers lived at little more than subsistence level many were enterprising, and were always on the lookout for a new and more profitable source of income. Towards the end of the 16th century many of them had begun to fish off Newfoundland in the spring (for most farmers were spare-time fishermen as well, though of course they joined larger vessels as crewmen for the Newfoundland work) and they would then come back in time for the harvest and the ploughing, leaving their womenfolk and children to see to the sowing when they had left again the following year.

Cider

In the early 1600s another profitable crop began to claim their attention, for we find the Lieutenant-Governor of the Island writing to Lord Conway (Secretary of State) in 1626, when war seemed imminent, asking that an order be given prohibiting the conversion of arable-lands to orchards.[3] That he should trouble to do so implies that the conversions were taking place at a fairly rapid pace, and he was no doubt worried about adequate supplies of corn in case the Island was cut off for any length of time. We have no trace of the Council's reply.

Farmers already had well over fifty years experience with this apple crop, for the Privy Council in 1573 gave permission for the importation into Jersey of 100 quarters barley or barley-malt, '...as the cider crop has failed these last two years.'[4] Just how much cider was made at this time, or for how long the orchards had been established, we do not know. There is, however, included in an inventory of provisions at Mont Orgueil Castle in 1533:

ij bariques de vin gascointz,
Quatre barriques de bière nouvellement apportée d'Angleterre,
xij pipes et demie de cydre neuf.[5]

This suggests that the cider was locally made, as it would be unlikely to be imported while new, and in both other cases it specifies that it was imported. This is seemingly the earliest reference to local cider.

It seems very probable that some of these Newfoundland fisher-farmers came to realise that an apple crop needed less attention than cereals, and must have given as good a return, or there would not have been this rapid conversion that gave the Lieutenant-Governor cause for alarm. There also appears to have been a further steady expansion of cider-making throughout the 17th century, for Poingdestre, writing in 1682, says that there was not a house in the whole Island that had not at least one apple orchard, and adds that in 1681 the crop was so heavy that there were not sufficient casks available for half the cider made.[6] Falle, writing in 1694, estimated that 24,000 hogsheads (1,260,000 gallons) were made every year.[7]

Truly the farmers had found themselves an admirable cash crop, but Falle deplores the fact that too much was drunk by many. If some did drink too much, many more must have improved their status from an increased income, and there is evidence in other quarters to suggest that this was the case. The number of orchards continued to increase during the following century, and it has been calculated that by 1795 19.5% of all enclosed land in Jersey (and nearly all arable land was enclosed) was entirely given over to orchards,[8] so that 2,000,000 gallons were being produced annually,[9] and somewhere around two-thirds of this exported.

Enclosure of fields had taken place in the first part of the 16th century, and the Island was almost wholly enclosed by 1550, leaving only the sand dunes and the cliff-tops as open land. No doubt due to the fact that most farmers owned their own land it seems to have happened without any of the problems or disturbances so common in England in some areas. Also, although sheep were numerous during the 16th and 17th centuries (with two and even three pairs of horns) there were no great landowning sheep-farmers. Each farmer kept a small flock to feed and clothe his family, and there was little wool left for export. Otherwise the farmer produced much the same as his English counterpart, but was in general more advanced in practice and technique.

Jersey farmers planting potatoes in recent years, showing how the maximum use has always been made of land

The principal crops grown, apart from apples, were wheat, rye, oats and barley (the latter for bread and beer), peas, beans and parsnips. Until the coming of the potato, parsnips were the principal dish of the inhabitants, and about 10% of the land was given up to their growth, while beans, which were often ground to make flour, were frequently sown between the rows of parsnips. The latter was a very popular dish when boiled and mashed with butter, and they were also commonly fed to pigs, which were very numerous, being considered the best possible diet for them. 'Turnops' were well established when Poingdestre wrote in 1682, some forty years before 'Turnip' Townshend introduced them into English farming. Hemp was commonly grown where the soil was suitable, and was used for making clothing, ropes, and sails for ships, but even by the early 1600s the crop was often insufficient. Livestock, as we have seen, consisted largely of sheep and pigs, but cattle were kept for the farmer's own use, and oxen for ploughing and similar work. As in England, horses were not yet commonplace, though most farmers owned one if they could, first as a means of transport, and only secondly as a working animal.

Tobacco

In 1628 the English Attorney-General was much disturbed to discover '...large quantities of tobacco planted in Jersey and Guernsey, to the detriment of corn-crops, and against proclamations',[10] and he recommended the Privy Council to order its destruction. His fears were in fact more in respect of the claims of the proprietors of the Plantations in America, and the loss to England of customs dues, than to any loss of corn. The Council seem to have been a bit slow in their deliberations, but finally wrote to the Lieutenant-Governor in 1632, ordering him to destroy all tobacco in the Channel Islands, and to allow no more to be planted. So ended another attempt at a good cash crop. If the farmers had little money they certainly had no intention of remaining in that situation.

The North Atlantic Ocean

The Newfoundland fisheries have already been mentioned. John Cabot had discovered North America in 1497, and Jacques Cartier, a native of St. Malo, explored the St. Lawrence River as far as present-day Montreal in 1535. As the Channel Islanders traded with both Bristol and St. Malo, but especially the latter, they must have soon been well-informed about these journeys. It is worth mentioning that Jerseymen who settled in Newfoundland centuries ago had a very strong tradition that Cabot had in fact been told about it by their own ancestors. Jersey ships were certainly recorded as fishing off the coasts of Iceland in the 14th century, a very long way from home, and a severe easterly gale could quite easily have resulted in one or more of them inadvertently repeating the voyage of Eric the Red, and landing up off the shores of

Labrador or Newfoundland. On the other hand, there was still a Norse colony at Greenland at this time, and ships made occasional voyages there, so that they may have heard about the place from these seamen. This is one of those folk-tales for which no proof has come to light.

Soon after Cartier's further voyages in the 1530s and 1540s the fishermen of St. Malo (the Malouins) began voyaging out to the New World to the cod-banks of Newfoundland, and as they and the Jerseymen were in general on friendly terms throughout the 16th and 17th centuries it would not be surprising if one or two Island ships were soon accompanying them. At any rate, a Jersey will of 1586 mentions a Jersey ship 'which is now unloading after her voyage to Newfoundland', and in the following year there was a dispute before the Jersey Royal Court about a cargo of Newfoundland cod. In 1591 there was a similar case, so the trade would seem to have been well established in late Elizabethan times.

The friendliness between St. Malo and Jersey is exemplified by the fact that at this period the Jersey 'Newfoundlanders' wintered at St. Malo, as there was no safe harbour for them in the Island. Guernsey had a good harbour, and it was closer, but the inhabitants of the two Islands had always held a strong animosity for each other, as so often occurred in these earlier times between adjoining communities of somewhat similar interests.

For the first half of the 17th century records of this trade are very sparse, but we have enough occasional references to know that it continued, sometimes up, sometimes down, but always there. In 1618 the Privy Council took the Lieutenant-Governor of Jersey to task, forbidding him to sell munitions, and especially gunpowder, to ships, or to local inhabitants for their own use, '…as has been done recently, especially for Newfoundlanders'.[11] The Council pointed out that it was imported on licence specifically for the defence of the Castles, and so of the Island.

Unanticipated problems

It is a possibility that the increase in orchards in the 1620s was the result of an increase in the fishing trade, though the records are insufficient to prove whether the latter did, in fact, increase at this time, but it received a severe setback when England and Spain declared war in 1624, followed by a further war with France in 1626. Not only were the ships now liable to attack, but the Catholic ports where they usually sold their fish were closed to Englishmen. It picked up quickly when both wars ceased in 1630, but was soon again in trouble. In 1635 a Jersey Newfoundlander was stopped by six Turkish men-of-war off the Scillies, but escaped by pretending to be French. (At this period the Arab nations were vigorously disputing control of the Mediterranean Sea, and were indiscriminately lumped together as 'Turks', though most came from Morocco).

On arrival at Weymouth they told officials that the Turks had said that they had twenty ships waiting to catch the English Newfoundland fleet, about two hundred ships which now sailed annually from various ports on the west and south-west coasts. Only six days later (September 26, 1635) it was confirmed that the Turks had taken 120 West Countrymen prisoner, within three leagues of the Lizard, and there were serious fears for the rest of the fleet.[12] A number of Channel Islanders were also captured at this time, for in 1639 it is recorded in Jersey that

> On 27th June 1639, Nicolle Effard returned from his voyage to Turkey (Morocco) at the request of the States to rescue those poor seamen who bad been taken slaves by the Turks. He left 4th Aug. 1638 and rescued seventeen, including his brother Pierre.

During the Civil War years of 1642-49 the fishing continued, at least during those years when fighting was not actually taking place, but the mariners had to pay a fine to gain exemption from militia duty. And at one period Parliament became so incensed with the depredations of Sir George Carteret's privateers that they sent especially to Newfoundland, and captured ten Jersey ships fishing there, as a retaliatory measure.

With the Restoration in 1660 the trade gained new impetus, and Falle records that at this time about twenty ships used to go every year to Newfoundland. Each of these would have carried about fifty men, taking the shore-based workers (gutting, salting, packing, etc.) as well as the actual fishermen. But by 1685 there was a severe slump, due largely to a French impost of a crown a quintal (100 lbs.) on all fish imported in English ships, for Colbert, principal Minister of France, was making great efforts to strengthen the supply of sailors to the

French Navy by encouraging the fisheries, and the war between Britain and France in 1689-97 brought the fisheries to a virtual standstill.

Thus the 17th century ended with the Newfoundland fisheries totally disrupted and virtually dead. Who could realise that within thirty years or so over two thousand Jerseymen, and one thousand Guernseymen, would be going out to 'Terreneuve' every year, and that by the end of the 18th century the Channel Islands would be in control of a major part of the whole fishing industry of the Atlantic seaboard of Canada? The waters off Newfoundland and the St. Lawrence estuary were fished by English West countrymen as well as Portuguese and French fishermen, but for almost a century – from about 1790 to 1870 – the majority of the fishermen on the banks off the Gaspé peninsula, off Cape Breton Island and some parts of Newfoundland were to be Channel Islanders, some going out every year, and thousands settling in the coastal villages which they themselves had created. The headquarters of several great fishing firms remained in Jersey and in Guernsey, and most supplies came from these Islands, but from 1873 to 1886 a series of bank failures in the Islands led to the failure of many of these companies, and resulted in riots in Canadian fishing ports, which necessitated Army intervention, as there was no money to pay the workers.

So much had this coast become a virtual 'colony' of the Channel Islands (though not Newfoundland, which was more in the hands of Westcountrymen) that people in the Islands rarely bothered to mention Canada. 'He is at the Coast' said in conversation was understood by all to mean not one of the Island's bays only a mile or so away, but a coast nearly three thousand miles away!

From an essay, 1971

The small spinning-wheel – the true Jersey or Guernsey wheel

13

Manufacture and Trade in the 17th Century

One would not normally expect to find a major manufacturing industry in islands such as these during earlier times, but knitting became such an industry during Elizabeth's reign, and continued throughout the 17th century and beyond. All of the Channel Islands, but especially Jersey and Guernsey, developed as centres of stocking manufacture to a truly astonishing degree, and no one quite knows why. One or two local historians have put forward the very feasible suggestion that it was first introduced by the Huguenot refugees of the second half of the 16th century, these being well-attested as having advanced knitting skills, but according to Richard Rutt, in *A History of Hand Knitting*, 'Channel Islands knitting was renowned in England when Queen Elizabeth came to the throne'[1] [1550]. Also, William Harrison in his *Description of England* (1587) spoke of 'women's diversely coloured stockings of silk jersey'.[2] There does not appear to be any record of silk being imported into Jersey, and it seems that the term 'jersey' was already a familiar one in England for a type of knitting or of knitted material, and this could only have occurred after the usage of many years. The Huguenots may have added to this reputation, but it does not seem that they introduced the trade, and we are left wondering what caused the expansion to a large industry.

There are several possible reasons for this, and it may be that a combination of these made for particularly favourable circumstances. The islanders were naturally a highly industrious people, and as we have seen were prepared to seize every opportunity to benefit themselves, both politically and financially. Secondly, the increasing population of the 16th century had created a new landless class, poverty-stricken due to lack of any form of industry, and a hand-knitting trade could well have been their salvation. Then, too, the voyages across the Atlantic were long and tedious, and the many men carried on the Newfoundlanders in the first few decades of this fishing trade had little to do to while away their time.

Knitting had earlier generally been a man's occupation, as a craft, but by the late 1500s was more of a cottage spare-time industry with women in England, adding extra income, though not yet something which women were expected to do as a useful pastime, as it later became. In the Channel Islands it was very rapidly to be taken up by both sexes, a proof of the lack of any form of guild organisation in general, and those farms which had been converted latterly to orchards left the wives, and children too, with more time available than most farm families, at least for long periods of the year, so that they could also add to the family income in this way. A fourth reason was almost certainly the age-old freedom from Customs charges on goods 'the produce or manufacture of the lslands', which must have helped their products to sell at a lower rate than similar goods made elsewhere, as they could export them to the continent more cheaply than English stockings, and export them to England more cheaply than continental stockings. By the 18th century the exports to France exceeded those to England.

But there seems to have been even a fifth possible reason, a matter of the quality of the knitting itself, about which there are tantalising glimpses, but nothing more. It is quite clear that in England 'jersey' came to mean knitted, as distinct from woven, as has been mentioned earlier, and Balleine quotes *Camden's Britannia* of 1586: 'The women make great gain by knitting hose, which we call Jersey stocks.'

In 1587 Amyas Poulet, gaoler to Mary Queen of Scots (and previously Governor of Jersey), describing her execution, says 'her nether stocke of worsted coloured watchett clocked with silver and edged on the topps with silver and next her leggs a pair of Jersey hose white....'[3]

An undated entry in the *Calendar of State Papers (Domestic)* placed as probably 1596, mentions the fact that there are three sorts of spinning-wool: 'On the big wheel, from whence comes woollen yarn, on the small wheel, from whence comes Guernsey or Jersey yarn, because first practised there, and on the rocks, when it is called worsted.'[4] (Rock.: 'A distaff together with the wool or flax attached to it' – *Shorter Oxford English Dictionary*)

Then in 1638 there is a further mention, this time to the effect that over 1,000 jersey spinners in Canterbury had been reduced to penury because of large amounts of yarn from Turkey.[5] There is no record of any large numbers of Jerseymen settling in this area, and this would have been a very large number indeed from the population of the Island at that time, so that it is reasonable to accept that it is the style of spinning referred to, as the earlier Elizabethan entry would suggest.

The States of Jersey stated in a 'Remonstrance' of 1679 that it was 'less than 80 years' since the manufacture of stockings began, with Jersey wool only, but the accuracy of this statement seems very doubtful, for in 1606 the Jersey Royal Court had had to pass a law making it illegal for the knitting of stockings to take place during harvest and *vraicing* times (the collection of seaweed for use as fertiliser) as farms were being neglected in favour of knitting, and this law was strengthened only two years later, while in 1607 all stockings made of 2-ply wool, instead of the standard 3-ply, were confiscated, and some years later inspectors were appointed to ensure the quality of stockings exported. A small number of waistcoats were also knitted, but stockings were predominant. Obviously the trade was already in full swing well before 1606, and profitable.

In 1619 Jersey was given a licence to import annually 400 tods of wool from England[6] (tod normally = 28 lbs), and in 1624 the States sent a petition to Parliament (why to Parliament, instead of the King, which was usual for petitions?) asking for larger supplies because 'more than 1,000 souls have no other means to get their living but by knitting stockings.'[7] These were exported to England, France and America, and during the war with France in 1626-30, when trade was stopped, despite the agreed neutrality of the islands, the Lieutenant-Governor, Sir John Peyton, and the Bailiff, Sir Philippe de Carteret, spent much effort in trying to persuade the Privy Council of the importance of re-opening this trade to France '...without the stocking trade Jersey would hardly exist.'[8] No doubt this was an exaggeration, but with a core of truth. The Council discussed these matters occasionally, but had more important things on their minds, and it was not until the reign of Charles II that Jersey got the extra wool asked for, while trade with France resumed as soon as the war was over.

The Remonstrance tells us that 400 tods were granted in the reign of James I, Charles I added a further 600 tods, and 'the Usurper'

(Cromwell) doubled the amount,[9] so that there was now licence to import 2,000 tods annually, an amount confirmed by Act of Parliament in the reign of Charles II. But if this was the permitted amount, a great deal more was in fact imported. Southampton acted as a staple port for this trade, and from Christmas 1627-1628 shipped 318 tods to Jersey, and 247 to Guernsey. Sixty years later, in 1686-1687 it shipped 3,406 tods (over 42 tons!) to Jersey, 1,736 to Guernsey, and 120 to Alderney.[10] Dumaresq, speaking of the trade in 1685, says:

> ... it will imploy four score toads [sic] weekly, double the number, of what we are permitted by Licence to Import; whereby, it does not only bring a kind of monopoly upon those Licences (under whose colour the merchants must Endeavour to bring greater quantities unlicenst by indirect ways) but also it comes to pass that ye Officers of his 'Majty's Custom of Southampton (the only port permitted) raise another kind of Impost, sometimes by conniving at, and sometimes by seasing and forfetting the said wooll.[11]

Poingdestre states that at this time 'that lazy industry' was exporting 10,000 pairs of stockings weekly and bases his estimate on the fact that there were many houses in which all the occupants, men, women and children from the age of five upwards, did nothing else but knit. He assumes their production at one pair per week per person, and though a good knitter should be able to finish two pairs a week it is likely that very few actually knitted full-time. Although he was Lieutenant-Bailiff, and should therefore have had access to some reasonable documentary evidence (though no adequate statistics existed as yet), it seems probable that this was a considerable exaggeration. He showed strong bias against 'that lazy industry', and he is implying that 10,000 people are wholly engaged in knitting out of the 15,000-20,000 population. In effect, if we assume that many knitters were the 'very poor', this would still mean more than half the farms lying derelict, and though the laws of 1606 and 1608 make it clear that at that time some farmers were neglecting their land in favour of knitting, Poingdestre's figure hardly agrees with his own statement of the cider production alone. Or was it that farmers turned their farms over to orchards, not so that they could go to Newfoundland, but so that they could knit? A doubtful supposition.

Manufacture and Trade in the 17th Century

Cider apples receiving their initial crushing (Dozens of farms had these circular troughs)

Fortunately Dumaresq brings some clear reasoning into the problem.

> Neither upon inquiry do I find the number of stockings made there, to amount to ten thousand pairs a week as some supposes, but believed by the most knowing to come to six thousand, one week with another, and allowing three pairs for one pound of wool, as the ordinary sort are it will imploy four score toads [sic] weekly.[12]

Four-score tods weekly will mean an annual requirement of over 4,000 tods, the 'tod' being of approximate weight of 28 lbs., though there were variations. If 6,000 pairs of stockings at three pairs to the pound is equivalent to 80 tods, as he suggests, then his tod is equal to 25 lbs., and not the more usual 28 lbs. If we therefore reverse the procedure, and suggest 6,000 pairs at three pairs to the pound, for 28lb. tods, the weekly requirement will be 114 tods, and the annual requirement about 3,700, which is nearer to the Southampton figure of 3,406. The question seems to revolve on how near to 28lb. the average 'tod' package weighed, for we know that it was a rough-weight measure only, not a scale-weight. Whichever, it means about 46 tons per annum, an astonishing amount. However, it seems clear that Dumaresq's statement of about 6,000 pairs weekly is much more probable than Poingdestre's 10,000, though it still means that about one-quarter of the population were knitters, even if we assume that about 700 produced two pairs a week.

As this figure especially includes the 'very poor' (it being agreed by many writers of the time that it was their only means of livelihood), and no doubt some of the fishermen and their families as well as farmers and their families, we can estimate that not too many of the farms were seriously neglected, but that such neglect as there was was very noticeable. This is still a surprising fact.

In a dispute between the States of Jersey and HM Customs, which was taken to the Privy Council in 1715, the plea of the islanders contains the following passage.

> The Inhabitants of those Islands are generally very poor, they have nothing valuable of their (growth) to send abroad, or to incourage strangers to fetch from thence: Their Chief ... [document damaged] ... Stockings, about which all their poor are imployd, but can hardly subsist thereby, it being soe much decay'd of late that maney doe not earn by it above Six or Eight pence each a week, so the better sort are forced to contribute to the releife of the poor, otherwise they must starve.[13]

In view of the fact that a Labourer's wage in 1634 was 5 or 6 sous (about $2\frac{1}{2}$p) a day, $2\frac{1}{2}$-$3\frac{1}{2}$p a week eighty years later was clearly a non-living wage even for the poorest. The plea does state, however, that the trade is '...soe much decay'd of late', and this agrees with the general pattern of the hand-knitted stocking trade throughout the whole of England, due to the introduction of the stocking-frame (a knitting machine) during the later 17th century. It is inconceivable that farmers would have begun to neglect their farms in favour of knitting unless the profit margin was substantially greater. It is also inconceivable that when this first became apparent, at the beginning of the 1600s, the farmers would have been prepared to neglect their farms for less than a labourer's wage. Therefore the absolute minimum which is likely to have been acceptable as a total weekly income for the family would have been the 3/0d. (15p) a week of the labourer, but at this sort of income even the worst farmers would have thought twice about forgetting their crops.

It seems likely, then, that for even some farms to be neglected the income must have been at least double this figure, and probably much more, until the intervention of the stocking-frame ruined the trade. Thus the price of a pair of stockings, at least in the first half of the century, would seem to have been around 1/- to 1/6d (5p-7½p) to the wholesaler, who then had to have them dyed for the upper end of the trade, though they would have been sold as they were at the lower end. As Jersey was exporting over 300,000 pairs a year this must have provided the Island with a very substantial income, while the total exported from the Channel Islands as a whole approached 500,000 in the latter half of the century. It is clear that they had a very considerable proportion of the export trade in stockings in north-western Europe, for in the vast majority of cases stockings were knitted in towns and distributed to the surrounding countryside only.

The costs and benefits of neutrality

Not very much is known about the more general trading of the Islands. Guernsey has already been shown to have had an extensive port-of-call relationship with the ships of the English wine trade, and large maturing cellars, but this was declining during much of the 17th century. That neutrality brought a great deal of trade is clear, but few details of this are available. There are no records similar to the port books of England, so that the only references are found in occasional disputes brought before the Court, mentions in correspondence with the Privy Council or in private letters, and the *Extentes* of the King's Revenue, which were compiled at roughly eighty-year intervals.

In 1558, when England and France were at war and the islands had additional military protection, the Privy Council had estimated that the profits on the Customs of English goods to Normandy, and French goods returned, would nearly pay for the fortifications and the 'entertainment' of the soldiers, this 'balance-sheet' referring to Jersey only. Obviously, therefore, it was a substantial amount, as the total annual pay of the soldiers alone was somewhere in the region of £400,[14] and again in 1587 the Council gave reasons for and against free trade:

For:
(1) The value of customs in England on cloths, kerseys, tin and lead exported to France, and linen and French wares imported to England.
(2) Inhabitants of the Channel Islands gain by considerable circulation of the money involved.
(3) More English than French merchants trade through the Channel Islands, they are reasonably safe from attack while doing so, and England gained plenty of useful information through this source.
Against:
(4) More imports to England than exports, through the Islands, and therefore a loss of coinage to the realm.

Although England and France were not at war at this time, as they had been so frequently over many centuries, it was the year before the Spanish attempt on England with the Great Armada. The Pope had declared that anyone who killed Elizabeth would be doing God's work for the Church, and the Islands, which were legally neutral in time of war, were used as transit centres by spies travelling in both directions, though most of them were more carefully watched than they realised.

It therefore seems reasonable to sum up the findings of the Council to the effect that though their trade left England with a deficit this was more than counterbalanced by the information flowing through them, and also, had their neutrality been cancelled in war-time, England would lose the opportunity of export trade to France, the Islands would be much more expensive to defend, and quite possibly the population would become so impoverished that they would become dependent on English subsidies. The loss to England would have been far in excess of the comparatively minor trade deficit.

In 1627 (in wartime) we find Secretary Conway sending a memorandum to Secretary Coke, to the effect that merchants and traders ought to be encouraged in Jersey, '...which is happily situated for trade, and having not many growing commodities, and certainly not enough to sustain themselves, they must trade.'[15]

Harbour problems

A major problem in this respect was the lack of a really effective harbour in Jersey. Guernsey had a good one at St. Peter Port, dating from the later Middle Ages, if not earlier, but this was because it had been built to enclose a suitable bay on the east coast of the island, which was sheltered from the prevailing winds. Jersey did not have a satisfactory bay in this respect, and as the 12th century Abbey of St. Helier had been built on an offshore islet for comparative safety from both enemy raiders and pirates the town of St. Helier had developed nearby, and needed a harbour.

It would be hard to find a more difficult situation, for the foreshore in this area is so flat, and the tidal range of forty feet so great, that the tide can go out more than a mile. This did mean that ships could go close inshore, being left high and dry as the tide receded, and so unload their cargo into carts on the beach. Nevertheless, by the end of the 16th century, St. Helier had had a wharf or pier of some sort for at least a century, and by 1585 the merchants were financing the building of a small new harbour, known as St. James, at the island where the abbey had once stood. The tidal movements made this a very great problem, and their harbour was still not finished at the beginning of the 1600s, but this shows very clearly that the merchants were in general very prosperous indeed.

In the late 1500s a fine new harbour was built at Havre des Pas, on the lee of the Mont de la Ville, possibly at the expense of the English government, although it had the serious deficiency of a very rocky approach. This left the old exposed harbour to gradually decay even more than it was already, and the St. James harbour to remain useable but unfinished, and this situation remained throughout the 17th century. Despite being well-designed the Havre des Pas harbour was clearly not favoured by the merchants, presumably because the approach was too dangerous, and it seems that it was deliberately dismantled early in the 18th century, the South Pier being again rebuilt, and most probably using the stone removed from Havre des Pas, though this whole situation remains unclear.

A new pier was also begun in 1670, attached to the islet on which St. Aubin's Fort is built, and this did have the advantage that it was not exposed to the prevailing winds, but it was not finished until 1700, just beyond the century on which this article is based. It was being paid for from part of the duties charged on the import of wines and ciders.

Guernsey, during this century, was declining as a port. It is probable that the improvements in both ships and methods of navigation had much to do with this, as coast-hugging voyages were less necessary, and the open Channel was now widely used. Eagleston states that piracy in the 1580s had so ruined the trade of Guernsey that no foreigners would trade there,[16] and this could well be a contributory factor. It seems likely that Jersey gained at the expense of Guernsey insofar as trade with the neighbouring coasts of France were concerned. The Civil War made no apparent difference, for although the Islands supported different sides both were granted the same trade privileges as before at the Restoration.

In 1619 Jersey had been granted licence to import annually a quantity of goods free of Customs charges, in addition to similar existing licences. Included in this new lot of goods were 20 broadcloths, 200 kersies, 200 pieces fustians and other stuffs, and £300 value of mercers', grocers', and haberdashers' wares.[17] Linens, roofing tiles, pottery and wine mostly came from France. It is interesting to note from the Council deliberations already mentioned the through-trade of goods, for the 'cloths and kersies' were principally destined for France, and the 'Linen and French wares' for England.

Coal imports

Quite large quantities of coal came from South Wales in the period 1550-1603 for which the Port Books have been published, and information from these relating to the Channel Islands has been made the theme of a careful study[18] by Trevor Williams. This was clearly a well-established trade, and must have continued during the 17th century, but the facts are not at present easily available. The Port Books are not entirely complete, and show an annual export to Jersey in the last twenty years of the 16th century of 100 weys, but the year 1600 appears to be more fully documented, and the figure is 191 weys for the period January to June only, which suggests that the 100 weys was in fact often exceeded, but not always recorded. Almost the whole of this trade was done in Jersey vessels.

Williams published an extracted list of ship movements to the islands during this period, in which the tonnage is usually given (and at this period tonnage recorded was always tons burthen) and the number of weys carried. Most of the ships sailed from Swansea, and Willan gives the Swansea wey as four tons,[19] but this does not agree with Williams' figures, which would suggest that the 2-ton wey common to many coal ports was also in use here.

Some of the ships would seem to have carried up to about 10% more than their stated tonnage (a feasible amount with a cargo such as coal) though the majority agree with the more usual ratio of 75-80%. This is using the two-ton wey: Willan's four tons would give cargo ratios from 150% to 220% of tons burthen, impracticable on a quiet river, let alone in the open Channel. This coal was for consumption in Jersey, not for re-export, for although the Island was fairly well wooded it could not possibly supply such a large population with its fuel demands. Right up to the 19th century many of the poorer inhabitants used dried seaweed, turf, or gorse as fuel, the first two being relatively good for cooking, but quite inadequate for heating. The shortage of fuel is exemplified by the fact that as early as 1340 we find in an inventory at Mont Orgueil Castle '28 qtrs. of sea-coal', valued at 3/0d. (15p) a quarter.[20] This is a very early date indeed for coal to be exported from England, though it had been mined for quite some time before this.

Southampton had always been the principal port in England for the Channel Islands' trade, and remained so during the 17th century. This was principally due to its importance in the wine trade in the earlier centuries, and now it had become the wool port specified, no other port being allowed to ship wool to the Islands, in order that a check might be kept on the licensed quantity. Apart from wool the cargoes were almost entirely general goods, of no especial significance or quantity. In fact the only items of any note are fairly large quantities of textiles, and the re-export to Jersey of hides, apparently sent to Southampton for tanning. In 1603 the States of Jersey sent a substantial donation to the town of Southampton when it was suffering severely from plague,[21] showing a very close link between the two places.

The actual number of ships owned in Jersey at this time is unknown, except for one reference in Dumaresq (1685):

> ... that is the disproportion of shipping in regard of the imployment the Island affords; for of forty Vessels with top sails

and decks, besides as many smaller crafts that now are in that Island, twenty are able to maintain the whole Commerce: as well for importing from England the materials of our manufactures, as of exporting the said manufactures beyond Seas; besides all ordinary necessaries; the rest if they want imployment from abroad, must study all means to imploy their vessels as now they do, in ransacking the markets to bring in all manner of provisions at a cheaper rate than the husbandmen here can afford them; whereby it comes to pass that husbandry is so much discouraged, that all the able youth, that did use to apply themselves to that calling finding no way to advance themselves, become seamen: to which the Late Warres among our neighbours gave no small encouragement, for the use they made of our shipping, to transport their goods: and that now failing, they either are forced to go in french Vessels, or to the Western plantations from whence they seldom return, but are wholly lost to the Island.[22]

The size of these ships can be gauged from Falle, who states that '...our trade does not require ships of more than 120-130 tons.' He also mentions that there are now only three or four Newfoundlanders, 'where there used to be 20', (because the French impost on English cod had killed the trade). Earlier in the century there must have been about a dozen or so Newfoundlanders, for Balleine states that around the year 1600 '...hundreds of Jerseymen were sailing to Newfoundland every spring', while Williams' coal-trade figures with South Wales list 31 Jersey ships between the years 1550-1603, an average number at any one time being six: these were mostly small coasters of around 20-40 tons.[23]

The Islands were fortunate in being legally exempt from the attentions of the press-gangs, though on a very few occasions, and particularly during the Commonwealth, this was ignored, and men were pressed. The exemption must have made for much more stable conditions among the ship-owners and crews alike.

From an essay, 1971

14
Blake's Attack on Jersey

Can you imagine the feelings of Jean Chevalier, a peaceable official of the Jersey Court, as he wrote in his diary: 'Today, the 20th October 1652, arrived in the Bay of St. Ouen eighty-four sailing ships, both large and small, bringing the army of Parliament to take this island.' The fleet had anchored off Sark the previous day, awaiting suitable weather to attempt a landing in Jersey, and it seems that no suspicions were aroused, for early the following morning it was discovered already gathering in St. Ouen's Bay.

In charge was Admiral Robert Blake, the principal leader of both Parliamentary army and navy, and with the conditions being unsuitable he sent a substantial part of the fleet to study the situation in St. Brelade's Bay and along the south coast, these then returning to St. Ouen, except for twelve frigates which remained at St. Brelade.

But why did the English go to this remarkable expense and effort to attack Jersey? It is true that the Island was still led and defended by Royalist supporters, and while there were both Royalist and Parliamentary supporters in the masses of the ordinary population we do not know enough to say in what proportions these were divided. It is nevertheless almost a certainty – as it is known that it was in England – that the majority would have preferred just to get on with normal living without having to side with anyone. In those days when travel depended on the wind the island seemed distant, so why not leave the Islanders to themselves, until the isolation caused them to alter their minds?

The reason was Sir George de Carteret, or Sir George Carteret as he was known to the English. He was not only the dominant Royalist in the island, he totally dominated it. He held Letters Patent appointing him as both Bailiff and Lieutenant-Governor (a combination so powerful that Balleine, in his History of Jersey, simply describes him as the Dictator).

Copy of a portrait by Peter Lely of Sir George de Carteret, Baronet

His support for the monarchy was unwavering, and as soon as the war began he saw a way in which he could be of use. At this time his uncle was Bailiff of Jersey, the position to which Sir George was appointed some years later. He had a galley built at St. Malo, armed it and crewed it, and sent them out to do as much damage to Parliamentary ships as possible. In no time they were so successful that ships which they captured were also converted to do the same, until he had a small fleet at sea. Because the Letters of Marque necessary to make them legal privateers could only be issued in London they were in effect an illegal Royalist navy, until Charles I appointed Sir George as Vice-Admiral of Jersey, which enabled him to issue such Letters.

He now needed some three hundred men as crew for his boats, but his autocratic manner made him unpopular, and he could not get enough crew in Jersey, so he filled the vacancies in his vessels, and especially the positions of master, with mercenaries. It was not long before these men began to misuse their position, feeling safe from discovery while at sea, and having no particular loyalty to anyone. They turned to attacking any and every ship in sight – plain piracy. De Carteret's appointment as Admiral was consequently revoked by Charles – King Charles II in Jersey, Charles Stuart, renegade, in England, who did not wish to be seen as financed by piracy, despite his extreme poverty at that time.

In fact, De Carteret was not alone in this field, for all through the 16th to 18th centuries many lords of the manors – especially in the West Country – had shares in or owned vessels which operated illegally, either as pirates or as smugglers, and some of the greatest nobles were also involved. Sir George's problem, if that is the right word, was that the actions of his 'navy' became just too blatantly and openly piratical.

It was thus both De Carteret and his fleet that needed to be eliminated in some way or other, and led to the attack on Jersey, the home port of the fleet, or, as Cromwell put it, 'that nest of vypers'. At the time that this was said it was probably a fair description!

On hearing of the arrival of the ships at St. Ouen Sir George hurriedly organised opposition, but everyone was unprepared. He assembled the parish militias on the sand-dunes facing the fleet, while leaving Grouville and St. Brelade's militias to guard their own areas. It was typical autumnal weather. The state of the sea was against a landing, it was raining heavily and continued to do so the next day, and with the movement of sailing-ships being so ponderously slow it was not until late in the evening of the third day that a landing took place. Over the whole of this time the militia-men were on the dunes, with no protection from the incessant rain, and no food or drink except for anything that they may have grabbed as they left home. There had been no time to organise any catering or shelter, and it is probable that an instant battle had been hoped for, not a delay.

Two thousand six hundred men and about eighty cavalry landed, led by Colonel James Heane, Commander-in-Chief of Dorset (whom Chevalier calls Haine). They met opposition, for Sir George had the parish cannons, but Blake had more and larger cannons on his vessels, and so was able to cover the landing easily. By this time Sir George had lost more than half of his men, many of whom, seeing that it was near night time, had gone home to get some sleep and food, and at least some of them would have returned the next morning, but it was too late. Those that remained with him withdrew to Elizabeth Castle, where they held out for a month, until a 40 lb. bomb, fired from Mont de la Ville, and from the greatest weapon of its type in existence at that time, hit the old Abbey Church at the Castle. It went through the roof and floor, and into the crypt, which was being used as a food and ammunition store. The resulting explosion destroyed the church, some houses, nearly all the supplies, and killed many of the garrison. About a week later the Castle was surrendered, the garrison being allowed an honourable withdrawal.

How is it that this battle so lacked the determination of the earlier period? In addition to the complete unpreparedness already described, most of the men, who were not armed to the same degree as the professional soldiers facing them, were simply hungry, thirsty, soaked to the skin, and tired, but apart from this the principal reasons had nothing to do with militarism. The islanders were not Englishmen (they mostly spoke a variant of the French language), but neither did that mean that they were, or wanted to be, French. They were simply Jerseymen, and mostly proud Royalists, in the sense that they held their independence directly from the sovereign, whichever family held the throne, not from Parliament, but they could not see the point of their Royalist leaders fighting the English, who had killed the King.

To most Jerseymen Blake's attack was almost certainly seen as part

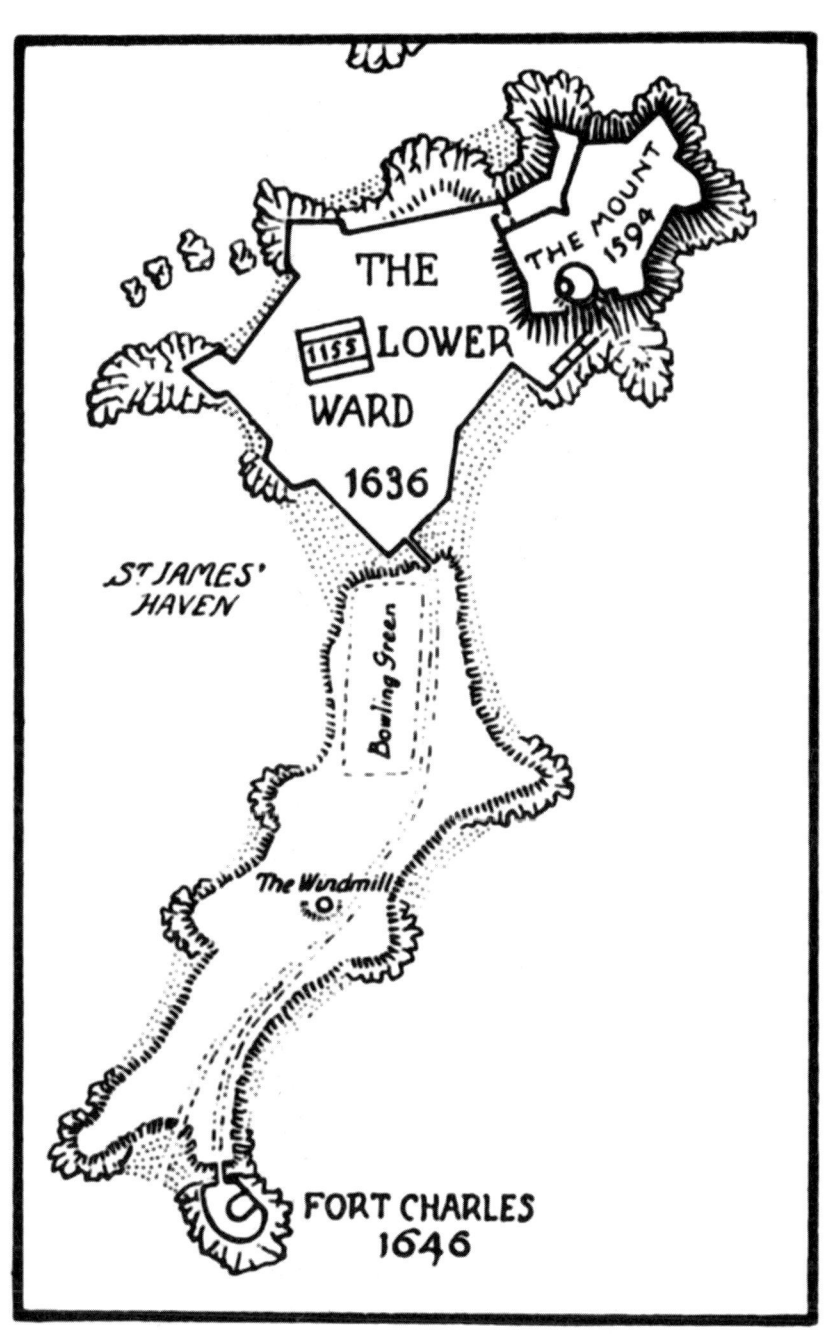

Plan of Elizabeth Castle, 1650

of a civil war taking place amongst Englishmen on the other side of the Channel, but into which they had been dragged by Sir George. It has been said that the Island leaders were Royalists but the people were supporters of Parliament. It was not that simple. The population was almost entirely Calvinist, a vigorously strong Protestant religion. They were no more happy with the variety of religious beliefs of Parliamentary members than they were with its anti-Royalism. In addition Charles I had supported the Church of England, the Queen had been a Roman Catholic. Prince Charles, proclaimed King Charles II in Jersey, was still only 22 years old, and it was not yet sure how much his mother had influenced his religious thinking. He was also just a poor fugitive in France.

The Islanders were confused and dispirited. For just what would it be worthwhile them getting killed?

The Reward
When Charles was able to return to the throne in 1660, he rewarded Sir George by granting to him, together with the Duke of York and two others, a very large area of land in America. He had almost no money, and had been almost immediately deluged with petitions from many hundreds who had supported the Royalist cause, and who had lost almost all that they had. (My ancestor was one of them!) The land cost the King nothing, the four men soon sold it in sections to would-be emigrants, but not before it had been named, and the name chosen was New Jersey.

Written for this book, 2007

15

Jersey Trade in the late 18th Century

Newfoundland

The background to this period is interesting in itself, and well worth recounting, as it undoubtedly had repercussions amongst local merchant and seamen. Jersey had many ships which in peacetime carried on two separate types of trade, the largest, both in type and in number, going to Newfoundland or thereabouts in early spring or summer for cod, and returning in autumn, usually via Spanish or Mediterranean ports. The smaller group carried out coastal trading (not forgetting to include smuggling) with English and French ports. In wartime a large proportion of these ships, especially the Newfoundlanders, carried Letters of Marque which enabled them to become armed traders, or privateers, and so to capture enemy vessels for their own profit. Without these letters all countries would have had the crew hung as pirates, but the system of Letters of Marque was an ancient international method of each country enlarging its own naval forces at no cost to itself when war broke out.

Some great changes had taken place in world affairs over the twenty years or so previous to the Battle of Jersey in 1781. In 1761 the British Government had awarded John Harrison £20,000 for his invention of a reliable chronometer. This at last enabled seamen to calculate longitude with accuracy, and Rear-Admiral Philip de Carteret, of Trinity Manor, set out in 1766 in HMS *Swallow* to map the Pacific Ocean, becoming one of the first British seamen after Drake to circumnavigate the world. He was followed a few years later by Captain James Cook, discoverer of Australia. Both made large areas of the Pacific Ocean accurately known for the first time. Further help to seamen was the publication of the first *Nautical Almanack* in 1767.

In 1763 the Seven Years' War had ended with the British acquisition of Canada from the French, and this particular event had immediate repercussions for Jersey, as it opened up an entirely new field for its fishermen. From the late 1500s ships had gone from Jersey and Guernsey to Terreneuve, or Newfoundland, almost every year for the cod which were to be found in great abundance around its shores. Now two brothers, Charles and Philip Robin, of St. Aubin, were among a very small number of British merchants who saw the possibility of thousands of square miles of new fishing-grounds in the Gulf of the St. Lawrence River, behind Newfoundland. They set up fishing-stations on the newly-acquired southern shores of the Gulf, in particular on the Gaspé peninsula.

Areas fished by Jersey firms, 17-1800s

In Newfoundland the ancient system still operated by which the master of the first vessel to anchor in a bay each year became 'admiral' of that bay, and others could only fish there if granted permission by the 'admiral'. It was a rough-and-ready method of policing, satisfactory when only a few ships were around, but quite inadequate when English, Channel Islands, French and Portuguese fishermen all aimed for a region in which fish in that particular year were plentiful. A few firms had managed to set up permanent settlements here and there, but the situation was very brittle, and fights between crews and shore-men were not uncommon, especially between those of different nationalities. Ships normally aimed to arrive off Newfoundland in early April, or in July, because of the heavy and persistent fogs in May and June. The fishing season was from June to October, and at the period we are discussing most Jersey vessels seem to have been aiming to arrive in the second half of July. Labrador, which was administered as part of Newfoundland, was almost uninhabited, but its coasts swarmed with fishermen in summer.

Newfoundland was still by far the most important area for local fishermen, but they were beginning to spread out now, and one commonly reads of ships which 'have left for Terreneuve, Nova Scotia or Canada'. In other words, destination subject to availability of fish at any given season. The Gaspé coast was being rapidly developed by Charles Robin, the driving force of the two brothers, who set up his first settlement at Paspèbiac in 1766, and almost immediately began to expand by the addition of further settlements along the coast. His work was seriously hampered by the American War of Independence (1775-1783) but from then on enlarged rapidly, until his firm had a virtual monopoly of the fishing-rights over an enormous area. A later historian of the area felt compelled to write:

> When Charles Robin came to Gaspé the fishing was scattered in small establishments without organisation. Though his purpose was to seek locations for new establishments on the capital he represented, yet the outcome was the development of a concern with interests so wide upon the coast and influences so commanding upon the greater part of the fishing industry as to practically consolidate and control the entire business without serious competition for nearly a century, and to set the pace for all future undertakings along this line.
>
> *Clarke's Sketches of Gaspé*

The firm was still in existence recently, under the name Robin, Jones and Whitman, though its Jersey connections were now very tenuous. (It was forced to close through bankruptcy in December, 2005.)

Newfoundland, on the other hand, became at this period largely peopled with fishermen from the Channel Islands, and their families, together with a number from Devon and Cornwall. According to Baker's *A Guide to Jersey and Guernsey*, 1839, 45 vessels were trading to Newfoundland and the surrounding regions from Jersey in 1771, while my own records show that 60 were working there from Jersey in 1786/87. Fortunes varied considerably from time to time, or from place to place, as a few examples from a single season will show. The following are quoted from the newspaper the *Gazette de l'Ile de Jersey:*

Some news from home

4th August, 1787   The *Liberty*, Capt. Philippe Dumaresq. News has been received of her arrival at Bonne Baye. She has suffered much from the ice.

20th October, 1787   The *Dauphin*, Captain Le Roux, arrived on the 16th from the Baye de Fortune, with 78 men, and has been less than 14 days on the journey'. [A very quick journey] 'The longboats of that bay have not taken, on the whole, more than 200 quintaux, although some have taken 300 or 320. [The quintal is a slightly unclear measure, being usually 100 lbs, sometimes 112 lbs, and even 128 lbs for the Brazil trade]

20th October, 1787   The *Adventure*, Capt Torré. Arrived from S. Sebastien on the 13th, where he has discharged his codfish. He sold most of his cargo at a very advantageous price, as high as 26-28 livres per quintal.

27th October, 1787   The *Beaver*, Capt Clé. Le Couteur. Arrived from Port Dauphin after an 18-day passage. The fish was very poor. The longboats have not taken 100 quintaux.

3rd November, 1787   The *Swallow*, Capt Heulin (sic). Arrived at Bilbao on the 29th October, where he has sold very well. She had not been on the bank at TerreNeuve for five days before she had caught 3500 cod, and since they did not have sufficient salt, they were obliged to stop fishing, although on the last day they caught 1500 cod. This ship met an English ship in the Channel, which pressed three men from them.

This last comment brings in a new factor. The press gang still operated at this time, and commanders of naval ships had the right to impress when at sea if necessary. The Channel Islands were exempt, except for naval deserters and non-native seamen found ashore in the islands, but Channel Islanders found on English ships or ashore in England were not exempt. Whether the three men impressed in this case were not Islanders, or whether the naval captain 'overlooked' the law is not clear, though Captain Huelin's comment sounds very matter-of-fact.

Codfish drying on flakes at Newport Islands, Quebec

Most of the cod was sold in Mediterranean ports, where there was a large demand due to the countries in that region being largely Roman Catholic, and having regular 'fish-days' every week. Cargoes of wine, brandy, dried fruit, citrus fruit and salt were brought back from these ports, and often taken straight to some English or Northern European port, then returning home to Jersey with a third cargo, though some came straight back to the Island. There was also heavy demand for fish in Brazil, and crews going there were paid danger money to compensate for the possibility of yellow fever. They brought back coffee and sugar, much of which went straight to Scandinavia, returning from there with masts and spars, which were in constant demand, as the average life of these on an ocean-going vessel was about three years. Some, however, called at Dantzic for a cargo of wheat or barley, or Holland for a cargo of brandy, cheese, roofing tiles and barrel hoops. The demand for the latter was also extremely high, barrels being the general form of container for almost everything. Cider was still a substantial export needing barrels, small casks were used for smuggling brandy, larger casks for use in the cod-fisheries, as well as for general agricultural storage.

Another new venture in America at this time was the mahogany trade. Britain had acquired British Honduras, or Belize, in the Gulf of Mexico, in 1783, and one or two local firms immediately moved in to trade there in hardwoods. Again, according to the *Gazette*, on the 30th September 1786:

> The *Henriette*, Capt Jam. Poingdestre, has arrived from the Bay of Honduras with a cargo of about 420 tons of Mahogany and Logwood. It is to leave here for London.

Logwood was similar to mahogany, but inferior, and with its principal use being to make dye it was imported as logs.

Also on 6th January, 1787:

> The *Betsey*, Capt De St. Croix. Arrived from the Bay of Honduras on the 4th. The vessel has been fifteen weeks on the journey [normally six or seven weeks] during which time they have suffered much from the bad weather. The crew have also suffered from lack of provisions, and one of the mariners died in Guernsey as a result of the fatigue and starvation during the voyage.

The cargo of mahogany was sold by auction in Jersey in the following month. This became a regular trade, and gave rise to the popularity of mahogany for furniture and stairways, etc., during the nineteenth century.

And assorted vessels

Almost all of the vessels trading with America were brigs or brigantines, and these terms were used very loosely, for the same vessel is often described in both ways when it is clear that no change of rig has taken place. This same looseness of definition also appears with the smaller vessels, which are often indiscriminately referred to at various times as either cutters or sloops (one reference in the *Gazette* actually stating that there was for sale 'the cutter or sloop now in St. Aubin's Harbour'). The task of ship recognition at this period is not made easier in consequence!

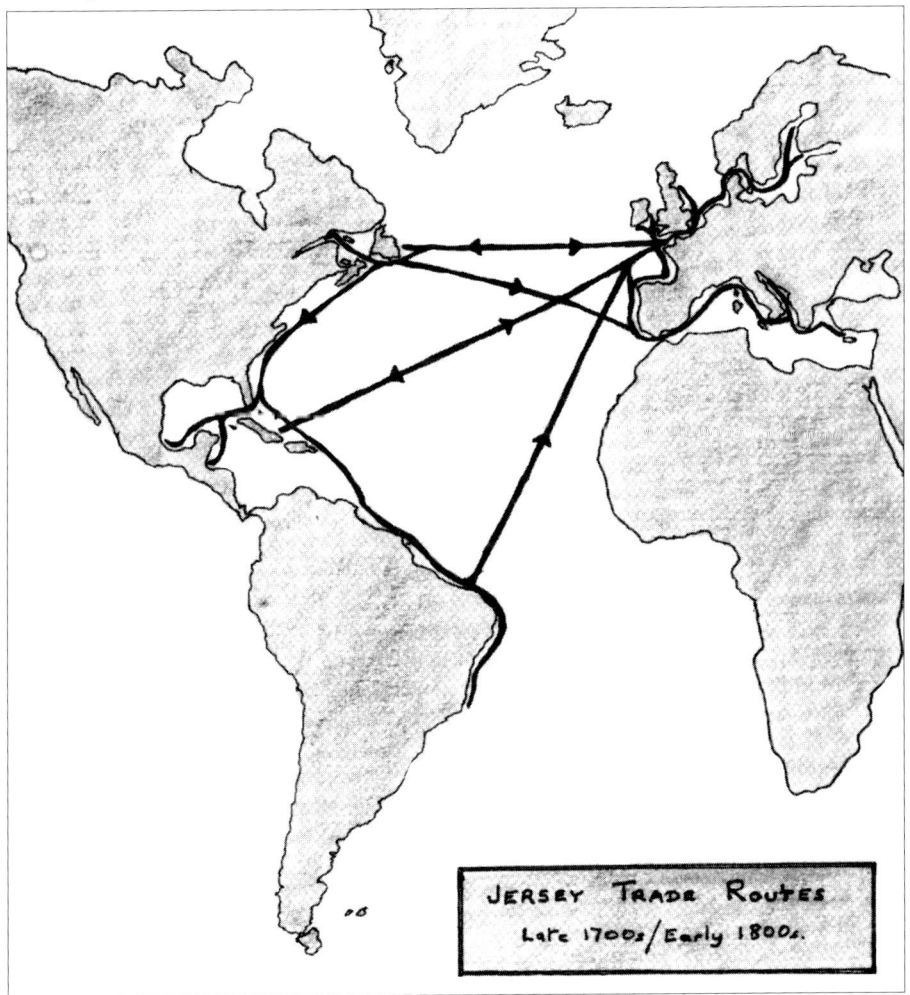

Map of Jersey trade routes, late 1700s-1800s

It was mainly cutters that traded to England, Ireland and France, bringing wine, brandy, oxen, fruit, linen, cotton and pottery from France, and also (a sign of considerable prosperity) quantities of young fruit-trees such as peach, nectarine, pear, pomegranate, gooseberry, etc. Flour, wool and coal came from England. The principal exports direct from the island were cattle and knitted goods, though the major export of Jersey businesses was the cod, sent directly to many countries from the St. Lawrence area of Canada. The knitting trade, now consisting of various types of garments in addition to stockings, had declined rapidly from the previous century, and consisted principally in supplying the many hundreds of islanders at work in North America, and though this was still substantial it was now rare to find anyone in the island who was financially dependent on it. In times of peace and when there was a good harvest substantial quantities of wheat were also exported, and the potato trade was just beginning, but the war conditions prevailing from 1776-1783, and later from 1793-1815, meant that the island had to become as self-sufficient as possible, and these trades then ceased.

There was also, after the American War, a surprising amount of passenger traffic, the *Fortune, Guernsey Packet, Liberty Packet, Postillon,* and *Southampton Packet* all running to Southampton, Guernsey or St. Malo/Granville as frequently and regularly as weather would permit.

Smuggling

It is well known that the Channel Islands were centres of smuggling during the eighteenth and early nineteenth centuries. At least in the first half of the eighteenth century the islanders did not look upon this as smuggling at all, but as a continuation of the centuries-old right to trade with England free of all duties. It is true that this right only applied to goods 'the growth and/or manufacture of the islands', which obviously excluded, for instance, taking French brandy to England. In the eyes of the islanders, but not of the English customs authorities, this was overcome by importing such goods from France, maturing them in the Islands, and then exporting them to England. This trade was principally operated from Guernsey, which had much better facilities in the way of cellar-storage than Jersey. Neither did Jersey boats do much as smugglers, though of course it did occur, but most of the smuggling from Jersey took place in English boats with the connivance of the local merchants who supplied the goods. A further reason why Jersey had a lesser part to play in this trade than Guernsey is simply that the run from the island to England was both shorter and less obstructed by reefs than that from Jersey, making the risks of capture less likely. Morality had nothing to do with it.

In 1767 the British Government had at last forced the Channel Islands to accept Customs Officers, which they had been trying to do for about forty years. The islanders had argued on two main counts: (a) that it was against their ancient rights of self-government, and (b) that if the 'trade' (smuggling) was lost to the islands it would be taken up by France, which would mean loss to Britain, as while it remained the profits made in the islands were spent largely in England. The latter may seem today a somewhat singular argument, but was nevertheless proved to be correct. As soon as the Customs Officers arrived in the islands in 1767 the French Government passed a set of laws making certain Channel ports 'free ports'. The principal one of these in the west was Roscoff, in Brittany, while Dunkirk covered the eastern end of the Channel, and smaller ones lay between. The loss of gold to Britain was almost immediately noticed, and after a year or two in the islands the Customs men simply vanish into oblivion, but the damage was done. The French 'free ports' remained a severe drain on Britain's currency until import tariffs on spirits were drastically reduced in the 1840s.

There appears to have been what might almost be described as a clear rift in Jersey between the merchants and the States in the second half of the eighteenth century. The merchants were clearly forward-looking and adventurous, out to seize every available new opening for more trade and profit. In 1768 they had formed the Chamber of Commerce only a few months after that of New York, which was the first of such Chambers anywhere in the English speaking world, though some did exist elsewhere in Europe. The Jersey Chamber spent much time trying to get the States to provide better harbour facilities, and they also badgered the British Government for better trade facilities, for at this period British Navigation Acts made it illegal, for instance, for them to sell fish in the West Indies and collect a cargo in return. They could sell their fish, for which there was great demand, but only for cash, and hence they had to go on to Brazil, Honduras or Spain for a return cargo. Neither were they allowed to export from Jersey olive oil, rum, molasses, or tobacco; not even sufficient for their own use on the voyage!

The States, on the other hand, moved very slowly indeed, and there seems to be reasonable evidence that they did so simply because they were not going to have any outside organisation telling them what was necessary for the island. In the 1780s the main harbour was still that at St. Aubin, and even this consisted only of the one (southern) pier, and the old pier at St. Aubin's Fort. The road now leading along the harbour-side towards the Bulwarks and the southern pier did not exist, this area consisting of a series of private wharves. Goods to and from the pier had to go over the sands, or at high tide by what is now known as Bulwarks Hill and the Rue au Moestre. Neither was the coast road from St. Helier to St. Aubin in existence until the early nineteenth century, the sands or a path through the then existing sand-dunes being considered adequate. At St. Helier the small pier existed, and though it was rarely in good condition greater efforts were being made from time to time to improve it. It was finally completely rebuilt and enlarged, and is now known as the South Pier. The improvements to the pier, however, still left far too small a harbour for some 50 or 60 ocean-going vessels, even though most of these were under 100 tons burthen.

At last, in 1788, the States really did move, and invited Smeaton, designer of the Eddystone Lighthouse and the leading harbour engineer of the day, to advise them. Not liking his plan they rejected it, and began, in 1790, the construction of the New North Quay in accordance with their own ideas. This was completed 25 years later, in 1815. By then the merchants were also building with their own money the other quay known as Le Quai des Marchands, now Commercial Buildings, using for infilling large quantities of stone removed from the Mont de la Ville as a consequence of the building of Fort Regent at that time. By the late 1820s they at last had a harbour.

A list of vessels at this period follows:

Name	Rig	Tonnage	Owners	Master	Usual Destination	Additional Information
AURORE				– De Caen	Baye Chaleurs	
BEAVER				Clément Le Couteur	NF, NS, or C	(See footnote)
BETSEY				Jean Balleine	NF or NS	
BETSEY		40	Fr. Journeaux?	– De Ste Croix	NF/Honduras	
CATHERINE				– Dumaresq	Iles Madame	
CHARMING NANCY			Ph. Winter?	Pierre Clément	NF	
CHÉTÉCAN			Ph. Robin			Wrecked at NF, 1786
COMMERCE	Brig'ne	127	Jacq. & Clém. Hémery	Germain Aubin	Labrador	Lloyds insured
CONCORDE	Brig	100	Pierre Le Brun	Th. De Ste Croix	NF, Quebec	
CORBET			Poingdestre & Robinson	– Neel	Labrador	
CORNWALL		100+	Janvrin?	Jean Vibert	Iles Madame	
CRUISER				Th. Tacker	St Malo	
DAUPHIN	Brig	141	Ph. Winter	Pierre Le Roux	NF, NS or C	Lloyds insured
DEUX AMIS				– Berteaux	NF, NS or C	
DISPATCH				– Cabot	Guernsey	
ELIZABETH	Brig	112	J. Villeneuve	David Mauger	NF, NS or C	Lloyds insured
ENDEAVOUR	Brig	73		Ed. Mourant	NF, NS or C	
EXPEDITION				Jean Le Couteur	Cape Breton	Lost off Spain 1787
FORTUNE		12		– Mourant	Granville	Mainly passengers
FRIENDSHIP	Brig'ne	78	J. & C. Hémery	Abm. Le Sueur	NF, NS or C	
FRIENDSHIP	Brig	41	Jean Le Feuvre	Jean Le Feuvre	NF, NS or C	
GUERNSEY PACKET	Cutter	27? 39		– Mourant	CI area	Mainly passengers
HENRIETTE		c.200		Jean Poingdestre	Honduras	
HERCULES	Ship	200		– Le Geyt	NF, NS or C	
HILTON	Brig'ne	175	J. & C. Hémery	– Bisson	NF, NS or C	
HOPE				– Dean	NF or NS	
INDUSTRIE	Brig'ne	123	Janvrin Bros.	– Pickstock	Labrador	
JENNY	Schooner	65		– Labey	NF, NS or C	Lloyds insured Built Dartmouth 1787

Name	Type		Owner	Master	Route	Notes
KENTON			Ph. Ingouville?	Ph. Ingouville	NF, NS or C	
KINGFISHER	Brig'ne	57		Jean Le Roux	Iles Madame	
KITE				– Le Mottée	Plymouth	
KITTY			Ferdinand Anley	F. Anley	London/C.I.	
LIBERTÉ	Brig'ne	90		Moses Steel	NF, NS or C	
LIBERTY PACKET			Jean Kerby?	– Simpson	Southampton	
LIGHTNING				Jean Vibert	NF, NS or C	
LIVELY				– Nicolle	NF, NS or C	
LYNX			Mallet & Gosset	Jean Du Heaume	NF, Labrador	
MAGDELAINE	Brig	38	Pierre Mallet	Edouard Noel	NF, NS or C	Lloyds insured
MAGOT		50	Ph. Robin	Fr. Le Feuvre	NF, NS or C	Lloyds insured
MAJOR PIERSON	Brig	172	Ph. Robin	Ph. Jean	Iles Madame	Lloyds insured
MARIE	Brig	90	Pierre Mallet	Fr. Noel	NF, NS or C	
MARIE	Sloop	25		Noël Messervy	St Malo	
MARY ANN	Brig	43	Ch. Renouf	Ch. Renouf	NF, NS or C	
MERCURE	Brig'ne	54	Ph. Robin	Clém. Hubert	NF, NS or C	Lloyds insured
MERCURE				– Malzard	NF, NS or C	
MOLLY	Cutter? Sloop		Jean De La Perelle & Jean Le Feuvre	Jean Le Feuvre	England, C.I.	
NANCY		64		Jac. Simonet	NF, NS or C	
NEPTUNE	Brig		Ph. Janvrin?	Dan. Hamon	NF, NS or C	
NIMPHE				– Messervy	NF, NS or C	Wrecked nr. Boulogne, 1786, crew saved.
PAIX	Brig'ne	72	Ph. Robin	– Bechervaise	Baye Chaleurs	Lloyds insured
PAIX				– Hacquoil	NF, NS or C	
PASPEBIAC		133	Ph. Robin	– Hacquoil	NF, NS or C	Lloyds insured
PEGGY	Brig'ne	70		Jean Chevalier	NF, NS or C	
PEGGY				– Dumaresq	NF, NS or C	
PIERSON	Brig			Ph. Vibert	NF or NS	Not same as "Major Pierson".
PILOTE	Cutter?		J. & F. Jeune	J. or F. Jeune?	Local	

POSTILLON	Sloop			– Le Ray	Southampton	
PRUDENT				– De La Perelle	English Channel area	
PRUDENT	Brig	57		– Le Quesne	NF, NS or C	
QUEBEC	Brig'ne	85		– Gaudin	NF, NS or C	
RÉSOLUTION	Brig'ne	71		– Gaudin	NF, NS or C	
St. AUBIN	Brig'ne		Remon & Du Heaume	– Noel	NF, NS or C	
St. LAURENS		145	Ph. Robin	– Fillieul	NF, NS or C	Lloyds insured
St. PIERRE		210	Ph. Robin	Ph. De Caux	Baye Chaleurs	Lloyds insured
SHIFT		49	Ph. Robin	– Fainton	Baye Chaleurs	Lloyds insured
SOLIDE		132	Ph. Janvrin	Laurens Remon	NF, NS or C	Lloyds insured
SOUTHAMPTON PACKET	Cutter? Sloop	40		Jean Neel	Southampton	Mainly passengers
SUCCÈS	Brig	110	Mallet & Gosset	Jean Le Riche	NF, NS or C	
SUCCÈS	Brig	150	Fred. Kerby	Elie Neel	NF, NS or C	
SWALLOW	Brig'ne	89	Mallet & Gosset	Amice Huelin	Gaspé	
SWIFT	Brig	95		Simeon Dubois	Labrador	
TRYALL (TRIAL)				Th. Falle	Labrador	
TRIO				Ph. Messervy	NF, NS or C	
TWO BROTHERS	Sloop	60	Henri Voye	Henri Voye	Bristol Chnl.	
UNION				George Neel	Baye Chaleurs	
UNION		55		Jean Lys	NF, NS or C	
		(one of these owned by Remon & Du Heaume)				
UNITÉ		400		– Poingdestre	Wrecked in St Aubin's Bay, 1786. Loss=30,000 livres.	
UNITY	Brig'ne			Pierre Janvrin	Iles Madame	
UNITY	Sloop	32		Jacques Barbier	C.I. area	
YOUNG-MARY	Brig'ne	70			England, C.I.	French-built

NF, NS or C=Newfoundland, Nova Scotia or Canada (Gaspé)

NOTES.

At this period newspapers used **English or French** indiscriminately, so that "Deux Frères" is also "Two Brothers", "Unité" is "Unity", etc. This has, **however**, been taken into account in compiling this list.

Also, what is known to be the same vessel is loosely described as either Brig or Brigantine, Cutter or Sloop. This has been impossible to confirm with certainty in some cases.

Société Jersiaise Bulletin, 1981

A type of cannon common on the many small provateers

Model of the Snipe, *the finest prize taken during the Napoleonic War*

16

Jersey Privateers in Napoleonic times

This chapter actually covers both the Revolutionary and the Napoleonic Wars, 1793-1815, but for simplicity I have given it the title by which the period is popularly known.

Privateers, of *all* nations, were normally not expected to be warships as such, but neither is it well known that they had a specific job to perform, which was to assist the Navy. Until about the mid-1700s most navies were inadequate when war came, and the job of the privateers was to make life difficult for the enemy by capturing as many of their vessels as they could, most of which were not armed, and so stopping trade. By the time privateering was internationally organised – during the mid-1700s – it was not greatly different – except in scale – to being an honorary policeman. It was too expensive to expect anyone to do it for nothing, so there was a reward available, but it was very chancy; you might hit the jackpot, which was rare, you might get nothing at all, which was not unusual, you might even get killed, though this, too, was much rarer than might be expected.

Until the mid-1700s larger Jersey vessels had usually over-wintered at St. Malo, because the harbours here were inadequate, and even in wartime they were not always unwelcome at St. Malo, for the Malouins (the people of St. Malo) considered themselves as Bretons, not as French.

Channel Islands privateers had had a long-standing unwritten agreement with the privateers of St. Malo that they would simply 'not notice' each other when cruising. There was some commonsense in this blind-eye arrangement, as well as a degree of mutual understanding, and often friendship. With Jersey and St. Malo being so close to each other – less than thirty miles – things could easily have led to stalemate, with ships not being able to use either port for fear of capture, while it could well have been your friend's vessel that you took prize.

During the Revolutionary and Napoleonic periods things were different, for the French had learnt their lesson from the previous wars, and this time they grabbed every Channel Islands' vessel that they could get almost as soon as the war began. This was partly due to a change in relationship with the Malouins, for in France the secret police were everywhere, and the Malouins were totally unable to carry on the old customs, even though they may have been willing to do so. Consequently the blind-eye policy died, and local shipowners had to take much more care.

War

In the first year, 1793, twelve Jersey privateers, or Letter-of-Marque ships are listed, but the *Queen* was unlucky enough to taken almost immediately. She was owned by Hemery Bros., and captained by Jean Le Feuvre. All the crew were imprisoned at La Rochelle, but lucky enough to be released within twelve months. On the other hand, François Janvrin's *Alligator*, captained by Philippe Hamon, took six French ships totalling 450 tons, as well as re-capturing the *Roze*, a brig (spelt with a Z!), while in this same year Philippe Lys was joint owner of four small privateers, which between them took four chasse-marées, each of about 30 tons, and two larger vessels. On the other hand the *Hazard*, captained by Elie Messervy, took nothing, and later in the year he was in charge of the *Enterprize* when it was captured, and all the crew imprisoned at Brest.

In 1794 things seem to have warmed up; for only six were out hunting, capturing four prizes and sinking another, although these were larger vessels, ranging from 80 to 300 tons. The largest, an American brig, was taken by George Dolbel in the *Défiance*, owned by Pierre & Thomas Mallet.

But during 1793, 94 French and Spanish ships captured two-thirds of Jersey's shipping, taking 900 sailors prisoner, though most of these were home again within a year or so, although in 1806 there were more than 200 Jersey residents who were still prisoners of war in France. This clearance of ships left the French virtually in charge in 1795, for we have little privateer activity listed for the next three years. There was a sudden Jersey upsurge again in 1798, when ten are listed, taking

29 vessels as prize, totalling about 1,400 tons, but it would be too tedious here to go through each year in succession up to 1815. 1800 was the busiest year, with 16 privateers out, taking 25 vessels ranging in size from 20 tons to 209 tons, and totalling about 1,500 tons. The average take throughout the twenty-two years of this war was ten vessels per annum, totalling an average of 805 tons, though there was very great variation from year to year, but this was not much more than one vessel captured per privateer per annum. The wars earlier in the century had made families rich, as the French navy was weak, but this time it was different.

In 1803 Jersey privateers operating were a Chasse-marée of 41 tons, a schooner of 72 tons, three luggers of 32, 55 and 97 tons, a sloop of 75 tons, and a brigantine of 157 tons – a total of 529 tons and of seven vessels. It shrunk in 1804 to two vessels, total 139 tons, in 1805 again two, total 152 tons, and in 1806 up to 472 tons.

What is surprising to us is the size of these privateers, for during the entire 22 years of this war only five are listed as being of over 100 tons. One of these was the *Vulture* (or *Vautour* if you are reading a French-language paper), a lugger of 104 tons, but giving us a puzzle to solve. In 1797 and '98, under the command of François Le Feuvre, and owned by Philippe and François Janvrin, it took seven prizes totalling about 400 tons, in 1800 it took a brig of 148 tons, in 1802 a brigantine of 52 tons, but from the end of 1802 to 1809 it just disappears, and the Shipping Register does not help as it only starts in 1803. (Vol. I from 1788, has been lost long ago). Then it reappears in 1809, under the command of Daniel Hamon, and in 1809 and 1810 it took six vessels totalling 604 tons. I believe that these were in fact two separate vessels. It seems probable, for many shipowners liked to keep a favourite name, but nowhere from the records can we answer this with certainty.

From 1803 to 1805, Philippe and François Janvrin were also operating the *Phoenix*, a lugger of 97 tons, with Daniel Hamon in command, and in 1808 the *Hope*, a lugger of 57 tons, Captain Elias L'Amy, the latter two vessels normally working together, but they were only reasonably successful in getting prizes.

By far the most successful was the *Phoenix*, just mentioned with the *Hope*. Owned by Philippe Janvrin & Co. (not Philippe and François) and with the irrepressible Daniel Hamon in charge, it took fourteen vessels as prize, totalling about 1,500 tons, between 1797 and 1805.

These included a 200-ton Brig, *Amiraux Désiré*, a ship, the *Betzy* (spelt with a z!) of 272 tons, and the *Mexicana*, which was pierced for twenty guns and of about 250-300 tons. This was almost certainly another full-rigged ship. With his lugger of only 97 tons Daniel Hamon was clearly quite a fighter, and a good leader of men into the bargain.

Owners

The principal owners were, without a doubt, the Janvrins, François and Philippe, who often operated separately, but sometimes together, their vessels not infrequently working together when at sea. The Janvrin family had been involved as ship owners for over a century, and had possessed some very successful privateers in the wars with France earlier in the 18th century. At times during the 1793-1815 wars the two Janvrins must have had to provide securities totalling well over a half-a-million pounds in present-day values.

Other prominent owners were Chevalier & Co., Elias Durell, George Hooper, Pierre & Thomas Mallet, and Remon & Co.

Masters

Germain Aubin was one of the most active masters, with seven captures in 1797 and '98, and though they were nearly all chasse-marées of about forty tons this was certainly a satisfactory result for his employers, Janvrin & Durell. I do not know what relationship there was with another Aubin, but he was decidedly less lucky, for it is recorded on 11th June 1799 that 'Capt. Jean Aubin died on Monday last, his death caused by fright when he fell into the sea from his ship.' Maybe the present-day term of 'shock' is kinder!

There is also an Aubin, probably one of these two, but he is only recorded as Capt. Aubin with no forename, and he has the distinction of taking four vessels, total about 180 tons, in one year, 1798. He managed this with one of the smallest of all the Jersey privateers, the *Globe*, of 16 tons, belonging to George Hooper, junior.

Philippe Hamon, working for François Janvrin, mainly in 1793, took eight vessels, mostly brigs and brigantines, averaging 85 tons each, but he was surpassed by Daniel Hamon, who in fact outdid every other master throughout the war. Were the two Hamons related? Working for Philippe Janvrin & Co. from 1797 to 1810 and in a 97-ton lugger *Daniel* took in all 20 prizes, concentrating on the larger vessels such as brigs and brigantines, and including three full-rigged ships, each of almost 300 tons. He accumulated a grand total of about 2,300 tons.

Other masters deserving a mention are François Hocquard, Philippe Le Cronier, who in a 25-ton cutter, the *Surprise*, belonging to George Hooper, took three vessels totalling 226 tons in twelve months, while François Le Feuvre, another of Janvrin's masters, managed to take nine vessels, mostly in one year, and though none of them were as large as his own ship, the *Vulture*, it was clearly a profitable year.

George Messervy took three vessels totalling 643 tons within one twelve-month period, in the largest of all the local privateers, the *Ceres*, a brigantine of 125 tons, which was a French vessel captured some time earlier, and finally Philippe Payn and George Wooldridge also deserve mention.

It was not always good going, however, as the following passage from the *Gazette de l'Ile de Jersey*, dated 26 February, 1814, shows:

Capt. Payn. Arrived from a cruise, 24th, badly damaged masts and superstructure, after an engagement with a French chasse-marée of 10 guns and 80-100 men. Jean Romeril (St. Lawrence) killed, Lt. Philippe Le Brocq, James Benest, John Biggs (seriously wounded), Thomas Williams, Philippe Bisson, Robert Champion (wounded).

This was Philip Payn's last voyage. Generally a successful master, this was one of the more disastrous of all the known voyages. It is possible – maybe probable – that there were worse, as in that period several ships are simply recorded as 'lost', without further comment.

The business-side of privateering

How did these men achieve such great profits that they are looked on as pirates?

The answer is that this story is substantially a fable. As in any business, some were successful, but it is a practical impossibility for all to be successful. There were many total failures, going cruising and returning empty-handed, and many others who made just about enough to cover their costs. It seems that there were two aspects. If you had one of the biggest of the privateer ships you had a lot more chance of capturing others (if you're rich it is easier to get even richer!) and alternatively if the master was a good leader and a dare-devil. Also, as I have said, the earlier wars had been different.

Let's look back at how you became a privateer. It was first necessary to apply for a Letter-of-Marque, which was a permit to buy large guns and ammunition from the government arsenal, and to fit them on a ship. This was only obtainable from the Board of Admiralty, and only during times of war. It was necessary to apply in person in London. In the case of Channel Islanders it was customary for local merchants having representation or offices in London to apply on behalf of Islanders. The Letter was issued to a named captain for a named vessel, and specified that only the ships of a named country could be attacked, usually, of course, France. But if another country, such as Spain, decided to join with France, then an additional Letter of Marque was needed. Often the merchants owned the named vessel, but it still involved a great deal of trust in the local captains, since at the time of application they had to provide two securities of £1,500 each (a total somewhere in excess of £50,000 in present-day money, and this for each new Letter-of-Marque).

A crew of roughly twice as many as would be usual for that type of vessel was also needed, so that if you captured anything a prize crew was put on board to sail it into any one of the ports where an Admiralty Court sat. Jersey and Guernsey courts sat as Admiralty Courts when needed and there were several along the south coast of England. Most privateers, including Channel Islanders, usually found their home port more convenient to use, this depending mainly on the weather. On board you would have as prisoners not less than two of the original captured crew, the rest having been ransomed for what you could get. When the Admiralty Court next sat you, as master, would have to appear, with all your documentation, together with the mate and a member of the crew. Your prisoners also had to appear, with documentation if available, to swear where they had been going, what they were carrying, and for whom. Without these witnesses you had no case.

If the case was proved the vessel and cargo were sold, usually by auction, and the money was divided into three portions, one for the king (presumably, in fact, to cover the cost of the Admiralty Courts), one for the owners, and one for the crew, who had all signed a document in advance stating exactly what share each would have in relation to their responsibility. But in 1856 privateering was abolished by international treaty, led by the greatest power at that time, Britain, so no longer could one get rich by prize-money. But hold on, that's not quite true. If you want prize-money, wait for the next war, join the Royal Navy, capture an enemy ship instead of sinking it, and you will get it, because it is still legal. The last lot, over £5,000,000, was paid out in 1949, from prizes taken during the Second World War.

Anticipation

Are you, like me, old enough to remember the uncertainty of the first few months of the Second World War, when nothing much seemed to be happening? Everyone knew that it couldn't last, that things were going to get much, much worse, but just what was going to happen was an uncertainty in itself. Then, in England, the Battle of Britain began, and in the Channel Islands, the German Occupation.

The atmosphere must have been very similar in the early 19th century. Normally the Channel was an exceedingly busy shipping area. When Captain Payn set out on his unsuccessful last voyage he had been aiming for a reported seven to eight hundred chasse-marées ready to sail at Bordeaux. But now, because of the possibility of a French invasion of Britain the Channel was almost bare of ships from 1804 to 1806. Both countries had tried to destroy the ability of the other to receive supplies, and had been so thorough that very few vessels dared to leave the Channel ports without naval escort, and this was in extremely short supply in the build-up to the battle of Trafalgar, in October 1805. The greater part of the English navy was blockading the French and Spanish navies in Brest, Cadiz, and the West Indies, leaving few vessels to guard the Channel. Eight hundred fishing-boats and river craft of the Sea Fencibles guarded the coast of England, armed with small cannon and manned by 15,000 volunteers, a maritime 'Home Guard'.

Imagine, then, the nervous anticipation of Britain waiting for Napoleon's army to invade. For well over a year everyone had known that the French were building several thousand barges and collecting other vessels in ports all along the Channel coast of France, to carry an invasion army of 150,000 men, thousands of horses, guns, and other supplies. Some Channel Islands privateers were going into French ports while pretending to be a French ship from Biscay or somewhere similar, their normal language being Jersey-French, not English, and on returning home reporting the number of vessels being built there, and any other military preparations. It was a very risky business, and more than one crew were caught and imprisoned.

So important militarily were the Channel Islands that the French Cabinet discussed the possibility of occupying them more than fifty times during the 18th and very early 19th century. (At a later date Hitler also knew it, and had more fortifications built in the Islands than on the entire Channel coast of France.)

Now change your viewpoint. No longer are you waiting in England for that invasion, you are here, in the Channel Islands, with the army of the greatest invader that there has been for centuries, gathering only a few miles across the water. What if Napoleon attempted to take the islands first, to safeguard his major attack? As early as 1761, in the Seven Years' War, 12,000 troops and about 150 flat-bottomed boats were gathered at St. Malo, but this attack never took place. Then just before this present war, in 1779 and 1781, there were two attempts, the first aborted because the sea at St. Ouen's Bay was too rough for a landing, the second culminating in the Battle of Jersey. In 1804, 10,000 troops were ordered to be ready to attack Jersey, but then Napoleon found that he needed them elsewhere. The anticipatory silence, stretched out over more than a year, must have been almost unbearable. What defence did the islands have?

Several thousand British troops were based in the islands at this time, but to counter a naval attack the answer was: their own navy. The famous 18th century politician Edmund Burke, speaking at this time, described the Channel Islands privateers as equivalent to a second-rate navy, and this description has since been confirmed by a leading naval historian as not unreasonable. (Second-rate being a naval technical term meaning that they had no battleships with more than seventy guns, these being classed as first-raters).

Guernsey privateers were on average about two-and-a-half times the Jersey tonnage. This was partly because they had the deep-water harbour, and partly because the war had taken away most of their trade, since they were not much involved in fishing. Jersey continued the Newfoundland fisheries almost uninterrupted, exporting to the West Indies and Brazil, though it lost all of its normal European trade.

There were naval flotillas in each of the islands. The larger vessels were in Guernsey, while in Jersey Philip d'Auvergne, Duke of Bouillon was in charge. (He was a Jerseyman and an admiral of the Royal Navy, who by a series of strange events had also inherited a French dukedom). He had no less than eleven English naval vessels at his command, which sounds grand, but the largest was a 44-gun frigate, so old that it was of no fighting use, and was used as the admiral's flagship, and as a store-ship for the others. The largest of the remainder was one of 20 tons, there were three of 18 tons, three of 10 tons, and three between these, a total of 138 tons. The Jersey privateers were four times the tonnage of the Admiral's flotilla! No wonder they can be classed as a second-rate navy!

Conclusion

Who and what were privateers? Chancers? Very probably. Most people trying to improve their situation have to take a chance now and again. Gamblers? – some undoubtedly were. Patriots? Again, many undoubtedly were just that, for very few made the sort of profit that would be considered desirable in normal times. Pirates? If you were to go back to the 1600s and early 1700s, before the laws were internationally recognised, you might be excused for the thought, but **the islands lay in a ditch between two of the world's most powerful sworn enemies, each wanting to possess them!** The Royal Navy did not have ships to spare, the islanders did. What were they supposed to do? In other words pirates? You're insulting some very courageous forebears!

Société Jersiaise Lunchtime Lecture, 2005

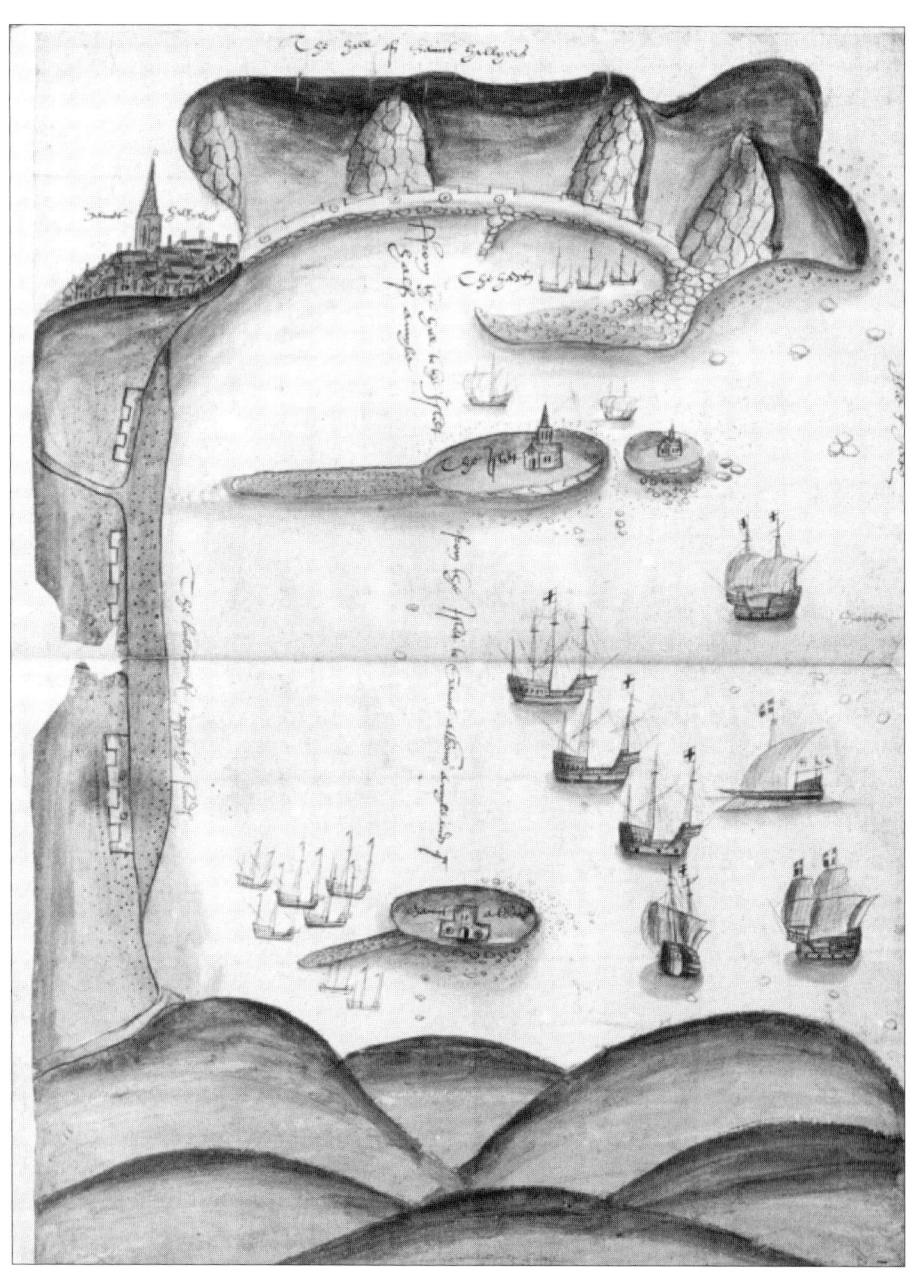

Map, 'The Haven of Jersey', c. 1545, showing clearly a built harbour at St. Helier

17

St. Helier Harbours to the beginning of the 19th Century

Introduction

In medieval times most vessels were small enough to come close inshore at high tide, drop anchor, and as the tide receded they were left high and dry on the beach, where their cargo was unloaded into carts. This was still common practice well into the early twentieth century. Any bay with a gently-sloping beach made a suitable harbour unless the approach was too rocky, while locally others acquired the name of *port*, *portelet*, or *havre* because they were sheltered anchorages, though they may not have been satisfactory for beaching. From very early times there have always been a lot of small boats using the little bays around the Island, and at the beginning of the thirteenth century, when the population of Jersey has been estimated at about 11,000, some 3,000 people were earning their living either by fishing or in the fish trade, which accounted for substantial quantities exported annually.

The first official map, the 'Richmond map', surveyed in 1787 and published in 1795, only shows piers at St. Helier and St. Aubin, and at the Hermitage Rock. It is known that other piers had existed before this date, such as those at St. Brelade, Gorey and Havre des Pas. There are piers at the two former sites today. Were they in such a bad state then that they were considered unusable, and have since been restored, or were they simply ignored as of no importance? The map was drawn up for military reasons by Army personnel, who at that period rarely saw that there might be a possible connection between themselves and the sea. It took the Napoleonic Wars, a decade later, to change that point of view.

The Harbour

No principal town of any island would be able to exist without a port, yet local writers and speakers, when referring to St. Helier and its harbour, still continue today to broadcast the fallacy which was best expressed by Balleine when he wrote:

> 'It seems extraordinary, for a seafaring community, that ships coming into St. Helier could find no better shelter than a broken-down jetty at 'La Folie', until the late eighteenth century.'[1]

The implication here seems to be that the inhabitants of St. Helier had never made any real effort to achieve a harbour adequate for their requirements, but were content to sit back and let the harbour at St. Aubin act as the main harbour of the island. Some 19th century writers argued that St. Aubin was at one time the capital town of the island, simply because they recognised the relationship between a port and a principal town, and St. Aubin had had a better port than St. Helier in some respects for over two centuries.

Amongst local historians only Philip Ahier came near to the truth with his article in the *Bulletin* of the Société entitled 'Col. Legge's Accompt of Jersey (1679)'[2], which is referred to in more detail later in this article, but he made the mistake of simply describing a harbour without putting the story into its full context, so that the significance of its construction was not fully appreciated by most readers at that time. This lack of appreciation may also be partly due to the fact that the harbour had disappeared so completely during the 18th century that it no longer even existed in legend or folklore, except for the use of the word *havre* in the name of the locality.

There is strong circumstantial evidence that St. Helier was a port as far back as the early 14th century, and probably before then, though it may well not have had a pier or jetty. Very few places did at that period, when beaching was the norm. According to the *Rolls of Assize* of 1311 there were 92 bakers and taverners in the parish of St. Helier in 1309,[3] compared with 280 in the other eleven parishes. St. Helier therefore had nearly four times as many as any other parish, with their average of 25 to 26 each. The population was fairly evenly spread throughout the island, though rather more thickly in the east than in the west, and the town of St. Helier had about half the population of the parish as a whole. Even allowing for the fact that the town held the weekly market does not explain such a large difference. Countryfolk throughout most of Europe did not normally buy their bread in towns, but baked it themselves, and it seems improbable that the very considerable difference can be taken up entirely with taverners, though they may have had wine while most country taverns would only have had ale. The difference can be easily explained, however, if several of these bakers and taverners were acting as ships' chandlers in a fairly busy port, and this number would imply a build-up over the years. Clearly they would not have appeared spontaneously at the date given.

An early pier at Gorey, though almost without doubt a reality in order to cope with the many demands of the castle and its garrison, and also an early pier at St. Helier, must remain conjectural, but despite this the first pier anywhere in the island of which we have satisfactory evidence was at St. Helier. There is a manuscript chart in the British Museum, dated at c.1545, and entitled 'The Haven of Jersey'[4] which looks to us rather amateurly drawn. The aspect of the hills and valleys is greatly overemphasised, but this was usual at this period, because the art of contour drawing was still in its infancy. The drawings of the ships, on the other hand, show that the artist was highly proficient, and may well have been the equivalent of a naval engineer or surveyor, for there are several types of vessel carefully portrayed. The larger vessels are seen where one would expect them at this time, at anchor in the shelter of Noirmont headland, where there is deep water, and close to St. Aubin's Tower, the building of which had been authorised in 1542 to protect that anchorage. The illustration, showing the whole of St. Aubin's Bay, also shows only one pier, and that is at St. Helier. The representation is of a strong stone embankment sheltering ships, composed of massive stones at the southern section, which faces the incoming tide, with the enfolding arm gradually tapering to smaller stones, while a little embankment nearer the shore would seem to be designed to protect the ships from the outward rebound of the waves. The latter in particular, if this interpretation is correct, clearly implies some knowledge in the art of harbour construction, though that experience may have come from elsewhere, while the detail shown in drawing the relative sizes of stones again suggests a technical specialist rather than an artist.

In 1552 fines imposed by the Royal Court were set aside towards the building of the *Havre Neuf* (New Harbour) at St. Helier.[5] This 'New Harbour' is the first that we can read about, and for local historians in general the words *Havre Neuf* came to mean no more than the name of that early Town Pier, as it was later called, where the present-day South Pier now stands. It did, in fact, retain that name for more than a century. But in my own lifetime, when referring to the two main harbours at St. Helier that existed up to the 1960s, before the substantial additions of recent years, we used to call them simply the 'Old Harbour' and the 'New Harbour', the latter being that enclosed by the Victoria and Albert Piers, and many other people did likewise. This also was more than a century after it had been built! No doubt our ancestors did the same, so that the term *Havre Neuf* could also simply mean the harbour most recently constructed. Does this not then also imply that an old harbour existed, or had existed?

By 1585 the States found it necessary to nominate as Collector for the Taxes on Wines and Spirits, Servais Le Vavasseur dit Bois, who was appointed to oversee the three harbours at St. Helier. These were the harbour at l'Islet, on which Elizabeth Castle was soon to be built, the Havre du Mont (or *Havre Neuf*, as it was still also called), and the Havre des Pas.[6] It might be argued that the Collector was collecting from beached vessels, but there is clear evidence that there was either a built pier or a pier under construction at each of these sites at about this time. Two years later a notice was published to the effect that a fine of 20 francs would be imposed on anyone taking stones from the Havre Neuf pier![7] This might imply either that builders were working on the pier, with piles of stones awaiting use, or, less likely, that the stonework of the pier was loose and unstable.

The harbour at l'Islet, known as the Havre St. Jaume, must have been usable by the time the Collector was appointed, but it was being built with voluntary contributions, principally from the merchants, and in 1599 it was still unfinished due to lack of funds. This disproves the long-held idea that it was built to serve the Castle, though at a much later date this became its sole use. It is mentioned as being in use during the Civil War (1642-1649, but 1643-1651 in Jersey)[8] and Dumaresq described it in 1685 as 'a small pier, unfinisht, under the Castle Walls, at the East side by a Sally port, where the Castle Boats are usually kept, and where greater Vessels may be safe, but the entrance is narrow and dangerous.'[9] This is therefore a different pier to that shown on the Richmond map, as mentioned on page 171.

The existence of a pier at Havre des Pas at this time remains somewhat of a mystery. There are too many rocks for a satisfactory beaching area, especially when this was so easily available between l'Islet and the town. It would seem that this pier, too, was usable by 1585, again taking the appointment of the Collector as a guide. Then Le Geyt states:

> En 1602, le 29 May. Aprés Record de Denonciateur d'avoir visité une piece de bois venue au Gravage du Fief du Mont de St.-Helier, entre le havre de bas et le havre neuf, sur le Fief de la Fosse, en presence de six hommes, ladite piece de bois fut mise en la possession d'Helier de Carteret, Sieur dudit Fief, à cause de sa femme.[10]

The phrase 'between the *havre de bas* and the *havre neuf*' must, in fact, refer to the Havre des Pas. The position stated suggests this, and no other reference to the Havre de Bas has come to light.

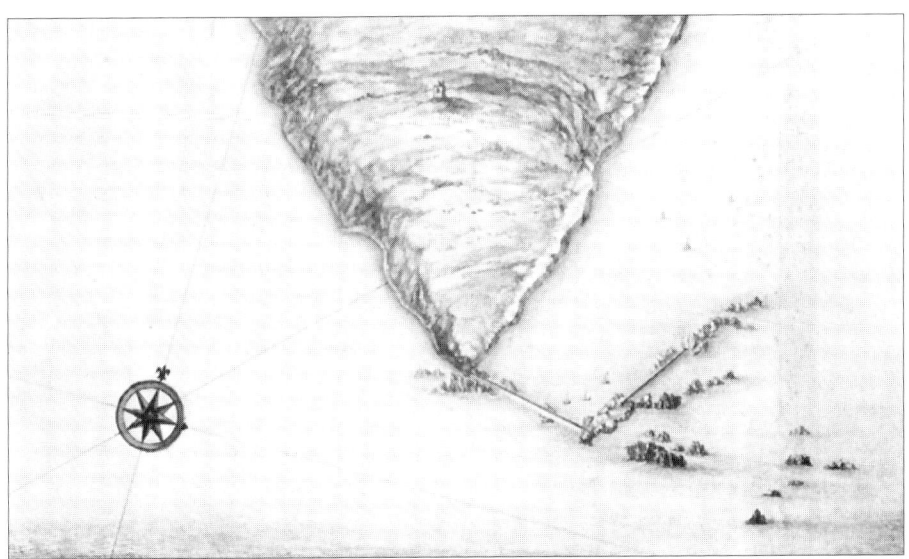

Plan for St Helier (Havre des Pas) harbour (Phillips, 1679)

In 1618 a petition was sent to the Privy Council requesting leave to levy an import duty of one *sou Tournois* on every pot of wine imported for local sale, and an import duty on 'commodities', 'to build a safe pier.'[11] This was approved by the Council, and again confirmed in 1628. It now seems clear that the harbour they built (or rebuilt?) was the Havre des Pas, which lasted for less than a century, and then decayed so rapidly, probably due to storm damage, that only its name remained. On the other hand, although it is on the lee side of the Montagne de la Ville, the best situation for a sheltered harbour, the area is very rocky. It may be that entry and exit was found so hazardous that the pier was deliberately dismantled, the stone being used to once again rebuild the Havre Neuf, or Town Pier, just around the end of the headland. This could account for its apparent total disappearance.

It was described in detail in 1680 by Lieutenant-Colonel George Legge in his Accompt of Jersey, accompanied by Phillips' map of the previous year, as under:

> At the outward head marked C' [the map is not, in fact, so marked] 'there is a 24-foot [sic] at high water, vessels of 50, 60 or 100 tuns may lye safe. The Peere is in length 5 chains 24 links [346 feet], in the seat 25 feet, at the top 12 feet and 10 feet high.... There are several other harbours about the Island as at Havre des Pas where the inhabitants of the Town of St. Helier are very earnest to have licence from His Majtie to build something...[12]

This account of Legge's, and especially his final statement, confirms my argument that the people of St. Helier had been trying for years to have a proper harbour, though without much success.

That this harbour had replaced the *Havre Neuf* as the principal harbour of St. Helier during most of the seventeenth century is clear. From Chevalier's *Diary*, written during the Civil War, there are references to its use during this period, and not one to the *Havre Neuf*. This is not to say that the *Havre Neuf* was not in use by small traders, but clearly the larger vessels were using the *Havre des Pas*. There is also only one reference to the *Havre St. Jaume*, already mentioned above, in which he tells how a patache (a naval tender) and a barque (one of Sir George Carteret's prizes) were both damaged beyond repair by a severe storm in March 1645/6 whilst in that harbour.[13] No doubt also, as Elizabeth Castle was virtually on a war footing during the period of the Civil War, that harbour was closed to normal use.

Chevalier's references to the *Havre des Pas* are as below:

1643, November 20th, General Lydcot ... embarked at Le Havre des Pas with his gentlemen.[14]

Sir Henry Killigrew ... died [at St. Malo] on Saturday, September 27th, 1646 ... His embalmed body was transported to le havre des pas, thence to St. Helier.[15]

1646/7, 1st February ... la compagnie des Jrrois (Irish troops) 'q estois en Jersey sanbarqua tant du vieux chastaux q du haure des pas ...[16]

Also during this period Prince Charles and his entourage are described in Chevalier as landing at Elizabeth Castle, but they came in a naval vessel far too large for any of these harbours, and would have come ashore in a shallop or cutter, what would nowadays be described as a naval pinnace.

William Trumbull, chancellor of Rochester diocese and later Secretary of State, visited Jersey in 1677 with his brother Charles, chaplain to William Sancroft. (Sancroft became Archbishop of Canterbury in the following year.)[17] Charles wrote a diary which has been published by the Société Jersiaise, and from its content they also are understood to have landed at Havre des Pas, though the wording is not specific enough to be certain.

There is a court record of a dispute dated 1677[18] between Philippe Dumaresq, seigneur of La Fosse, and the Connétable of St. Helier, over possession of a cottage described as *la Maison du Guet* (meaning 'the Watch-house') situated at what is now called Mount Bingham. This cottage still stands in the La Collette Gardens, and does appear to be of 17th century origin, but it awaits an archaeological survey before it can be dated with reasonable accuracy. According to the document it was built by the Parish of St Helier 'pour l'usage de guet'. There is a small double aperture at the eastern end of the south-facing wall, and it has been suggested that the use of this somewhat unusual aperture was for placing signal-lamps for shipping. In fact the cottage is situated just to the north of the entry to the Havre des Pas, so that while its title does infer merely a watch-house its situation suggests rather a pier-head control for that harbour. On the other hand, the

1679 Thos. Phillips

1737 Peter Meade

1783 'An Officer'

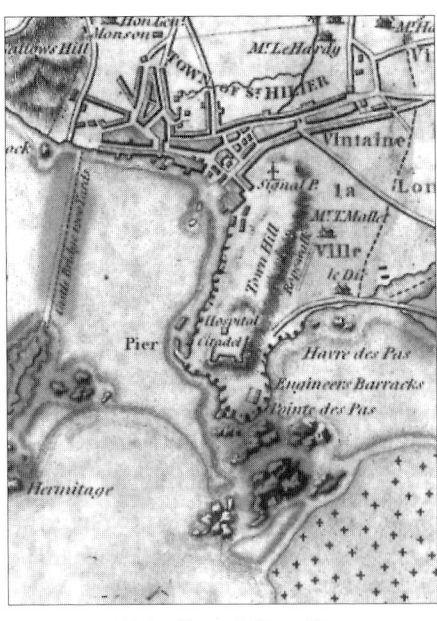

1799 Stead/Bouillon

interpretation of the court record could well mean that it was probably new in 1677, which would seem a late date to be adding to this harbour's facilities, unless it was to replace a former one.

Lt.-Col. Legge's account of 1680, accompanied by Phillips' map, has already described this pier, with no suggestion that it was in decay. Phillips was a Master Gunner, and his job here, under Legge, was to survey and advise on the fortifications, so that we can assume that his map, which clearly shows a built harbour at the Havre des Pas side of the Montagne de la Ville, is reasonably reliable, but it is in fact both helpful and yet posing some problems. He only shows four piers in the island, at Gorey, Le Hocq (of which we have no other reference), the Havre des Pas and in St. Brelade's Bay, the latter being clearly marked as *La Chaussée*. But it is also the only one so marked, and as it is fairly close under the churchyard, but clearly not a part of it, exactly what is he illustrating? He shows no pier at all either at the site of the *Havre Neuf* or at the *Havre St. Jaume*, and in view of the fact that they are not mentioned by Chevalier it does seem feasible that both were so decrepit that they were no longer of use except to shelter small boats.

South-west prospect of St Hellier's town in Jersey (Note the long extension under construction to the Town Pier)

He does not show the pier at St. Aubin's Fort on his map, but this was only in the very early stages of construction, and in his detailed drawing of the Fort he shows it as a long rubble mound, which to my mind confirms that he was most careful to be accurate.

In 1685 Philippe Dumaresq, Seigneur of Samarès and of La Fosse, on which fief the Town Hill is situated, passed contract before the Royal Court with the procureurs of the Vingtaine de la Ville, who were to raise the funds '*a estre employé au bastiment d'une chaussée au Havre des Pas*'[19] *Bastiment* appears here to mean 'in the building of' rather than its definition of 'building trade'. No dictionary that I have found (not even one of the early 19th century) defines the word as a jetty or pier. It can be a road, a carriageway, or a sea-wall, but Phillips does use that term for what seems to be a jetty at St. Brelade, and in 1706 the States formed the *Comité tenu pour l'avancemt de la Chaussée de St. Hellier* specifically to rebuild the Town Pier. It would seem, therefore, that this use of the word was, and still is, strictly local, and that the vingtaine's responsibility was to work on the existing pier at Havre des Pas.

Only six years later (1691) it is somewhat differently described by Dumaresq:

> About half a mile from the Town, there was once a Peer designed, and begun at the waterfront of the Town Hill, called Havre Neuf, aforementioned, but found inconvenient, and so laid aside, as since another at the South point of the said Hill, called Havres des Pas (sic) was intended for greater vessels than those it is now fit for, which use the St. Malo's trade: but its entrance is also so narrow, and full of rocks that it discourages the bestowing of any charges about it.[20]

This clearly implies that it was still in some use by the smaller vessels, but in general abandoned as inadequate, but where does Dumaresq's contract of 1685 with the procureurs of the vingtaine fit in? He was foregoing his rights in the vingtaine, but in exchange there was a proposal for some building work seemingly related to the harbour, though the exact meaning of the wording is not at all clear, and we have no further knowledge of any such work. There was never a proper road to the pier, though what is now called the La Collette Walk may have been originally constructed for the use of the carters employed when the harbour was in course of construction. The pier does not appear at all on Meade's Survey map of 1737, and today its remains are no longer visible from the shore, though they still showed very clearly on an aerial photograph taken in the 1930s when a map of the Island was being prepared. In this photograph, under the sea, which appeared black, was a white L-shape joined to the land, of a size which would appear to agree with Legge's description, and just beneath the Victorian tower on the headland. Unfortunately this photograph, which used to be on display in the Map Room of the former Société Jersiaise Museum, has since disappeared.

Cartographical evidence from the late 17th century is not fully trustworthy on this subject. Neither Lemprière's map of 1694, which shows the pier at St. Aubin's Fort, but no other pier or jetty anywhere in the Island, nor Norden's, of 1695, shows anything relating to maritime requirements anywhere, which would seem to imply that they were only interested in the natural structure of the island itself, not in man-made additions.

During the 17th century, and especially after the Restoration of King Charles II in 1660, Jersey had built up a substantial fleet for use in the fishing-grounds off Newfoundland and Canada. There were too many of the larger vessels used in this trade for them to shelter off the coasts of Jersey, and they had to winter at St. Malo in Brittany, where there was a large natural harbour. Some vessels were even owned jointly by merchants of St. Malo and of Jersey, and even in times of war relations between the Malouins and Jerseymen normally remained amicable. Nevertheless there was an obvious need for a new harbour at St. Helier, made even more urgent by a political change in the status of the Channel Islands. From the year 1483 onwards the islands had had the right to be neutral in times of war, and though there were occasional breaches of this neutrality they had enjoyed a considerable degree of peace and prosperity, but in 1689 William III ordered the discontinuance of this privilege. As a consequence of this edict these vessels could be liable to seizure should war break out between France and England, as it had done periodically over many centuries. More harbour accommodation in Jersey was imperative.

The States decided that once again the Havre Neuf should be rebuilt, and work began in 1700, as soon as the pier being built at St. Aubin at

St Helier Harbour, c. 1770, showing the original Pier Road before the land was cut away to build Fort Regent

St Helier Harbour, c. 1900

that time was finished. By 1703 short-term loans were being raised from local merchants and others, repayment to be made from the Impôt duties. It is probable, though not certain, that the first work done was the dismantling of the old pier, which was clearly in a very decrepit state, and possibly of the Havre des Pas pier also, to re-use its stones in the new work. The 'Great Storm' of 26/27 November 1703, in which some 8,000 people were drowned all along the south coast of England, must have seriously affected whatever work had been done so far.[21] On the 18th March 1706 a States' committee was appointed to take charge, the *Comittée tenu pour l'avancemt de la Chaufsée de St. Hellier.* By the time of its second sitting, on 7th April 1706, only three weeks later, it seems to have enlarged its own powers, and was known as the 'Comité pour les Chaussées'.[22] The oldest of all the States' committees, (which shows the importance that they have always attached to the harbour facilities of the Island) it has been responsible for the upkeep and creation of Island harbours ever since that date.

At the first meeting Abm. Dumaresq (later described as Gent) was engaged as barge-master, Tho. Nicolle for 'placing the stones of the pier', and Jean Denise for 'work with the cart and otherwise as is deemed necessary'. These were, of course, not the actual workers, but rather the principal employers. Barge-crew were engaged later, the stone being brought by sea from Ouaisné, and Ph. Le Gallais, Connétable of St. Helier and a member of the Committee, was authorised to oversee the work and pay the men. In 1708 it seems that work began to speed up. Jean Le Gallais was appointed as chief mason, with Ph. Romeril as assistant, there were also four *inspecteurs* and five quarrymen for cutting stone at *Whesnel*, later *Whaisney*, nowadays Ouaisné. Most of these men were paid 20 sous a day, except the barge-men, who had less. The workforce was increased in 1711 with the addition of Jean Le Cornu 'and his horse' (17 sous), Jean Bisson 'and his horse' (15 sous), and eleven labourers, mostly at 10 sous, while in 1712 there were seven masons, four men 'with horse', four quarrymen at 22 sous with four assistants at 12 sous. There was either a halt or a considerable slowdown not long afterwards, for after 1713 there are no further references in the Committee Minutes, though it is known that the States issued 50,000 *livres Tournois* in notes in 1720 'on completion of the work.'[23]

Men 'with horse' acted both as tractor for moving the stones and as crane for lifting the heavy blocks. This would have been done with the use of a pulley suspended between two spars lashed together in an A-shaped frame, propped against firm footings, and used in the same manner as the jib of a crane. The fact that there were more men 'with horse' in the later stages would be due to the laying of the very heavy parapet blocks,[24] these having to be lifted high and placed with great accuracy. A team of horses would have been necessary to raise them to the required height. By this stage there may have been a crane, but its existence is very doubtful, and in any case it would have been fixed, as all cranes were at that time, and so unable to deal with the parapet-blocks. Cranes were a rarity in most ports until the nineteenth century. Unloading of ships was usually done using their own spars and tackle.

There is a drawing of the harbour made shortly after this period by John Bastide and Charles Lemprière. Bastide was a government ordnance engineer, working at Elizabeth Castle from 1730 to 1734,[25] and it would seem probable that he drew the harbour and Lemprière added the ships. If you study the picture carefully you will notice that there is a long extension of the pier at just above tide level, while the end of the pier seems not well finished. If, as it appears, they laid the foundations for the entire length and then began to build upwards, they in effect created a temporary reef. It may have been that Bastide was illustrating storm damage, but there is no record of this, and this method of building has been recorded elsewhere. On the other hand, it is known that a second 'Havre Neuf' was being constructed in 1735, this being the square quay on which the La Folie Inn is situated today, though there was an earlier La Folie Inn at the landward end of the original pier. Meade's map of 1737 shows the 'Town Peer' as a rather thin structure like half an octagon, but not the Havre Neuf, with a comment 'not finished and very unsafe'[26]. There is no reference in the Minutes of the Committee as to either pier being not properly completed, so which one did he mean?

On 11th January 1749/50 the States passed an Acte for the raising of a Public Lottery (a customary way of raising funds in the eighteenth century) to pay for more 'work to be done on the Chaussée de St. Helier',[27] and George II gave £200 also.[28] Hamilton's map of 1781 shows that the seaward end has been substantially strengthened, though only three of the four sections of semi-octagon remain. He also shows a small pier, which does not appear in other evidence,[29] just to the north of the Town Pier, and no Havre Neuf. It does not seem to be logically situated, except to break the backwash from the shore, and it seems possible that it is simply a badly drawn Havre Neuf. But who knows?

In February 1768, only a month after its foundation, the Jersey Chamber of Commerce recommended to the States that a new quay should be built along the shore northwards from the Town Pier,[30] but nothing came of this for many years, despite the fact that in 1779 there were no less than 71 ships owned or registered in Jersey, averaging about one hundred tons each.[31]

In November 1787 the Chamber of Commerce again pressed for harbour improvements, and presented to the Governor, Bailiff and Jurats, who had agreed to meet them, several plans for the improvement of both St. Helier and St. Aubin's harbours, with a recommendation that that of Mr. Clement Hemery for the harbour of St. Helier was, in their opinion, the best.[32] The plans were passed to the Harbours Committee, which after long deliberation called in John Smeaton to advise them. He proposed plans for St. Aubin, which the merchants there did not accept due to inadequate access by road, and also put forward plans of his own for St. Helier,[33] and though these plans for St. Helier were not carried out, on the advice of local sea-captains, the States decided to enlarge both harbours.

So once again it was the fear of war with France that led to the States' decision to enlarge the harbours. The Battle of Jersey was only six years in the past, and the Revolution was raging in France. Beginning in 1790, the old Town Pier was almost completely rebuilt, both strengthened and lengthened, and later became known as the South Pier, while the North Pier (nowadays known as the New North Quay) which was begun at the seaward end and gradually extended towards the shore, was worked on for some time, remained for some thirty years as a disconnected breakwater, and was finally joined to the land about 1834. The harbour builders had at last unintentionally got the right idea, the necessity to shelter the English and French harbours, as they are known, from those fearsome south-westerly gales, rather than to improve the harbour itself. The breakwater at Elizabeth Castle ultimately achieved that goal, but it was not begun until 1872, and so is outside the scope of this article, except to say that it would have been extremely expensive and much more difficult to construct a century earlier.

Conclusion

Returning to the criticism of local historians regarding the 'broken-down jetty near the inn called La Folie' it is clear that though St. Aubin had for a time become the leading commercial port, this view has not taken into account the full facts. The merchants and the States had been struggling for three hundred years to provide a safe harbour at St. Helier, though the States were at times somewhat tardy, and there is little doubt that they were defeated principally by the necessity to build a harbour in one of the worst sites in the world. It was open to the full force of gales from the south and south-west, as the breakwater at Elizabeth Castle did not yet exist to shelter the town shore, and it had to withstand the massive tidal range of up to 40 feet, as well as the fact that these tides reversed direction around the island four times in every twenty-five hours. When one takes into account these facts, one is left full of admiration for what they had actually achieved. The abortive attempt to build on the lee side of the Mont de la Ville, at Havre des Pas, had clearly shown that that area had too many rocks for the larger ships to use in safety. The lee side of Noirmont would have made a better harbour, but the depth of the water in which to work would have involved enormous costs. On the other hand, neither the expertise nor the finance had been available to build a structure at Havre Neuf strong enough to last for many years. Guernsey had managed to achieve a fairly safe harbour as far back as the late sixteenth century, but they were luckier in that St. Peter-Port is well-sheltered from the west. Even so, Ansted describes their harbour as being 'in course of construction for two centuries, from 1580 to 1780... '[34] so that it is clear that they, too, had much difficulty.

Jersey was not alone in this. One reads in many sources of similar ports in England, especially in the south-west, where the words 'broken-down' or 'decayed' are the most frequent description of the piers up to this same period, and most of these ports only had about half the tidal range.

Written for 'People of the Sea', 1986
Société Jersiaise Bulletin, 2001

18
Shipbuilding in Jersey

Like dwellers by the sea all over the world Jerseymen have always been sailors, but history is almost completely blank on one aspect of this sea-roving community – who built their ships, and where? It is obvious that even in quite early times they would have built their own small fishing-craft, for even the most primitive peoples do this today. It is a different task altogether to build a ship of forty tons or more, which we know that they possessed at least as early as the 14th century, for on more than one occasion Edward III ordered the Channel Islands as a whole to send ships of this size to join in military convoys during the period of the Hundred Years' War. By the end of the 16th century Jerseymen were journeying regularly in their own vessels to the cod banks of North America, which they continued to do right up to the early years of the 20th century.

The first men to have crossed the North Atlantic regularly were the Norsemen, who by the end of the 14th century were making periodic trips to Greenland, where they had an established settlement, and who are reputed to have travelled even further west on occasions to the somewhat inhospitable coasts of Labrador. It is interesting to find that the first men to use the Newfoundland cod banks regularly for fishing, early in the 16th century, if not before, were the fishermen of Normandy and Brittany. The banks were first reported by John Cabot in 1497, who had sailed from Bristol on a voyage of exploration. (Cabot, incidentally, was the son of a Venetian, and not a Jerseyman as has occasionally been suggested). The fact that the Normans and Bretons seem to have taken to visiting Newfoundland regularly at such an early date in much greater numbers than the English, who claimed its discovery, may be explained in that they were the direct descendants of those sea-roving Norsemen who had so often raided the Channel coasts in the 9th and 10th centuries. They were a race of fearless, seafaring men, and undoubtedly they would have known all about the

Ship under construction, almost certainly at Clarke's yard, West Park. The closely packed ribs show that it was being built in anticipation of meeting ice, probably in the St Lawrence estuary

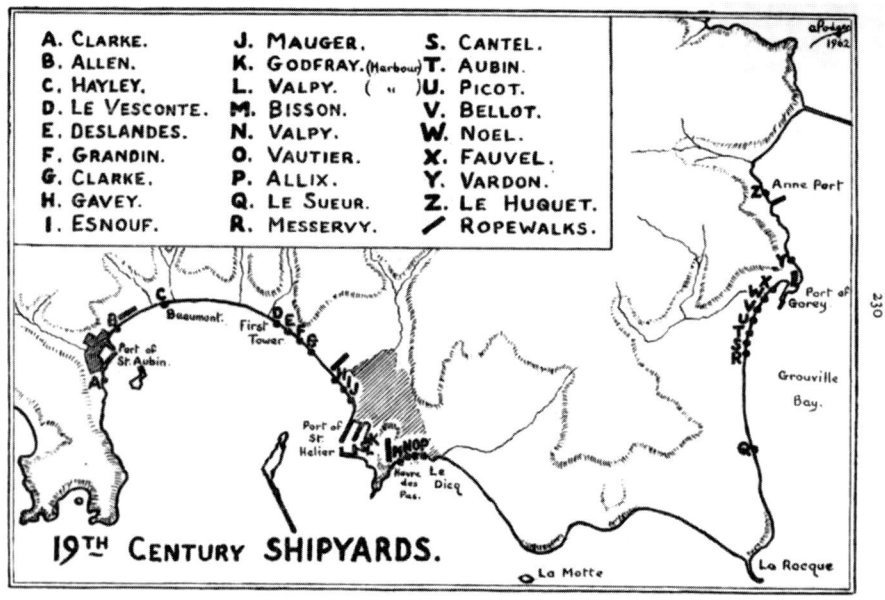

Map showing the locations of 19th century shipyards

journeys made by their kinsmen to Greenland. Thus to them Cabot would have merely opened up a new route to the west, of which they were already aware.

So far we have no proof of Channel Islanders being among these very early visitors to Terre Neuve, as it has been known locally ever since, but it seems highly probable that they were no slower than their contemporaries across the Bay at St. Malo and the other small ports along the coast. G F B De Gruchy makes a strong claim that the natives of the Channel Islands are also direct descendants of these same Norsemen, and it is noteworthy that on more than one occasion Channel Islanders and Frenchmen fishing off the coasts of North America have been described indiscriminately as 'Normans'.

There seem to be no records extant of any sort of shipbuilding taking place in Jersey in medieval times, but even if we choose to doubt the statement that our ancestors were probably visiting Newfoundland within a decade or so of the discovery of America by Christopher Columbus we know for certain that they were doing so during the 16th century. There is a will in existence made in 1582 which refers specifically to a Jersey-owned vessel 'now unloading after her voyage to Newfoundland', and in 1618 the Privy Council had to direct the Governor not to allow stores from the castles to be sold to the Newfoundland fishers, as the depletion of these stores was likely to imperil the inhabitants in times of emergency. Thus we are now faced with the problem of the origin of these locally owned ships, which would have been of a size somewhere in the region of 100 tons.

[Since writing this it has been discovered that a man named Wace, who may be the father or grandfather of the Jersey poet, was building ships in the Bouley Bay/Bonne Nuit area in the later years of the 11th century, and is believed to have supplied one or more towards William's fleet to invade England.]

It would be easy to take for granted that they were bought outside the island, but there are sound reasons for disputing such a suggestion. The inhabitants had been fishing for centuries, and must have had considerable experience in the construction of small fishing vessels. Any suggestion that they also purchased these small fishing boats is quite unthinkable when one considers the facts of medieval life. There was, close to hand, ample quantities of wood from which small boats could be quickly made, for the island was fairly well wooded, and fishermen at that time would have had almost no money with which they could make such a purchase. It seems reasonable to assume, therefore, that in the very early times they would have occasionally made some attempt to build a larger vessel when this was required, and merely through trial and error over the centuries would have discovered what pitfalls to avoid, even if they knew little of real design.

The first actual mention we have of the construction of a boat is in 1468, when Mont Orgueil Castle, occupied by Lancastrian supporters, was being besieged by a small fleet under the direction of the Yorkist Vice-Admiral, Sir Richard Harliston. The occupants of the Castle are described as building a boat in full view of the besiegers, but one day an arrow fired from the Castle was found to bear a note from a Jerseyman who was working there, stating that they were in fact building two boats. The one on view was only a decoy - the other was nearly ready for use. Needless to say it was captured as soon as it was launched.

There follows a lapse of nearly three centuries before our next reference, when Falle mentions that 'most wood (in Jersey) is knotty, but here and there sticks are found fit for the building of good ships'. It is reasonable to take this as meaning that these 'sticks' were actually used for the building of such ships, but we have another wait of over fifty years before we again find a direct description of a ship being built. This time, however, the evidence points very strongly indeed to the fact that Jerseymen were already well-versed in the construction of quite large vessels, for the *Gazette de l'Ile de Jersey* records the building of the 280-ton *Elisha Tupper* at Bel Royal in 1789. This was built in the parish of St. Lawrence from oak grown in that parish, and it was owned by the Janvrin family, who were at that time the shipping magnates of the island, owning several vessels.

The paper contains a glowing account of this venture, referring to the forthcoming launching on the following Monday, and stating that enough extra oak was cut on this occasion to build a somewhat smaller ship and a small boat. It goes on:

> The principal inhabitants of St. Lawrence say that in spite of the quantity of oak that was cut down on this occasion there is still, in that Parish, more than one hundred times as much, fit to fell, if it is not to die of old age.

The writer then goes on to claim that the other parishes are all equally-well wooded, and though such a statement is obviously an exaggeration, especially in view of Falle's statement only fifty years earlier, it seems that Jersey was beginning to consider seriously the possibilities of setting up a permanent shipbuilding industry. It must also be remembered that this was the era of civil commotion and revolution all over Europe, with consequent dislocation of normal trading, and this was therefore probably built to confirm that Jersey grown timber would be satisfactory if other sources of supply were closed. It is interesting to note that this particular ship was named after a prominent Guernsey merchant of the time. Was it at his suggestiuon, was he a partner in the venture? Who knows? [It has since been confirmed that he was he was a partner in this effort.]

In many places, and notably in the West of England, it was customary for teams of shipwrights to travel to any place where a vessel was wanted, and build it on the most convenient beach to hand. This method, like a modern builder hired to build your house for you, continued there from medieval times well into the 19th century. It is probable that this may also have applied to the Channel Islands, though owing to difficulties and expenses incurred in travelling we may have to look for some more local method. As I have said earlier it was quite possible to find the right way to build merely by a slow process of trial and error, but a marriage of these two systems would be a simple matter, in that where a large vessel requiring some specialised knowledge was to be built a small team of expert shipwrights might be hired, acting as foremen over the less experienced local men. This is, as yet, a matter for conjecture, but it would explain the seeming total absence of any permanent shipyard in Jersey until the 1820s. It is, incidentally, also for this same reason that it is so difficult to find any archaeological proof of medieval shipbuilding in many countries – not only were there no permanent shipyards, except in one or two rare instances, but whatever traces may have been left in most places would have been lost in the tides long since.

However, another fact has recently come to my notice which would appear to explain even more decidedly the lack of yards in Jersey until this date. The Jersey Register of Shipping, commencing at 1803, shows at the very beginning a substantial number of locally owned ships to have been built in 'British Plantations', or in North America. It is a known fact that later on, during most of the 19th century, it was normal practice for Jersey firms operating in North America and Newfoundland to send their retained men out to the forests during the winter months when fishing was not possible there. They would cut down trees in some creek or a short way up river, and use them to build the small schooners which were used on the Banks during the remainder of the year. Many of the schooners were built this way, and it would therefore seem from these Registers that this was a custom of some duration, and that some of the local firms which had been established in the New World since the early part of the 18th century had been building their own ships for many years, not in Jersey, but in North America and Newfoundland. I have not yet been able to make any extensive search into this question, but there are at least three pointers to its probable truth:

(a) The almost complete absence of any reference to ship building in Jersey itself, despite the large number of ships owned here.
(b) The fact that while there was not a great deal of wood in Jersey suitable for shipbuilding (with apologies to the writer in the *Gazette*!) there were enormous forests in Canada and Newfoundland growing almost to the water's edge, and which in the 18th century at least must have been virtually free for the taking.
(c) The spare labour that was available through the winter months, as mentioned above, due to the fact that it was customary to indenture certain types of labour for a term of years (usually five) in the New World. This saved the companies the cost (and risk) of transporting numerous men there and back each year, and also ensured a permanent staff in a way that would not have been possible with seasonal labour.

There has also been discovered in Newfoundland the remains of a shipyard which has not been used for some centuries. According to the local legend Jerseymen set up this yard as far back as the 16th century, but as no real archaeological survey has yet been made of this site we shall have to await such a development before we can accept the legend as fact. [Since this was written, some years ago, a survey has been carried out, and it is now believed that this was set up by Norsemen, most likely in order to make repairs to their ship, rather than for building a new one.]

As the cod-fishing trade expanded so new markets had to be found both for the fish, and for the produce usually purchased as a return cargo after the fish had been sold. At the commencement of the 19th century it became apparent that wood could be imported cheaply from the Baltic and, with a world in the process of rapid and continuing economic expansion, more and more ships were needed.

The Channel Islands were in the very fortunate position of being able to fix their own import dues, and yet pay no such dues on goods going into Great Britain, provided that they had been manufactured in the islands. The result of this privilege, which dated back to the Middle Ages, was to give Jersey shipbuilders a tremendous advantage over their English contemporaries. Ships were built here of the finest wood available, and rigged with the best Russian hemp and, as Great Britain at this time was imposing a high import tariff on these materials the Jersey-built ships could be sold in England at a lower price than English-built ships on which lesser-grade materials, had been used. There was also, of course, a considerable demand from the many expanding local companies, and a new industry was soon established.

George Deslandes appears to have set up the first permanent yard in 1821, but in the next decade or so several others followed his example, and the number continued to increase until the 1860s, at which time there were eighteen yards distributed around the coasts of the island. The map (see page 188) shows altogether the sites of 26 yards, but it must be understood that these were not all in existence at one and the same time. They all appear at some time or other during the 19th century, but eighteen was the highest number operating at any one time. Three rope-yard sites are also shown, at St. Aubin, Kensington Place, and Havre-des-Pas. These were, of course, an essential part of the industry, while there were many sail-lofts, the majority in the Commercial Buildings area.

The shipyards situated on the east coast, in Grouville and St. Catherine's Bay, were small, and were in fact set up to cater for the needs of the oyster fishery which operated from Gorey. Their output consisted almost entirely of Cutters, with occasionally a small Schooner, but they were prepared to carry out a larger order if necessary. Picot, for instance, built at least one Brig and a Barque in addition to smaller vessels, but it was at Havre des Pas and in St. Aubin's Bay that most of the bigger vessels were built. The yards there were quite extensive. The largest, F C Clarke, stretched from Kensington Place to West Park Pavilion, right across the area now bounded on the north by the Triangle Park. Other yards were situated all along the shore as far as First Tower, and their sites are now largely buried under Victoria Avenue. Although Clarke's was the largest yard, Daniel Le Vesconte and Co. at First Tower, hold the record for the largest number of vessels on the stocks. In 1864 they had under construction at one time three Ships (each of about 900 tons), two Barques (100 and 300 tons), one Brig (250 tons) and two Schooner-Brigs (each 100 tons).

Shipyards near Gorey

The largest vessel ever built in Jersey was the *Rescue* (1187 tons) and Miss Julia Marett mentions the *Evening Star*, of about 1,000 tons, built on the land adjoining the Bulwarks at St. Aubin. This is described in the article as a 'Clipper-barque', an unusual term which I have not previously encountered, but as the vessel was employed on the Australian emigrant trade, returning with wool, she was probably given a finer hull than usual, a clipper hull in fact, to enable her to compete with the fast vessels she was likely to encounter in both of these trades.

At the commencement of 1865 there were thirty-four vessels recorded as being on the stocks, with an estimated tonnage of 12,460, but suddenly the whole industry collapsed. Only fifteen years later even the laying-down of the keel of a cutter was a matter for newspaper comment, and by 1890 nothing was left except for a couple of repair yards. This failure was almost entirely due to the rapid expansion of the steam-boat industry, coupled with the replacement of wooden hulls by iron. There are no facilities in Jersey for large-scale iron-foundry work, and the cost of importing iron instead of wood was prohibitive. It is astonishing that the repercussions of such a rapid decline in an industry were not catastrophic. Although at this period there were some substantial banking failures in the island they appear to have been due to the overall decline in the sailing-ship industry, and the loss of the shipyards alone does not seem to have had any major effect on the local economy.

Except for one or two of the merchants' stores on the Esplanade and at St. Aubin, which were originally built as part of these shipyards, a wooden stake in the sand here and there where a keel was laid down, and an occasional memory in the mind of a few old folk, nothing now remains.

Since writing the above a few records have come to light of shipbuilding in the later years of the 18th century, and these are listed here.

For the first three listed we have only the name and tonnage, but AG Jamieson, editor of *A People of the Sea*, has dug out a little more information, as below:

1st Reg.	Vessel	Tons	Rig	Built by
1794	DE JERSEY	200+	Ship	Unknown
1798	ROWCLIFFE	344	Ship	do.
1800	SPEEDY	71	Cutter	do.

Then, coming from the Registry of Shipping, we have:

1806	PEACE	8	Cutter	M Le Boeuf
1807	BETSEY	16	Cutter	P J Le Neveu
1809	SYLPH	19	Cutter	F Grellier
1810	GENERAL DON	12	Lugger	M Le Boeuf
1813	VENUS	65	Chasse-marée	F Grellier
1814	PRINCE OF BOUILLON	48	Schooner	J Gavey

1815	PALLAS	120	Brig	J Gavey & F Grellier
1815	CALISTA	26	Smack	F Grellier
1815	LORD SIDMOUTH	132	Brig	M Le Boeuf

Société Jersiaise Bulletin, 1962

19

Life at sea in the 19th Century

When my wife and I were first married, in 1949, we already had two small boys from her previous marriage, her husband having been killed whilst in the Navy. We also used to take in two or three visitors in the summer to make the finances go a bit further, as I expect at least some of your families may have had to do at that time. Come washday that meant that there were several sheets to be dealt with, at first entirely by hand, after a little while with the aid of a Hoover Twin-Tub washing machine. What an enormous difference that made! But there was still the matter of getting the sheets dry again. We lived in a house in the Parade in St Helier, now demolished, which was fine for us, but had only a small back-yard with high buildings on three sides of it, and single-storey extensions to the house against two of them. So the clothes-line was about twelve feet up, otherwise the wet sheets and things would have been gently caressing the guttering of those extensions!

To hang out the sheets you went to the wall at one end, undid the rope from its cleat – shall we call it the halyard? – until the line was low enough, re-cleated the halyard, pegged on the sheets, undid the halyard again, hauled up the line, re-cleated the halyard, then did the same at the other end of the yard. It was usually OK in summer, but with children as well there were sheets to hang out all year round. Have you ever tried rushing outside in a sudden hailstorm or squall to get the darned things in again when you knew that they were dry a moment ago, and before they got too wet again uncleat the halyard, mind the things don't blow against the gutter, unpeg them, haul up and cleat, rush to the other end and repeat!

But we never had to climb sixty to eighty feet or more up a rope ladder, which wasn't fixed to solid ground, and was probably swaying wildly in a squall, then stand on a wire rope with two or three others, and sidle along for many feet, bending your stomach over the equivalent

The Royal Navy recognised the value of Channel Islands sailors. The 'ship', in a field adjoining Faldouet dolmen, has gone, but the officers' and cadets' quarters remain as a private building.

of a horizontal tree-trunk, while you hung on to anything graspable. Below you was a thick, wet, heavy canvas sheet as big or bigger than one of the walls of this room, flapping wildly, and which it was your job to control before it knocked you into the sea? Haul it up by the little bits of rope fixed to it at intervals for reefing the sail, tie that round the yardarm that you were leaning on that's one reef taken in, then down to the next, do the same again perhaps four or five times before the whole sail was neatly tied, then probably down twelve to twenty feet to do the same to the sail below. Hands almost unusable by now, they were so frozen, but it's sidle back to the rope ladder, try to hang on for dear life as the ship sways in the storm, and somehow get down to the deck again.

It's true that that was fairly normal all too often, but as humans we do like to dramatize, either verbally or in our minds. Life at sea was very commonly not like that. Do you think that there would be round-the-world yacht races if the weather was like that all the time? Of course not. Life at sea can be very pleasant, even for working sailors, for many days at a time, and the owners of sailing vessels generally tried to have them in port, having repairs done, during the worst weather months, but weather does what it likes and when it likes.

The type of vessel made a difference as well. If you were on a full-rigged ship, a barque, or a brig, you had those sails to furl and unfurl as I have described, but there was a fair-sized crew of twenty or so for a full-rigged ship down to nine or ten for a brig. On the other hand schooners had no yardarms, everything was done from down on the deck like a modern yacht, so only half-a-dozen men were needed, and if the worst came to the worst two men and a boy could cope in normal weather, but not for weeks on end. Square-rigged vessels were the norm for the first half of the nineteenth century, and they were good in ocean voyages, but fore-and-aft rig schooners (like modern yachts) became more common as the century progressed, being more manoeuvrable when approaching land, and less costly in manpower.

Whatever type of vessel it was, one of the crew had to be cook. On the larger vessels this was not usually too much of a problem, though one might hear some choice words if he turned out to be inadequate. On the schooners, however, the boy was usually given the job, initially advised by anyone with more experience, but he had to become a very fast learner, or suffer whatever the crew might literally throw at him. While the master might on rare occasions take his wife with him, who would almost certainly have been a better cook, women on board were generally looked on as certain to bring bad luck.

Up to the end of the 19th century almost all vessels were equipped with a coal-fired range, so familiar to us older ones in pre-war houses. Cooking at sea requires a stove with a low 'wall' around each burner or around the heating area, to stop the pans from going over the edge as the ship rolls. It was also advisable to use only half-full pans, unless the weather was very calm. Come meal-time for those not on watch it was a case of going to the galley, get your plate/dishful, and if the weather was rough try to get to the focsle without getting your dinner drowned as a wave washed inboard, or losing it altogether by falling on the slippery deck in your rush to get it safe.

Incidentally, canned food was invented at the request of Napoleon, to feed his armies on the march, so that it was not commonplace until fairly well into the 19th century. Neither, of course, were there refrigerators, so the cook's job could be quite a problem. I do not know if Jersey ships followed the West of England custom, but it is probable that at least some of them did so. That is to say, each week started with a new stock of food in the galley – I'm not sure if the start was Sunday or Monday. So what happened to the odd left-overs from the previous week? They all went into a large saucepan to make a rather unusual sort of steamed pudding or thick stew, depending on the contents. By all I mean ends of meat, flour, marmalade, suet, cabbage, jam, fish, the lot! It's supposed to have been fairly popular, no doubt due to the fact that if you're working hard and it's cold almost anything goes down with satisfaction.

It has been pointed out that in some ways British sailors were better off than most other workers. A form of social insurance was devised for them during the reign of Charles II, so that for a few pennies a month deducted from their pay whilst at sea they would not have to beg if they suffered too severe an injury to be able to continue, or their widows would have some compensation, however small it might be, if their death was related to their work. This idea had followed a fund set up after the defeat of the Spanish Armada, to assist sailors who had been in the battle (or their widows) and to prevent them becoming unemployed vagrants, as they would no longer be needed by the navy.

Also a law passed in 1729 meant that they had to have a written contract before commencing a voyage, which no landsman had, and in addition to this, because the size of any crew was necessarily limited, there was more chance of advancement at sea than anywhere else. But of course these advantages carried with them the risk of never seeing home again.

Paying this tax in England towards the sailors' insurance was not really practicable for Channel Island vessels, and the Jersey Merchant Seamen's Benefit Society was formed in 1835 to operate just such a system in this island, and it remains in existence today, though almost redundant because of the official Social Security, except for the fact that there is still one person receiving a pension from that Society today (2006). It is, however, in process of having its terms restructured to allow it to continue, as it still has money in hand. In 1902 it had 200 pensioners on its books, both sailors and widows of sailors, and they were each receiving £2 per annum. For the average working man at that time this would have been equivalent to about two or three weeks' wages.

If they were involved in the cod-fisheries of North America there was one danger that I have not mentioned. The actual fishing was done by men sitting in small boats, dories, with long lines overboard, and when they had sufficient they returned to the mother-ship (usually a schooner) to unload. Cod weighing 20lb. were quite normal. A mother-ship would have anything up to a dozen dories at sea at a time, but thick banks of fog were, and still are, liable to roll up very quickly, due to ice-floes coming down the coast from Greenland, that sometimes last for days. Conch-shells were carried for use as fog-horns, but sound in fog can be misleading, and though loss of life was unusual it did occur.

Even nowadays fishing can be a dangerous occupation, but at least they do have the advantage of really waterproof clothing, and neither are they any longer reliant on the wind. The sea is a different matter, and probably always will be. Fishermen are tough, and when at sea cannot sit back and rely on someone else to keep them in comfort, they have to learn to act quickly and decisively when in difficulty. As a result they breed sturdy offspring of independent mind, and if their home is an island so much the better, for they can bring that independence into being as a community. And this is how the Jersey of today was born.

Talk to Channel Islands Family History Society

Early reclamation at St Aubin

First reclamation site at La Collette

20

Land Reclamation in Jersey: Past and Present

It seems an appropriate time to attempt to put the matter of land reclamation into perspective, in view of the many differing comments and arguments now prevailing. The purpose of this article is therefore to give a brief history of such events locally and to glance into the future.

Probably the first reclamation in Jersey was when a seawall was built to protect the town of St. Helier. This wall, which ran from the Town Church in a straight line down towards what we now call Castle Street, will have enabled small tidal coves behind it to become available for building, though it was principally for tidal protection. We do not know exactly when it was built, but it was in existence in the late 17th century.

It seems that sometime during the early 18th century the land area was extended outside of this wall, taking in much of the beach and creating the area now covered by lower Mulcaster Street and Conway Street. Wharf Street presumably led to a wharf, or was itself a wharf, which no longer exists. Not even the oldest inhabitant would ever think of this as a reclaimed area without prior knowledge that this was so.

St. Aubin comes into this picture at the end of the 18th century when the owners of the houses under Noirmont, who were mostly merchants, got together to ask permission from the Crown to build a jetty in front of their properties. This was granted, and Le Boulevard (the Bulwarks) came into existence. Behind that jetty the land was infilled, creating the long gardens and some of the built-up area behind it. Some time later the whole sweep of land on which the St. Brelade's Parish Hall (the former railway terminus building) and the harbour were built, the reclamation being paid for by the States.

Here I must take issue with remarks made by a local speaker in a talk about St. Aubin given to the Société Jersiaise, at least as mentioned in the *Jersey Evening Post*, for I was not present at that lecture. He is reported to have said:

> Reclamation will damage the wholeness of its character, and destroy the unified pattern of centuries of valid development. So don't interfere with fundamental lines.

Yet he had said earlier:

> ...the original cliffs were shown at last being pushed into the background as the shoreline changed by infilling towards the sea.

In other words, what we now see as the attractive little town of St. Aubin is built on reclaimed land, but because the majority of buildings on it have that timeless look that granite gives we see it as a natural growth. This is not to say that land reclamation should be encouraged there, and certainly not merely for a car-park, but if it were to take place it would probably be as acceptable to future generations as that town is now.

At the beginning of the 19th century, when Fort Regent was being built, massive quantities of stone became available, which was being cut from the hillsides of the Mont de la Ville to make those hillsides unscaleable in case of assault. A group of merchants did as had been done at St. Aubin, and asked the Crown for permission to build their own quay, using this stone. They built and infilled the entire site of the Merchants' Quay (Le Quay des Marchands, now Commercial Buildings), and the large stores on it. There was no Planning Department to tell them what to do in those days, though they were ordered by the military authorities that the buildings should not rise above the level of Pier Road, in order not to impede the lines of fire of the guns at Fort Regent. Nevertheless they clearly did their own planning, for the stores were built to a standard pattern for almost the whole length of the quay, though this is not so easily apparent today.

The States followed by building the Esplanade, and then when the Albert Pier was built in the late 1840s the area between the Esplanade and the top of the harbour was infilled and the Abattoir buildings constructed, while the terminus building for the railway to St. Aubin was added shortly afterwards.

The sea wall towards St. Aubin was begun in 1865, making the former unusable sand dunes suitable for building. But, apart from comparatively minor filling as the sea wall was built, there was no more until 1929, when the top of the Old Harbour was filled in, covering the area from the present Route de la Liberation down to the harbour wall, on which the Customs and Immigration buildings and all the surrounding roads now stand. [Since this was written, in 1994, this area has now become the steam-clock park area.]

This takes us to the present group of reclamations, starting south of the Victoria Pier, then west of the Albert Pier, then west of that area again as far as West Park. Now beginning south of Mount Bingham and the first of these modern sites, being described as 'south of La Collette'.

Reclamation West of Albert

Two things seem to be clear from this account, namely that private funding can do as good a job as States' funding, and while reclamation affects the people at the time that it is taking place it seems to become accepted very quickly once completed. Provided that there is pride in one's surroundings, which there clearly was both with the merchants at St. Aubin and those at Commercial Buildings, then an excellent result can be achieved, while the States' contribution of the Abattoirs buildings with a frontage on the harbour having character and quality showed that same pride, so common in the Victorian era throughout Britain. Nor must it be thought that all of these merchants were true Jerseymen, for amongst them were men whose recent forebears had come to Jersey because it was a good place in which to make money.

We now come to the future, to the Waterfront Plan. Michael Day, in his paper on the Waterfront policy, has stated that 'prettification of inappropriate architecture' would be anathema, and that the waterfront should 'look and feel part of the island that has created it'. He considers that the waterfront should be 'different and innovative and an inspiration for the future. Jersey is one of the most prosperous places in the world, and it can afford to do these things properly.'

It will be easy for many to say, as I am sure that they will, that 'good Jersey architecture' means 'granite buildings'. In this situation this is not so. The waterfront gives an ideal opportunity to create architecture for the twenty-first century, not gimmicky but of imaginative high quality. Some granite here and there in the more public buildings will help to tie the future to the past, but only if it is top-quality work, not mere random facing as done on many buildings at present, and not out-of-scale imitation farmhouses!

The proposal for an hotel on the edge of the marina, if carried through, will also demonstrate the feelings of those responsible for the island. It could be that most selfish of tourist requirements, a medium or high-rise building on the foreshore, but even a five-storey flat-roofed building in that situation will destroy the view of Elizabeth Castle, or much of it, for most of the houses on the northern slopes of the town. This, just for the benefit of people who come for a few days, then move on elsewhere! On the other hand, a low-level hotel, though much more expensive in land-use, can be an imaginative attraction, as can be found in the eastern Mediterranean and other areas.

The example set by the States on the quality of design and funding of public buildings on the site will determine how money from private funds is spent in this area, and setting this standard will require a very substantial investment, but it will be of lasting benefit. Pride has been entirely lacking in the States' approach to reclamation in the last few years, but there does seem to be a change of heart recently, encouraged by public interest. It is essential that this change takes effect if future generations are to look back on us with gratitude and respect, rather than with regret at an opportunity lost.

Talk to University of the Third Age Social History, 1994

POSTSCRIPT

There is one aspect of history that has surprised me, and that is the way in which at least 80% of writers of English history stick strictly within the coastline for their field of knowledge. In the 1950s a nine-volume paperback history of England was published by Penguin Books Ltd., a reputable firm, written by eight of the leading historians of the period, and totalling over 2,000 pages. Apart from one sentence in Volume 5, (the Tudor period), which lists the existence of the Isle of Man, the Scillies and the Channel Islands as Crown Dependencies, there are no other references to them whatever. The Orkneys, the Shetlands and the Hebrides were and remain Scottish rather than English dependencies, though becoming involved after the Union, but even so get no mention either.

Almost the same ratio applies to the majority of histories of Britain, irrespective of the period being written about, and despite the fact that all of these places are parts of the British Isles. It is not due to shortage of information, for there are many hundreds of entries in the *Close Rolls, Acts of the Privy Council*, and other official records of this type, and which must be available in many libraries, as they are here in Jersey. It would seem not unreasonable to expect one sentence in 500 pages or so, especially in respect of the Viking period, and of the 11th to 15th centuries, whichever of these dependencies is the subject involved.

Using an admittedly exaggerated simile it is as though, writing your own 2,000 page autobiography, you say, round about page 850, '... and I have three teenagers, James, Mary and Arthur' and that is the sole reference. In no way whatsoever has anything that has happened to them at any time, or anything that they have done, impacted on your life! A strange viewpoint.

AP
September 2006

NOTES

Abbreviations
BSJ   *Bulletin* of La Société Jersiaise
HIJ   *History of the Island of Jersey* (Balleine)
CSP   Calendar of State Papers
APC   Acts of the Privy Council
OJH   *Old Jersey Houses* (Stevens)

3: Saint PETER'S MARSH (Goose Green Marsh)
1 *The Molendinary System of Queen's Valley* BSJ. Vol.25, 1990, p.297. (re the chapel of St.Nicholas)

4: LIVING IN PRECARIOUS TIMES
All information in this article came either from the Lettres Close (Close Rolls) or from Ancient Petitions.

11: THE SOCIAL LADDER
1 Since writing the above I have noted two passing references to husbandmen: '... for many poor husbandmen can better spare their carts' (two days a year carrying stone. A.P.) 'than pay a Crowne in money'. *Remonstrance* of 1679. B.S.J.Vol.11, 1888, p 277, and the passage quoted on page 124 from *Dumaresq's Survey.* B.S.J.Vol.XII, 1935, p.418
2 *A Biographical Dictionary of Jersey*
3 *H.I.J.* (Revised edition) p.161
4 *C.S.P. (Dom). (1625-1649/Addenda)* 26-1-1627/8
5 Dumaresq's '*Survey*'. BSJ. Vol. XII, 1935, p.418
6 *Extente* of 1607, p. 66-68
7 *Extente* of 1668, p. 62-63
8 Some Land Use Statistics BSJ. Vol.XV. 1952, p.444
9 Jersey and the European Economic Community, Table 6, p.155
10 *H.C.L.* p.102
11 *H.C.L.* p.105
12 *A.P.C. (1623-1624)* 30-6-1624
13 *H.C.L.* p.112
14 *Social Life in the Seventeenth Century*, BSJ Vol.III, 1941, p.79
15 *C.S.P.(Dom)* (Add.*James I*, Vol.42, No.7)
16 *Reparations for his M_ties Castles* BSJ Vol.VII, 1912, p.147ff
17 *La Cloche Memoirs* BSJ. Vol III, 1890, p.501
18 Compiled from dates given in *Old Jersey Houses* (Vol.I)

12: FISHING AND AGRICULTURE
1 *Medieval Land Tenures In Jersey*
2 *C.S.P. (Dom). (1580-1625/Addenda)* 10(?)-12-1593

3 *C.S.P. (Dom)*. (1625-1649/Addenda) 20-3-1625/6
4 *A.P.C.* (1571-1575) 15-3-1573/4
5 *Mont Orgueil Castle* p.176
6 *Caesarea or a Discourse of the Island of Jersey* (Quoted in OJH, p.38)
7 *Caesarea, or an Account of Jersey* (Quoted in HIJ, p.230)
8 *Some Land Use Statistics*   BSJ. Vol.XV, 1952, p.442
9 *O.J.H.* p.38
10 *A.P.C.* (1628-1629) 15-9-1628
11 *A.P.C.* (1617-1619) 24-6-1618
12 *C.S.P. (Dom)*. (1635) 20 & 26-9-1635

13: MANUFACTURE AND TRADE
1 *A History of Hand-Knitting*   Richard Rutt. p.185
2 Quoted in *H.I.J.* p.92
3 Quoted in *H.I.J.* p.91, being part of a letter from Robert Wyngfield to Lord Burleigh, in the British Library
4 *C.S.P. (Dom)* (1580-1625/Addenda) Undated (1596?)
5 *C.S.P. (Dom)* (1637-1638). 31-1-1637/8
6 *A.P.C.* (1617-1619) 23-3-1618/9
7 *H.I.J.* p.130
8 *C.S.P. (Dom)* (1625-1649/Addenda) 11-5-1627
9 *La Remonstrance des Etats* BSJ.1888, p.260
10 *The English Coasting Trade* p. 150-152
11 *Dumaresq's Survey* BSJ. Vol.XII, 1935, p.419
12 *Ibid* p.419
13 *The Case of the Inhabitants* BSJ. Vol.IV, 1897, p.57
14 *C.S.P. (Dom)* (1547-1565/Addenda) 1559(?). p.494
15 *C.S.P. (Dom)* (1625-1649/Addenda) 11-2-1626/7
16 *The Channel Islands under Tudor Government, 1485-1642* A.J.Eagleston.   Cambridge 1949
17 *A.P.C.* (1617-1619)   23-3-1618/9
18 *Trade Relations between Jersey, Guernsey, and Welsh Ports in Elizabethen Times* D. Trevor Williams. BSJ. Vol.XV, 1934
19 *The English Coasting Trade* p.64
20 *Mont Orgueil Castle* p.160
21 *Caesarea, or an Account of Jersey* p.291, Note 32
22 *Dumaresq's Survey* BSJ. Vol.XII, 1935, p.418-419
23 *Trade Relations between Jersey, Guernsey, and Welsh Ports in Elizabethen Times* D. Trevor Williams. BSJ. Vol.XV, 1934, p.261ff

18: SAINT HELIER HARBOURS to the beginning of the 19th century
1 *H.I.J.* p.198
2 Ahier *Col. Legge's 'Accompt of Jersey'* p.238 et seq.
3 *Rolls of Assize* 1311. (Quoted in De Gruchy. p.96)
4 Manuscript chart in the British Museum, dated at c.1545, and entitled *The Haven of Jersey* BSJ Vol.VI, 1908, pp.334-5
5 *Royal Court Rolls* 1552
6 *Actes des Etats* 27th May 1585, pp.49/50
7 *Actes des Etats* 1587

Notes

8 Chevalier *Journal de Jean Chevalier* p.271.
9 Dumaresq *A Survey of the Island of Jersey* p.432
10 Le Geyt *Le Geyt sur la Constitution, Lois & les Usages de Jersey* Vol.1, p.342
11 *A.P.C.* 24th June 1618
12 Chevalier *ibid* p.271
13 Ahier *Col. Legge's 'Accompt of Jersey'* p.238 et seq.
14 Chevalier *ibid* p.105
15 Chevalier *ibid* p.370/371
16 Chevalier *ibid* p.407
17 *Concise Dictionary of National Biography* Vol. III (see individual entries)
18 *Royal Court, Cour de Samedi*, 5th May 1677
19 *ibid* 20th February 1685 (These two drawn to my attention by Jean Arthur)
20 Dumaresq *A Survey of the Island of Jersey* p.432
21 Haydn *Dictionary of Dates*
22 Comité pour les Chaussées Minutes
23 *Actes des Etats* 3rd May 1720, pp.68/9
24 There is a crude sketch in the Société library, drawn in 1870, signed T.L.B.T., purporting to show the development of the harbour, (which includes 'La Crane,1738' situated on the eastern side of the La Folie quay), but it unfortunately gives no references; the La Folie inn is sited on the earlier pier.
25 As (24) above
26 Nicolle. *Mont Orgueil Castle.* p.89
27 Nicolle. *The Town of St. Helier,* p.31
28 *Actes des Etats* 11 Jan. 1749/50, p.39 et seq.
29 *Actes des Etats* 18 Nov. 1751, p.63 et seq.
30 BSJ. Vol.XVII, 1959 (between pp. 258 & 259)
31 Jersey Chamber of Commerce Minutes
32 Jersey Chamber of Commerce Minutes
33 Comité pour les Chaussées Minutes
34 Ansted, *The Channel Islands* p.36.

The principal references to the pier during the 18th century, in date order, are utterly confusing.

1730s Drawing by J.Bastide & C.Lemprière, engraved C. Toms, shows a fairly long pier, not showing apparent signs of neglect.

c.1735 Havre Neuf constructed, i.e. the La Folie Quay not the Town Pier reconstructed

1737 Meade's map shows a thin semi-octagon, but 'not finished and very unsafe', and does not show the La Folie quay.

1749/50 States vote for 'more work to be done on the pier'.

1755 Bellin's map shows no pier at all.

1762 Painting by D. Serres shows what appears to be a sound structure, seen from the town.

1768 Chamber of Commerce recommend a new quay along the shore north from the Town Pier

1770 Sepia drawing similar to Bastide and Lemprière's of the 1730s, but from a different

Notes

viewpoint, shows large vessels tied up against the long pier, suggesting at least reasonable stability

1781 Hamilton's map shows a pier similar to Meade, with another new arm from shore, and no La Folie Quay, unless his new quay is a distortion of it.

1783 'An Officer's map shows apparent ruins of Meade's/Hamilton's pier, with more solid and shorter pier built on that site, and square La Folie quay has appeared

1787 The Richmond map, which as the first Ordnance Survey map, has to be the most reliable, but comes in almost too late for most of this period. It shows a pier similar to Meade's, of 1737, except that it is (now?) curved rather than angular, and the pierhead is fully circular. It also shows the square La Folie Quay, and a clear roadway from the town to the pier.

1790 Town Pier was almost completely re-built and lengthened, and the New North Quay begun from the seaward end, but only a few yards constructed to date.

1799 Bouillon/Stead's map is an amalgam of Hamilton's and 'an Officer's, but with the seaward end of the New North Quay now apparently re-built.

BIBLIOGRAPHY

Public Records (English) published by HM Stationery Office, London:
Acts of the Privy Council of England (APC)
Calendar of Home Office Papers
Calendar of State Papers (Domestic) (CSP Dom)
Calendar of State Papers (Domestic)(Addenda)
Journal of the Commissioners for Trade and Plantations
Register of Papal Letters
Lettres Close. Early volumes In Latin. English translation of all references to the Channel Islands available at the Lord Coutanche Library, the Société Jersiaise, Jersey)
(All available in the Jersey Library Reference Section, St. Helier, Jersey)

Public Records (Guernsey)
Actes des Etats

Public Records (Jersey)
Jersey and the European Economic Community (Report of the Special Committee of the States of Jersey, 1967)
Jersey Chamber of Commerce Minutes
Jersey Merchant Seamen's Benefit Society – Voyage Volumes
Le Geyt, P: *Le Geyt sur la Constitution, Lois & les Usages de Jersey* (4 Vols) published by States of Jersey, 1846
Rolls of Assize, 1311 (Quoted in De Gruchy, G F B: *Medieval Land Tenures In Jersey* published Bigwoods Ltd., 1957
Rolls of the Royal Court of Jersey
States of Jersey, Comité pour les Chaussëes, (now Jersey Harbours) Minutes
States of Jersey Register of Shipping

Published by the **Société Jersiaise**
Actes des Etats
Ancient Petitions
Chevalier, Jean: *Journal de Jean Chevalier, 1643-1651* (9 Vols) published 1906-1914
Extente de l'Ile de Jersey, 1607
Extente de l'Ile de Jersey, 1668

In the **Annual Bulletins** of the **Société Jersiaise** (BSJ)
Le Procés entre les Etats et le Gouverneur Lanier – La Rémonstrance des Etats (1679) BSJ, Vol.II, 1888
Proclamation of Charles II: BSJ, Vol.XV, 1952
Reparations for his Maties Castles of Mount Orgueil and Elizabeth in the Isle of Jersey (1634-l637) BSJ, Vol.VII, 1912
Sir John Peyton's Booke of Disbursements upon the Castells of Jersey (1617-1619) [from State Papers (Domestic)] BSJ, Vol.IX, 1921

The Case of the Inhabitants of the Islands of Jersey, Guernsey, Sark and Alderney (1714) BSJ, Vol.IV, 1897.
Ahier, Philippe: Col. Legge's 'Accompt of Jersey' (1679) BSJ Vol.XIX, 1967
Ahier, Philippe: Sir Thomas Morgan. BSJ, Vol.20, 1969.
Aubin, C N: The Molendinary System of Queen's Valley, BSJ, Vol.25, 1990
Balleine, G R: Social Life in the Seventeenth Century, BSJ, Vol.XIII, 1941.
Dumaresq, Philippe: A Survey of the Island of Jersey, 1685. BSJ.Vol. XII. 1935
Dury, G H: Some Land use Statistics for Jersey in the late Eighteenth Century, BSJ, Vol. XV, 1952
Ellis, M F H: The Channel Islands and the Great Rebellion, BSJ. Vol. XIII, 1937
La Cloche: Memoires de la Famille, BSJ. Vol. III, 1890
Marett, Miss J M (edited by): Some Letters of the Seventeenth Century, BSJ. Vol.XII, 1935
Mills, D A: Cartographie Jersiaise, BSJ. Vol.VI
Nicolle, E T: La Hougue Bie, in Legend and History, BSJ. Vol.
Nicolle, E T: The Neutrality of the Channel Islands during the Fifteenth, Sixteenth and Seventeenth Centuries, Jersey Pamphlets, Vol. 87.
Poingdestre, Jean: Caesarea, or a Discourse of the Island of Jersey (1682), BSJ, Vol. II, 1889
Williams, D Trevor: Trade Relations between Jersey, Guernsey, and Welsh Ports in Elizabethan Times, BSJ, Vol.X11, 1934

Useful books
Ansted, D T, & Latharn, R G (Revised E T Nicolle): *The Channel Islands*, W.H.Allen & Co., Ltd., London, 1893
Baker, T: *A Guide to Jersey and Guernsey*, London, 1839
Balleine, G R: *A Biographical Dictionary of Jersey*, Staples Press Ltd., London, 1948
Balleine, G R: *A History of the Island of Jersey*, Staples Press Ltd., London, 1950
  Listed in Notes as HIJ
Balleine, G R: *History of the Island of Jersey*, revised by Marguerite Syvret and Joan Stevens, 1981, Phillimore & Co., Chichester, England, for the Société Jersiaise. Listed in Notes as HIJ (Revised edition)
Burnett, John: *A History of the Cost of Living*, Penguin Books Ltd., Mddx., 1969 (HCL)
Davis, Ralph: *The Rise of the English Shipping Industry*, Macmillan & Co., Ltd., London, 1962
De Gruchy, G F B: *Medieval Land Tenures in Jersey*, Bigwoods Ltd., 1957
Duncan, Jonathan: *History of Guernsey*, Longman, Brown, Green & Longman, London, 1841
Eagleston, A J: *The Channel Islands under Tudor Government 1485-1642*, Cambridge University Press for the Guernsey Society, 1949
Falle, Philip (revised E Durell): *Caesarea, or an Account of Jersey 1694/1837*
Haydn: *Dictionary of Dates*, 25th edition, Ward, Lock & Co. London, 1910
Huisinga, J: *The Waning of the Middle Ages*, Penguin Books Ltd., Mddx. 1924/1965
Mollet, R: *A Chronology of Jersey*, Société Jersiaise, 1949
Mumford, Lewis: *The City in History – its origins, its transformations, and its prospects*, Secker & Warburg, London, 1961/1963
Nicolle, E T: *Mont Orgueil Castle, Jersey*, The Beresford Library Ltd., Jersey, 1921
Nicolle, E T: *The Town of St. Helier*, J T Bigwood Ltd., Jersey, 1931

Bibliography

Paxman, Jeremy: *The English – a portrait of a people*, Penguin, London, 1999
Poingdestre, J: *Caesarea, or A Discourse on the Island of Jersey*, 1652
Rutt, Richard: *A History of Hand-Knitting*, B T Batsford Ltd., London, 1987
Stevens, Joan: *Old Jersey Houses* (Vol.I) Privately, Jersey, 1965
Vicomte du Gibon: *Les Iles Chausey, L'Ancre du Marin*, St.Malo, France, 1918
Vincent, B (Editor): *The Concise Dictionary of National Biography Vol. III*, The Softback Preview, Oxford University Press, 1994
Willan, T S: *The English Coasting Trade, 1600-1750*, Manchester University Press, 1938/1967

INDEX OF PEOPLE

Alexandre, 59, 91
Allix, 104
Amy, 91
Anson, 100
Ashbrooke, 113
Asplet, 91, 102
Aubert, 99
Aubin, 164

Bailhache, 52
Baker, 150
Balleine, 68, 73, 105, 107, 130, 140, 141, 157, 172
Bechervaise, 91, 158
Becket, 21
Becquet, 91
Behuchet, 42, 68
Benest, 91, 101, 165
Berteaux, 157
Bertrand, 42, 44, 68
Biggs, 165
Bisson, 103, 107, 157, 165, 183
Blake, 91, 141, 144
Bois, 174
Bor, 86
Bruce, 41, 68
Brun, 157
Bruton, 100
Burke, 90, 168
Butt, 102

Cabot, 72, 124, 157, 187
Carter, 28
Carteret (see De Carteret)
Cartier, 124, 125
Champion, 165
Charles I, 131, 143, 146
Charles II, 31, 131, 132, 143, 146, 181, 200
Charles VI, 25
Chevalier, 77, 141, 144, 158, 164, 176, 177, 179
Chiverton, 103
Clarke, 73, 78, 149, 194
Cofynet, 25
Coke, 136

Colbert, 126
Collas, 74, 100
Columbus, 81, 189
Conway, 121, 136, 203
Cook, 147
Cornish, 26
Coutanche, 69, 103
Cromwell, 91, 132, 143

d'Aubigny, 21
d'Auvergne, 169
Dancaster, 59, 60, 61
Day, 206
De Caen, 157
De Carteret, 26, 27, 31, 37, 83, 86, 107, 111, 114, 131, 141, 143, 147, 175
De Caux, 159
de Cheney, 85
de Cobham, 83
de Games, 46
De Gruchy, 16, 23, 89, 189
De la Perelle, 158, 159
De La Rocque, 72
De Penhouet, 45
De Pontbriand, 45
De Quetteville, 74
De Ste Croix, 99, 152, 157
De Vienne, 45
Dean, 157
Deslandes, 78, 193
Distelfeld, 83
Dolbel, 90, 91, 101, 162
Dorward, 100
Drake, 81, 147
Du Guesclin, 44, 49
du Heaume, 55, 61, 62, 158, 159
du Port, 21
Dubois, 159
Dumaresq, 32, 89, 109, 111, 112, 132, 133, 134, 139, 150, 157, 158, 174, 177, 180, 183
Dumouriez, 89
Duneville, 25
Durell, 100, 164

Eagleston, 138

Index of People

Edward I, 77, 83
Edward III, 41, 44, 87
Edward IV, 25, 85, 86, 93
Effard, 28, 126
Elizabeth I, 22, 26, 81, 129, 136
Eustache the Monk, 22
Even, 86

Fainton, 159
Falle, 20, 77, 109, 120, 122, 126, 140, 190, 191
Fantris, 87
Fillieul, 159
Finch, 86
Finlaison, 57
Finnie, 103
Fiott, 88, 89
Fruing, 74

Gallienne, 88
Gaudin, 159
Gavey, 195, 196
Germain, 157
Ginot, 86
Gosset, 158, 159
Gray, 103
Grellier, 195, 196
Guerin, 88

Hacquoil, 91, 101, 158
Haine, 144
Hamon, 90, 158, 162, 163, 164
Hampton, 103
Harliston, 190
Harnett, 101
Harrison, 129, 147
Hastein, 56
Heane, 144
Hemery, 99, 157, 162, 185
Henry VI, 47
Henry VII, 72
Heraux, 101
Heulin, 150
Hitler, 168
Hocquard, 165
Hooper, 164, 165
Hubert, 158
Huelin (see Heulin)

Ifan, 44
Inglis, 78
Ingouville, 158

Jackson, 102
James I, 106, 131
James II, 32, 107
James, Jonas, 86
Janvrin, 74, 90, 100, 157, 158, 159, 162, 162-165, 190
Jean, 158
Jeune, 158
Journeaux, 103, 157

Kerby, 88, 158, 159
Knocker, 63

l'Amy, 90, 163
La Cloche, 69, 116
Labey, 157
Laffoley, 91
Laurens, 37
Le Bas, 74
Le Boeuf, 195, 196
Le Brocq, 165
Le Brun, 91, 157
Le Caux, 100
Le Clerk, 25
Le Cornu, 58, 64, 67, 183
Le Couteur, 150, 157
Le Cronier, 88, 165
Le Feuvre, 101, 157, 158, 162, 163, 165
Le Geyt, 52, 91, 157, 175
Le Gresley, 90
Le Lievre, 78
Le Maistre, 63, 67, 69
Le Masurier, 88, 89
Le Mountais, 28
Le Neveu, 195
Le Quesne, 26, 102
Le Ray, 159
Le Riche, 159
Le Roux, 150, 157, 158
Le Sueur, 157
Le Vesconte, 79, 90, 194
Lempriere, 89, 181
Longsword, (see William)
Louis XI, 86, 93
Lys, 159, 162

Index of People

Mahaut, 55
Mahe, 99
Mahy, 102
Mallet, 28, 158, 159, 162, 164
Maltravers, 56
Malzard, 158
Marett, 194, 210
Martin, 102, 104
Mary, Queen of Scots, 130
Mathurin, 56
Matthews, 103
Mauger, 157
Maugier, 87
Maulevrier, 47
Meade, 32, 181, 184
Messervy, 87, 88, 90, 158, 159, 162, 165
Misson, 102
Mollet, 63
Montbrun, 91
Morrison, 28
Mourant, 90, 102, 157

Neel, 157, 159
Newman, 99
Nicolle, 28, 102, 126, 158, 183
Nino, 45, 46
Noel, 103, 158, 159

Osbourne, 27
Owen, 44, 49

Paisnel, 32, 34
Paulet, 26
Payn, 165, 167
Perchard, 102
Perree, 101
Perrot, 103
Peyton, 86, 87, 131
Pickstock, 157
Picot, 103, 193
Piquet, 63
Poingdestre, 15, 56, 67-69, 109, 122, 124, 132, 134, 152, 157, 159
Poulet, 130
Prouings, 101
Purchase, 101

Remon, 159, 164
Renouf, 57, 158

Richardson, 104
Robin, 73, 74, 148, 149, 150, 157, 158, 159
Robinson, 157
Roissier, 91
Rollo, 71
Romeril, 90, 165, 183
Rutt, 129

Selous, 63
Sequin, 25
Servais le Vavasseur dit Bois, 174
Shares, 86
Sherlock, 104
Simon, 99
Simonet, 158
Simpson, 158
Sinel, 59, 67
Slany, 86
Slous, 91
Smeaton, 156, 185
Snow, 87
Speed, 29
St. James of Compostella, 22
St. Jaume, 174
St. Mary, 17, 37
St. Nicholas, 31, 37
Steel, 29, 158
Stevens, 23, 37, 58, 116

Tacker, 157
Torre, 90, 150
Townshend, 124
Trevele, 25

Valpy, 74, 101
Vibert, 28, 63, 157, 158
Villeneuve, 157
Voisin, 99
Voye, 159

Wace, 18, 77, 189
Wallis, 55, 67
Wethereall, 86
Willan, 139
William, Longsword (Duke), 71
William I, Duke of Normandy,, 18, 189
Williams, 138, 140, 165
Winter, 157
Wooldridge, 165

INDEX OF SHIPS
[2] Indicates two vessels of *same na*me on that page.

Active, 99
Adventure, 150
Aigle, 90
Alezan, 87
Amiraux Desire, 164
Alligator, 90, 162
Aurore, 157

Beaver, 150
Betsey [2], 157, 195
Betzy, 164

Calista, 196
Catherine, 157
Concorde, 157
Ceres, 165
Charming Betty, 88
Charming Nancy, 88, 157
Chetican, 157
Commerce, 157
Concorde, 157
Corbet, 157
Cornwall, 157
Courier, 103
Cruiser, 157

Dapper, 99
Dart Packet, 103
Dauphin, 150, 157
De Jersey, 195
Deux Amis, 157
Diana, 102
Dispatch, 157
Dolphin, 101
Duke of Argyle, 99
Duke of Wellington, 102

Elisha Tupper, 190
Elizabeth, 87, 157
Endeavour, 132
Enterprize, 162
Evening Star, 194
Expedition, 157

Fleur, 52

Fly, 104
Fortune, 154, 157
Friendship,[2], 157

General Don, 195
Globe, 164
Guernsey Packet, 154, 157

Hazard, 162
Henriette, 152
Hercules, 157
Hilton, 157
Hope, 90, 99, 101, 157, 163

Industrie, 157
Integrity, 101

Jenny, 157
Jersey, 88
Jersey Sloop, 87
Joseph & Benjamin, 102

Kenton, 158
Kingfisher, 158
Kite, 158
Kitty, 100, 158

Le Heraux, 101
Liberte, 158
Liberty, 102, 150
Liberty Packet, 154, 158
Lightning, 158
Lion, 103
Lion's Whelps, 27
Lively, 88, 104, 158
London Packet, 89
Lord Sidmouth, 196
Lotterie, 90
Lynx, 158

Magdelaine, 158
Magot, 158
Major Pierson, 158
Marie, 158
Mars, 89, 99, 100

Index of Ships

Mary, 101, 104
Mary Ann, 158
Mary & Ann, 100
May Flower, 102
Mercure [2], 158
Mexicana, —
Molly, 158

Nancy, 100, 158
Nelson, 101
Neptune, 158
New Eagle, 103
Nimphe, 158
Nostra Senora la Virgin del Carmen Dolores y Providad, 90

Olive Branch, 100

Paix,[2], 158
Pallas, 196
Papillion, 100
Paspebiac, 158
Peace, 195
Peggy,[2], 158
Phoenix, 88, 90, 163
Pierson, 158
Pilgrim, 87
Pilote, 158
Postillon, 152, 159
Prince of Bouillon, 195
Prudent,[2], 159

Quebec, 159
Queen, 162

Rambler, 102
Rescue, 194

Resolution, 159
Rover, 100
Rowcliffe, 195
Roze, 162

Sea-gull, 102
Shift, 159
Solide, 159
Southampton Packet, 154, 159
Spartan, 103
Speedy, 195
Spright, 101
St. Aubin, 159
St. Laurens, 159
St. Pierre, 159
Succes, 159
Surprise, 165
Swallow, 150, 159
Swift, 159
Sylla, 103
Sylph, 195

Trio, 159
Tryall (Trial), 159
Two Brothers, 159

Union,[2], 159
Unite, 159
Unity, 159

Vautour, 90, 163
Venus, 195
Vulture, 90, 163, 165

Young-Mary, 159

Zeus, 103

GENERAL INDEX

Abbey, 17, 19, 137
Africa, 28
Aghios Elias, 37
Alderney, 42, 132, 214
Anjou, 20
Aquitaine, 39, 51, 84, 85, 119
Astarte, 37
Attacks on the C.I., 17, 40-45, 81, 84, 93, 136, 141-144, 168

Battle of Hastings, 77
Bay of Biscay, 22
Beaumont, 29
Bel Royal, 29, 190
Biarritz, 20
Black Death, 43, 48, 69
Board of Admiralty, 166
Bordeaux, 39, 84, 167
Bretons, (attacks by) 44, 45
  (fishing-boats) 72
Brittany, 18, 39
  (attacks on Jersey by) 45
  (attacks from Jersey on) 85
  (exports to) 20, 120
  (fishermen of) 72, 187
  Jersey boats winter in) 181
  (Roscoff in) 95, 155

Cape Breton, 45, 72, 74, 75, 102, 127, 157
Castel Sedement, 49
Castle Cornet, Guernsey 39
Castles, (see Elizabeth, Gorey [Mont Orgueil], Grosnez)
Chapels, 17, 31, 37
Chausey Islands, 16, 26
Chemin Public, 63
Cherbourg, Normandy 49, 89
Cocos Island, 28
Coutances, 57
Customs, (Great & Little) 20
  (H.M.English) 95, 132

dragon-ship, 32, 34

Elizabeth Castle, (breakwater at) 185, 186
  (destruction by bomb) 144
  (engineers at) 86, 184
  (harbour at) 174, 176
  (Prince Charles at) 177
English Channel, 15, 27, 28, 34, 58, 71, 159
Esplanade, 46, 195, 204
Exports, 77, 119, 130, 136, 154

Forest at St.Ouen, 55, 56, 59, 60, 61, 67

Gascony, 20, 39, 51, 84, 85, 119
Genoese galleys, 42, 68
German Occupation, 42, 167
Goose Green Marsh, 29
Gorey Castle, [Mont Orgueil] (attacks on) 42, 44, 47, 190
  (Irish troops transferred to) 177
  (provisions for) 122, 139
Granville, 17, 91, 154, 157
Grosnez, (smuggling at) 98
Grosnez Castle, 44
Grouville, 47, 49, 78
  (ship-building at) 193
  (smuggling at) 98
Grouville Militia, 143
Grouville Windmill, 52
Guernsey, 17, 39
  (attacks on) 41-45, 47, 68
Guernsey, fisheries) 124, 125, 127, 129, 130, 132, 135, 137, 138, 148, 150, 152
  (harbour) 137, 138, 186
  (pirates at) 25, 27
  (privateers) 83, 87-89, 94, 166, 168, 169
  (ship-building) 191
  (smugglers) 94-96, 98, 100, 102-104, 154
  (stocking-trade) 129, 130, 132, 135

Haiti, 24
Harfleur, 25
Holy Land, 21
Holy Trinity, (parish of) 18, 46, 77, 103, 105, 147
Hundred Years' War, 41, 187

General Index

Imports, 77, 84, 131, 136, 138
Insurance for sailors, 200
Isle of Wight, 26
   (ships built in) 99, 100, 102, 103, 104
l'Islet, 19, 45, 175

Jersey Merchant Seamen's Benefit Society, 75
Jersey Register of Shipping, 191
"Jersey spinners", 131

La Brequette Forest, 63
La Brequette Manor, 49, 55, 56, 61-64, 69
La Brequette reef, 59, 61, 62, 64, 69
La Brequette, (Rue de) 63
La Croix de la Bataille, 47
La Croix de St. Nicholas, 47
La Hambye, 32
La Haussiere, 55, 59, 61, 62, 67, 69
La Hougue Bie, 32, 34, 35
La Moye, 62
La Rocco Tower, 57
La Rocque, 16, 59
La Saline, 63, 64
Le Cotentin, Normandy 57, 58
Le Dicq, 29
Le Havre de Bas, 175
Le Havre des Pas, (pier at) 32, 137, 171, 174-177, 179, 180, 183, 186
   (ship-building at) 78
Le Havre Neuf, 32, 174, 176, 179, 180, 181, 184, 186
Le Mont de la Ville, 137, 156, 186, 204
Le Rue du Craslin, 29
Le Vinchelez de Haut, 55
Les Ecrehous, 16
   (chapel at) 17
Les Hurieaux, 63, 64
Les Laveurs, 59, 60, 63
Les Mielles, 58, 60, 64
Les Minquiers, 16, 17, 22
Les Moitiers d'Allonne, Normandy 57
Les Quennevais, 56

Melcombe Regis, Dorset 43
Militia, 42, 47
Mills, 41, 42, 58, 68, 76
Mont Mado, 62
Mont Thiebault, 61

Morocco, 28, 126

Pirates, (at Les Minquiers) 17
   (Jerseymen as) 45
   (17th century in English Channel) 72, 120
   (Pope condemns) 85,
Pirates, (Sir George Carteret's) 143
Pirates, (see also Item 2, p.24-28)
Plague, 43
Population, (13th century) 19
   (14th century) 40
   (17th century) 105, 106, 109, 111, 112, 120, 129, 131, 132, 134, 136, 139
   ("always in a state of war") 89
   (effect of enemy raids on) 41, 42, 43, 48, 49, 68
   (effect of plague on) 43, 69
   (unemployment rare, 19/20th centuries) 80
   (view of the Civil War) 141, 146
Portelet Inn, 58
Portsmouth, 21, 27, 102
Portugal, 76, 81
Portuguese sailors, 25, 81, 83, 127, 149
Poseidon, 37

Ransoms, 22, 44, 47
Reef, (pier built like) 184
Reefs, (see Les Ecrehous, Les Minquiers, Paternosters)
Rochester, Kent 21, 177
Roscoff, Brittany 95, 155
Rozel, 26, 105

St. Aubin, (harbour at) 73, 137, 153, 171, 185, 186
   (merchants at) 88, 148, 195, 206
   (piracy at) 26
   (rope-yard at) 193
   (ship-building at) 78
St. Aubin, (Le Boulevard - The Bulwarks) 194, 203, 204
St. Aubin's Bay, (wreck in) 157
St. Aubin's Bay, (ship-building in) 193, 194
St. Aubin's Bay, (sea-wall) 205,
St. Aubin's Fort, 173
   (harbour at) 137, 180, 181,

General Index

St. Aubin's Town, 109, 111, 148, 194, 195, 203, 204
St. Brelade, 28, 58, 73, 203
   (Parliamentary fleet at) 141, 143
   (pier at) 171, 179, 180
   (smuggling at) 95, 96
St. Clement, 16
St. Helier Town or Parish, 57, 184
St. Helier, (harbours) (see Essay, pp.171-186)
St. John, 18, 77, 99, 100
St. Lawrence, (crew-man of privateer killed) 165
St. Lawrence, ("St. Germain" in) 56
St. Lawrence, (ship-building at) 190
St. Lawrence Marsh, 31, 32, 35, 36, 37
   (dragon at) 32, 34, 35
St. Lawrence River, Canada 124, 127, 148, 154
St. Malo, Brittany 120, 177, 181
Ste. Marie de Valricher, 17
St. Nicholas, 31, 37
St. Ouen, (ancient forest) 59-61, 63
   (loss of land at) 55-59, 64, 69
   (see also "La Brequette")
St. Peter's Valley, 29, 31
St. Peter-Port, Guernsey 39, 83, 84, 86, 137, 186
St. Pierre d'Allonne, Normandy 57
Sandybrook, 29, 31, 36
Santiago de Compostella, Spain 22
Sark, 22, 24, 26, 42, 141,
   (captured by French) 42
Sark, (Parliamentary fleet anchor off) 141

Sea Fencibles, 177
Slaves, 28, 80, 126
Southampton, (H.M. Customs at) 94
   (importance to wine trade) 39, 84, 85
   (named ship arrested at) 100
   (named ships built at) 99, 101, 102
   (named ships trading to) 158, 159
   (trade with) 95, 132, 134, 139, 154
Spaniard, 45
Streams, 16, 36

Tax, 20, 21, 40, 71, 95, 109, 119, 200
Turkey, 28, 126, 131
Veneti, a tribe in Brittany, 18
Vikings, 18, 34, 71
Vingtaine, 31, 111, 180

Wales, 44, 49, 138, 140
Warden of the Isles, 18, 21, 25, 45, 56, 83
Wars of the Roses, 26
Waterworks Valley, 35
West Indies, 24, 76, 155, 167, 168
West Park, 46, 194, 205
Weymouth, Dorset 43, 101, 126
Wind, 17, 79, 141, 201
Wine, 76
Wine trade, 39, 135, 139
Winter of 1334/5, 16
Winter of 1777/8, 73
Winter refuge for boats, 31, 36 97, 181
Winter, (farming in) 108, 120
Winter, (work for fishermen in Canada) 192